W9-AHT-765

International Direct Marketing

Manfred Krafft · Jürgen Hesse · Jürgen Höfling
Kay Peters · Diane Rinas (Editors)

International Direct Marketing

Principles, Best Practices, Marketing Facts

With 71 Figures

Center of interactive Marketing
and Media Management (CIM)

Siegfried Vögele Institut
Internationale Gesellschaft für Dialogmarketing mbH

UNIVERSITY LIBRARY
GOLDEN GATE UNIVERSITY
536 Mission Street
San Francisco, CA 94105-2968

Springer

Dr. Manfred Krafft
Chaired Professor of Marketing
Institute of Marketing
Marketing Center Münster (MCM)
University of Münster
Am Stadtgraben 13-15
48143 Münster
Germany

Dr. Jürgen Hesse
CEO
Professor of Management
Siegfried Vögele Institut
Ölmühlweg 12
61462 Königstein
Germany

Jürgen Höfling
CEO DHL Global Mail
Charles-de-Gaulle-Str. 20
53113 Bonn
Germany

Kay Peters
Director
Center of Interactive Marketing
and Media Management (CIM)
c/o Marketing Center Münster (MCM)
University of Münster
Am Stadtgraben 13-15
48143 Münster
Germany

Dr. Diane Rinas
Deutsche Post AG
Charles-de-Gaulle-Str. 20
53113 Bonn
Germany

ISBN 978-3-540-39631-4 Springer Berlin Heidelberg New York

Library of Congress Control Number: 2007934291

This work is subject to copyright. All rights are reserved, whether the whole or part of the material is concerned, specifically the rights of translation, reprinting, reuse of illustrations, recitation, broadcasting, reproduction on microfilms or in any other way, and storage in data banks. Duplication of this publication or parts thereof is permitted only under the provisions of the German Copyright Law of September 9, 1965, in its current version, and permission for use must always be obtained from Springer-Verlag. Violations are liable for prosecution under the German Copyright Law.

Springer is a part of Springer Science+Business Media
springeronline.com

© Springer-Verlag Berlin Heidelberg 2007
Printed in Germany

The use of general descriptive names, registered names, trademarks, etc. in this publication does not imply, even in the absence of a specific statement, that such names are exempt from the relevant protective laws and regulations and therefore free for general use.

Typesetting: Druckpress GmbH, Leimen

Printed on acid-free paper
SPIN 11852902 43/3180ba   5 4 3 2 1 0

Foreword

Dear readers,

Globalization continues at a fast pace. National markets are merging more and more each day. One key example of this is the expansion of the European Union (EU). Fifty years after European economic integration was initiated with the Treaty of Rome, the EU has grown into an economic powerhouse of twenty-seven countries, and an end to the expansion is still nowhere in sight. At the same time, the Asian giants, China and India, continue to develop into markets of enormous potential.

While rapid globalization and market liberalization are opening up attractive new opportunities for all kinds of businesses, the pressure on profit margins is increasing. Tapping into new customer segments beyond national borders is a way for companies to meet growth objectives and improve profitability in what has become a very competitive environment. It is not enough, however, for customers abroad to simply recognize the presence of a foreign company. Trust needs to be established and enthusiasm generated for a company's products and services.

Creating awareness through advertisements in conventional mass media does not usually pose any major problems to a company entering a new country with a different cultural background. The real challenge lies in turning attractive prospects into active customers in unfamiliar markets–customers who are willing to purchase the advertised products and become loyal customers over the medium term. This is where dialogue marketing comes into play. Just like in the domestic market, dialogue marketing is essential for successful communication with target groups in foreign markets. It has proven its value in the acquisition of new customers and as an important tool in customer relationship management. This book offers expert advice and best-practice case studies to support international direct marketing campaigns.

As Deutsche Post World Net's international mail specialist, we at DHL Global Mail* are pleased to have taken part in the making of this book. Together with the other authors, we have contributed our expertise to help make your international campaigns a success. We hope the book will prove useful to you in your daily work and give you a competitive edge.

We wish you success in seizing new opportunities and developing new markets.

Yours faithfully,

Jürgen Höfling
CEO DHL Global Mail
Deutsche Post AG

---

* The brand name DHL Global Mail is used by subsidiaries of Deutsche Post World Net, which offer products and services abroad, in the name of and on behalf of Deutsche Post AG. These subsidiaries of Deutsche Post World Net are referred to as DHL Global Mail in the sections that follow.

Preface

International direct marketing is of ever increasing importance for entering and maintaining foreign markets. As in domestic markets, direct marketing is the instrument of choice for companies when communicating personally with prospects and customers. Much like history's explorers – from Marco Polo and Alexander Humboldt to Meriwether Lewis and William Clark – companies are often entering unknown terrain with a high level of uncertainty. However, none of these explorers embarked on their missions without a master plan. To the contrary. They compiled all the information they could get hold of before leaving with every intention of returning safely from a successful mission. Like those explorers, companies entering overseas markets are striving to get hold of the best information available on their target markets to assure a successful launch while simultaneously minimizing their risk. International direct marketing is a highly effective instrument for opening up overseas markets while controlling the associated risks. This book addresses the needs of companies going abroad with direct marketing instruments and helps managers navigate the move, keeping their companies a step ahead of competition.

International Direct Marketing – Principles, Best Practice, Marketing Facts is a publication that combines easy-to-read scientific findings and successful case studies with up-to-date facts and information. For us, however, this book also contains an important core message, which is at the heart of every campaign – there is no one-fits-all medium that will ensure the success of international one-to-one communication. Like in an orchestra, the interaction of the individual advertising "instruments" is the key to creating an advertising symphony from a simple communication melody. Integrated direct marketing campaigns are therefore crucial. Despite the growing role of electronic media, traditional mailings still dominate the field of direct marketing in domestic and international markets throughout the world. So it comes as no surprise that in many of the successful examples presented in this book, mailings remain the core element. Other advertising media always complement the integrative campaign approaches. Without them, mailings could not work as effectively as they do.

Along with the latest expertise, achieving success with cross-border communications also requires a full understanding of both the foreign target group and the target market. To this end, the book provides an overview of 24 important foreign markets in North America, Eastern and Western Europe and Asia. Drawing on a proprietary consumer survey, the book not only contains general economic data and trends on these countries, but also shows how different forms of advertising and direct marketing instruments are currently perceived by the consumers. This kind of information is crucial for any international expansion plan and also helps avoid expensive errors as early as in the preparation stage.

This English edition builds on earlier editions in German and French which were so successful they sold out. We gratefully acknowledge the support of our teams and the many experienced practitioners who provided us with valuable insights and helpful recommendations for improving the book. For this edition we also received support from our academic colleagues at major US universities, the Direct Marketing Association of America (DMA) and the Federation of European Direct and Interactive Marketing (FEDMA). We are highly indebted to all of them. We intend to develop this book over time. One direction is the inclusion of more case studies from North America and Asia, another is the integration of interactive media. We are also considering taking the data section online and making it configurable according to user needs. We invite you to share your ideas and recommendations with us at internationalDM@uni-muenster.de.

We hope you enjoy reading this book and we wish you success in putting its ideas into use.

Manfred Krafft
Jürgen Hesse
Jürgen Höfling
Kay Peters
Diane Rinas

Table of contents

Expert statements on international direct marketing

"Traditionally, the finance, auto and insurance industries have been the most apt to use direct marketing, but different industries are using the medium as they grow accustomed to integrated marketing; at the same time, agencies are getting more projects/briefs targeting stakeholders other than end users — another opportunity to use DM in other stages of the relationship process. Generally speaking, the DM industry is realizing the importance of consumer emotion and thus is moving away from its historic focus on informational/rational offers. At the same time, marketers are demanding insight-driven creativity, which is causing an interesting twist: DM is being used to build brands while advertising is being used to drive response. Failing to understand consumers' values, needs, hopes and fears – while continuing to bombard consumers and see them merely as people to "sell to" – will have a negative impact on DM messages: They'll be blocked by the consumers themselves, by protective legislation, or both.

The principles of direct marketing (fostering one-to-one communication and direct response) are more important than ever considering the fragmentation of media, growing demands for measurable marketing, and the increasing power among consumers to control how they receive information. Direct marketing — traditionally limited to slower-moving analog direct mail and late-night infomercials — is now comprised of personalized interactive websites, email, online customer service centers, SMS, and sophisticated promotions with electronic-based elements that can capture an amazing level of data about buying habits, personal information, and consumer preferences. As marketers demand results from their media spend, they are increasingly pursuing holistic marketing solutions, and direct marketing is playing an increasingly important role in the mix. Pockets of innovation are currently springing up in the far corners of the world (text messaging leads in Asia, for example), which means clients are increasingly hiring global networks to leverage new direct-marketing solutions and include them in the holistic marketing mix."

Maurice Levy
CEO and Chairman, Publicis Group, Paris, France

"In Hungary Direct Marketing has only 15 years of history, and it did not reach that importance as in Western Europe or in the USA yet. But the growth of DM is even quicker than in some other countries as more and more companies recognize its value. The Hungarian economy is still growing substantially and the communication is also in a developing phase. The companies recognized the importance of the integrated communication, and it helps the development of the Direct Marketing. The development of the internet communication is quicker than the traditional one, so year by year it reaches record growth which also helps the development of the Direct Marketing

In my opinion the development of Direct Marketing will continue. Its role within the Marketing will be bigger year by year. The main reason is that there is such a strong „communication noise" by traditional mass media. So the importance of individual communication is increasing. Likewise, the advertisers can reach their targets better by a higher level of personal communication. The internet is also a great tool for Direct Marketing, and its share of the „advertising cake" is rapidly increasing. Overall, Direct Marketing can be the leading communication tool in Hungary very soon.

Since Hungary joined to the EU consumers receive more and more international direct mails. Before Hungary joined to EU our Association received 4-5 company requests for information as they wanted to enter into business in our country. In the last months every month we have 4-5 requests. About the neighbor countries I do not have specific information, but generally in those ones which also joined to EU (e.g., Slovenia, Slovakia, Czech Republic, Poland) the developments are similar."

Péter Hivatal
President, Hungarian Direct Marketing Association "Direkt Marketing Szövesteg (DMSZ)", Budapest, Hungary

"The most important trend in the US is the concern over privacy. This is the result of the internet motivating marketers of all types, sizes and experience to engage in the medium without understanding the importance of following the self-regulation standards set up by the Direct Marketing industry. This will hasten poor business practices, bringing about extensive government regulation. As regulation becomes tighter, utilization of data will become more difficult. This means that targeting will be less possible, negating one of the chief advantages of the database era.

As labor cost rise, efficiency and productivity will be more and more important to gaining superior profit margins. In an era where marketing creativity will be of less importance to consumers due to the ever increasing availability of goods and services, consolidation will be even a more important trend.

Internet marketing will be growing at a faster rate than any other medium, which will mean consumers will search at an unprecedented rate for the lowest price. This will drive profit margins lower, reducing ROI for most marketers. It will put a premium on the marketers who understand the importance of differentiation and know how to implement strategies of creativity, uniqueness, service up-grades, etc. so as to make price a secondary consideration due the better benefits offered. Value is still important but not to the extent where profit margins are lowered to meet the lowest cost provider in the category.

Due to even greater global free market conditions, there will be increased international marketing across boarders to keep the expansion profiles of companies aggressive. This will make for greater competition, more choices for consumers, and more competitive pricing. It is doubtful that percentage margins will increase, but margin dollars of profit should grow due to greater volume."

Ted Spiegel
Professor of Direct Marketing, Medill School of Journalism, Northwestern University, Evanston, USA, and fourth generation member of the Management of Spiegel, Inc.

"In France, direct marketing accounts for the largest share of corporate communication expenditures. The budget dedicated to direct marketing is rising faster than the overall advertising market itself. This may be attributed to the customer base being the most valuable resource of companies.

What trends should be expected in the near future? Gone are the days of mass media campaigns. They will be replaced with fewer mailings which will be aimed at the specific groups identified by analysts.

Customer data, complemented with the historic data of transactions, will enable direct marketing campaigns to be customized to the individual customers' return. The detection of high potential prospects will be conducted by matching them against look alike profiles.

The next years will see an extraordinary growth of international direct marketing campaigns. This is due to both increased demand from advertisers, who nurture cross-border or global brands, and the growing supply of international service providers arising from freer trade in services.

Companies require integrated customer data bases, homogenous technological infrastructures, as well as consistent processes and reporting systems. But they must also refrain from designing purely global strategies: The full centralization and harmonization of marketing strategies put close customer relationships at risk.

Direct marketing is the art of defining very small target groups."

Sandrine Macé
Professor of Direct Marketing, ESCP-EAP, Paris, France

"The most important trend in the U.S. is the movement away from the traditional forms of direct marketing (mail, phone, fax) to electronic (e-mail) and wireless (cell phones, PDAs). This increased ability to deliver rich messaging with the electronic media blends the traditional advantages of TV (creative messaging) with the targeting capabilities of direct marketing. The clouds on the horizon are that consumer protection groups are concerned about privacy issues. While the U.S. has more liberal privacy laws than most countries, this could change in the near future."

Russ Winer
Professor of Marketing, Stern School of Business, New York University, New York, USA

"As CEO of an internationally active company I will concentrate on the local and regional trends in Asia and Latin America. In my opinion Brazil offers a very favorite environment for direct marketing. Direct database marketing activity is relatively high in Brazil and will continue to remain so, as Brazil's Internet use and PC penetration are the highest in Latin America. Additionally, half of the advertisers are using or considering some type of direct-marketing communication (Source: AAAP/ Internet Advertising Bureau). Another regional hot spot for interactive/direct marketing is Venezuela: Research suggests that internet use in Venezuela will increase some 300 percent in the next five years, while cellular phone penetration is 23% (compared to Argentina's 19% and Brazil's 13%). In Mexico, there are growth opportunities, as most marketing disciplines are growing in the double digits while traditional advertising is stuck at a 1.5% growth rate. The direct CRM industry is somewhat developed, while the interactive marketing industry is barely developed, compared to sales/promotional marketing and PR, which are highly developed. Yet there is virgin ground in Latin America, especially in Argentina – the economy permitting – as the internet represents only 1% of total investments (Source: AAAP/ Internet Advertising Bureau).

In the Asia-Pacific region, Australia has seen an increase in DM spend in the last few years by companies that have not traditionally invested in direct marketing, particularly FMCG companies investing in loyalty programs. However, some Australian marketers are reluctant to invest further in direct marketing, as they only see it as a direct-response media to generate leads and don't acknowledge the role direct marketing can play in building brands. Generally, Australia's DM industry is in good shape and the potential for the market is huge, particularly if agencies can migrate marketers' thinking beyond pure "direct response." In Japan, mobile phones are the key to effectively reaching and engaging consumers in promotions. There are 87 million mobile phone subscribers of which approximately 90% use mobile internet capabilities to surf the web, email and play mobile games.

Generally, demands for accountability and breakthrough, engaging creative mean new career opportunities for industry professionals: Some of the most competitive and talented people in marketing – both on the creative and analytical sides – are increasingly attracted to the direct and interactive fields. As technology drives contact possibilities (websites, email, SMS, etc.), marketers have more consumer data to digest than ever before: Fast, accurate analytical teams are and will continue to be a marketer's competitive advantage."

Nick Brien
CEO, ARC Worldwide, Chicago, USA

"Direct marketing in the U.S. is now mainstream. The DMA's annual econometric study for 2005 Direct Marketing: Economic Impact discloses that direct marketing now accounts for some 48% of the advertising spending in the U.S., and contributes an uplift to the country's gross domestic product equivalent to 10.6%, some $1.8 trillion worth of goods and services. Among the thriving and important media used in the U.S. are, in order of spend ($ billions): Telephone ($47), Direct Mail ($31), DRTV ($21.5), Catalog ($18.8), Internet Marketing ($12.6). The words "below the line" are heard in the U.S. only from the mouths of visitors, since DM is now a fundamental and critical element in the strategic planning of all companies.

Why this ascendancy of the direct marketing discipline? There are three major reasons. First, the digitalization of information creation, transmission, manipulation, and storage has enabled marketers, especially direct marketers, to gain an unprecedented reach and impact. Digitalization and its offspring, multiply communication channels, information sources, planning tools, and the ability to test-test-test. And since testing is the circulatory system of direct, and testing can increasingly be done in real time, there can be a real-time impact, or nearly so. Even with direct mail it is now possible to generate letter or postcard copy and art digitally in a few hours, upload to a service provider who generates and posts personalized materials in a few hours which are delivered in 48 hours to drive traffic to a prospect or customer's personalized web-site. Idea to order in less than 3 days with direct mail!

Second, general advertising doesn't seem to be effective in a population of consumers and business buyers who are stressed for time, overloaded with information, and engaged in global competition, which we all indeed are. Lord Saatchi, of the same firm, has noted that retention rates for television advertising have dropped from 35% to 18% in the last 20 years because audiences either don't or can't concentrate. Direct solves that problem, delivering targeted messages to multi-tasking people who want them, at the time that they want them.

Third, digitalization and competition have driven companies to multichannel marketing and the data-generation and control challenges implicit therein. For example, the DMA's annual Multichannel Marketing Report shows graphically how many tools are now used by DMA-member merchants: 93% used e-catalogs and websites, 90% e-mails, 87% paper catalogs, 83% search keywords, 71% direct mail, 69% search engine optimimization. Success depends increasingly on a refined view of a changing target audience, obtained by response generation, data control and analysis. These are core strengths of direct.

Globally, direct marketing will go in this direction at the speed that each country's market and economic development level will tolerate, with some convergence in the industrialized countries and in the "upper middle class population worldwide." I say "some convergence" because the privacy laws and media choices of different countries have a dramatic impact on the introduction and development of direct, as does the size of each market itself. The U.S. is fortunate in having a market of some 300 million, low-cost communications access, and a predilection for freedom of commercial communication, with a privacy regime based on preventing injury, not preventing commercial communication in the disguise of enforcing a "human right". This has enabled a rapid-fire dialectical development process as size gives greater statistical reliability and faster evolution. Of course, this also gives rise to "industrial-process direct", with attendant negatives feedback from the consumer population, increasingly sensitive to poorly targeted materials.

Countries that look very much like the U.S. in many respects, and in which direct should prove successful, and will develop rapidly with the economy, include Brazil, India, China and Russia. Brazil already has a well-developed database industry, a vastly improved postal system, and a growing urban middle class. China and Russia look in many respects like the 19th century mid-western United States, where cataloging thrived, although the vast urbanization of China makes it less of a catalog market than Russia. India has possibilities, but is hampered with a lack of payment systems, effective postal system and a dirth of lists.

 Direct is even now becoming mainstream in the larger European markets, Germany, UK, and France, and the combined Anglo-phone Scandinavia. Mobile marketing is of particular note in these markets and Scandinavia and Japan probably lead the world in innovative uses of mobile telephony. Direct will be more a retention tool than a prospecting tool in the more privacy-conservative countries of Central Europe, like Poland, as it is in Italy and Spain."

Charles A. Prescott
Vice President and Director of Global Knowledge Center, Direct Marketing Association of America, New York, USA

"In the UK, traditional media have seen significantly different trends in usage rates. For example, telemarketing is coming under considerable pressure in the UK, partly because of legislative changes and partly because of the misuse of automated dialing equipment. However direct mail usage is continuing to show healthy growth in the UK. While CRM will continue to increase in sophistication, a more recent trend is the emergence of personal data management services, with some analysts and industry observers predicting that it will become even bigger than the CRM space over the next decade. Personal data management services are enabled by personal knowledge banks that give individuals ownership and control of their own data. Personal knowledge banks are a powerful concept in direct marketing because they overcome many of the challenges posed by traditional database marketing, such as, among many others, the problems inherent in data quality maintenance, increased customer resistance, response rates, intrusion and privacy, opt-in versus opt-out and the rise of new communications channels such as e-mail and text messaging.

The desire for customization of products has now become a world-wide phenomenon. But efficient customization requires detailed knowledge of and intimate familiarity with customer preferences, current usage rates, brand choices, purchase frequencies, response to promotional offers and the relative importance of different design attributes. These factors tend to increase the demand for direct marketing. But at the same time, worldwide, there is increasing concern about issues such as invasion of privacy, confidentiality, spam, junk mail, and unsolicited phone calls. Smoothly reconciling these conflicting trends will be a key challenge for direct marketers around the world."

Kalyan Raman
Professor of Marketing, Loughborough University, Loughborough, UK

"In the USA, direct marketing will be developing along several interdependent trends. On one hand, models and guidelines will be developed that allocate marketing resources more profitably across communications channels. Customer lifetime value (CLV) will be at the heart of these efforts for all, targeting, customer acquisition and retention. The CLV metric will be increasingly forward looking, as the importance of backward looking customer performance metrics like RFM, historic profits, etc. decrease. Based on this trend, the execution of efficient and effective cross-selling/up-selling campaigns will become the norm for most of the firms that sell multiple products and services. Across all communication channels, the most popular form of communication will be via email for most firms to reach their customers, followed by direct mail. Also, the interactivity of customer dialogs will increase substantially as contacts are ever more customer-initiated with the firms, either for complaining or for seeking information on products and services. At the same time, companies offering multichannel shopping will employ multichannel communication strategy, constantly looking for synergy between all channels. For both, B2B and B2C firms will increasingly rely on more powerful statistical tools to manage their customers across channels in a profitable manner.

Internationally, the role of the internet and web-based marketing will rise significantly. The concept of database marketing will become widespread as more forms worldwide realize the benefits of using a customer database to practice CRM strategy. This also holds for small and medium-sized companies. Parallel, the increased reliance on marketing analytics increases the need for skilled people in these areas. At the same time the demand for internationally trained people will rise, as multinational companies employ web-based marketing strategies for international consumer or business segments across several countries or continents. With respect to international DM expenditures, retailing, telecommunication and other service industries will lead the growth. An accompanying trend in international DM will be an increase in outsourcing of international direct marketing efforts to achieve cost efficiency. This trend partially compensated by a shift from mass marketing to segment level marketing in less developed nations, and from segment level to one-to-one marketing in more advanced nations. Finally, the increasing employment of CRM and (international) DM strategies will be reflected in more educational institutions seeking expertise to develop corresponding curriculums as the demand for DM experts worldwide rises."

V. Kumar
ING Chair Professor and Executive Director, ING Center for Financial Services, University of Cennecticut, Storrs (CT), USA

The editors and authors

From 1983 to 1991, **Thomas Curwen** worked with leading European advertising agencies for clients in B2B markets, particularly in the financial services industry. From 1991 to 1998, he worked exclusively in the IT sector and his skills include an excellent knowledge of digital marketing. He knows how customers react to both old and new technologies, whether they are consumers or companies.

At Publicis, Thomas Curwen ensures that all Internet projects are in line with the business strategy of its customers, while meeting both customer expectations and the requirements of the market.

Professor **Jürgen Hesse**, PhD, has been the director of the Siegfried Vögele Institute, the international company for dialog marketing, since 2002. Dr. Jürgen Hesse, with a doctorate in marketing, began his career at the GfK Gesellschaft für Konsumforschung, one of the largest market research companies worldwide. In 1981 he was appointed professor of business administration and marketing at the German Institute of Higher Education for Mail and Telecommunications.

In 1995 he created and headed up the Institute for City Marketing in Dieburg, Germany. He has been a visiting professor at the University of Xi'an, known as the "Institute of Post and Telecommunications" in the People's Republic of China, since 1998.

Auke van den Hout has worked for the Acxiom Corporation (formerly Claritas) since 1997. After working as a business development manager in Europe and Asia, a country manager for Italy and as director of the international Internet division at Claritas, he is now a seasoned member of the European management team. With a master of business economics from the Erasmus University in Rotterdam, The Netherlands, he has gained extensive experience in the financial industry. He played an integral role in the purchase and transfer of Claritas to the Acxiom Corporation, and today holds the title of Continental Europe Leader. The Acxiom Corporation, with its head office in Little Rock, Arkansas in the USA, is a globally successful business and a leader in customer data management.

Jürgen Höfling studied business administration at the University of Würzburg in Germany and at the State University of New York at Albany in the U.S.A. His degree in business administration was conferred by Würzburg in 1989. From 1989 to 1995 he was employed by Werner & Mertz Group in Mainz, Germany and in Paris, France.

He began working for Deutsche Post in 1995 as Director of International Marketing, in the capacity of head of product management and marketing for international mail.

In 2000, he was appointed to the Divisional Board Express, with responsibility for Marketing Express Germany, Marketing & Sales Euro Express Europe and Deutsche Post Fulfilment.

On January 1, 2003, he assumed the position of Managing Director Marketing & Sales DHL Express Europe, and on October 1, 2005 that of CEO DHL Express Nordics.

From January 1 to March 31, 2007 he served as CEO DHL Global Mail Europe, and took on the position of CEO DHL Global Mail and Chairman of the Divisional Board Deutsche Post Mail International as of April 1, 2007.

Professor **Manfred Krafft**, PhD, has been the director of the Institute for Marketing (IfM) at the University of Münster, Germany, since early 2003. Trained as a banker, after his education at the University of Kiel, in 2000 he was appointed to the Otto Beisheim Chair of Marketing at the WHU Wissenschaftliche Hochschule für Unternehmensführung in Vallendar, near Koblenz, Germany.

At the University of Münster's Institute for Marketing, the main focus of his research is on customer relationship management, direct marketing, sales and marketing management. Through his participation in numerous projects in cooperation with academic colleagues from the USA, his research and teaching have taken on an international dimension. His publications range from numerous contributions in anthologies, to articles in scientific journals (including Interfaces, Journal of Marketing, Journal of Marketing Research, and Marketing Science).

Thomas Nagel, drawing on some 15 years of professional experience in international direct marketing, is an established direct marketing specialist who advises businesses both at home and abroad. His expertise lies with B2C markets – acquiring new customers in the mail-order business and developing market entry strategies using international direct marketing.

Apart from numerous published trade articles and columns on direct marketing, Thomas Nagel also has several specialist books on this subject to his credit as author and co-author. He also works as a guest lecturer and consultant at various international educational and professional institutes.

Rosegret Nave served as Director of Marketing of MAIL International at Deutsche Post AG until 2006, and Director of Marketing at DHL Global Mail UK until August 2007. Starting in 1997, she held various positions of responsibility in the mail marketing area of Deutsche Post.

Rosegret Nave studied business administration at the University of Cologne, specializing in marketing and product procurement. She began her career in the field of business planning at a health insurance company, where she systematically established and headed the marketing area.

Kay Peters collaborates on scientific matters with Professor Manfred Krafft at the Institute for Marketing at the University of Münster. Since 2004, he is CEO of the Center for interactive Marketing and Media Management (CIM) at the University of Münster. His main areas of research are interactive direct marketing, customer relationship management and international marketing. A marketing graduate from Kiel, Germany, he worked with a variety of international companies across Europe and Latin America – including a software company which he founded and managed – before returning to his scientific activities.

Kay Peters has published a series of articles and specialist contributions on his main areas of research in scientific magazines and anthologies.

Anita Petersen, PhD, has worked in market research since 2004 with the Market Research Service Centre (MRSC) of Deutsche Post World Net Business Consulting GmbH. Her main areas of research are in dialog marketing and mail communication.

A graduate in psychology, from 1995 to 1999 she studied at the University of Cologne. She then spent time as a scientist, both researching and teaching at the University of Cologne's Psychology Institute, Germany, where in 2001 she was awarded her doctorate. In 2002 she moved into institutional market research. She is the author of "Interpersonal Communication: an Intermedia Comparison".

Diane Rinas, PhD, is an expert in international direct marketing, international communication and target group marketing, with a particular focus on intercultural marketing. Since 1999, these areas have also been at the center of her work at Deutsche Post AG. Additionally, she often gives presentations on her subject at congresses, in workshops and universities and has also published a number of professional articles.

A holder of graduate degrees in business administration and economics, Rinas wrote her thesis at the University of Cologne on "Segment-oriented Marketing by Private Television Companies." A trained banker, she worked in various areas of the media and was also a lecturer in marketing before joining Deutsche Post.

Alastair Tempest was appointed Director General of FEDMA in September 1999, having been Director General of FEDIM from February 1992, and of the European Advertising Tripartite since 1989. From 1992-94 he was Director European Affairs, Readers' Digest, and from 1980 to 1989 he was also Director of External Affairs for the European Association of Advertising Agencies. He has a Masters degree in European Economic Studies from the College of Europe, Bruges. He has made his career in European public affairs strategy and policy of commercial communications.

Jon Williams is the interactive creative director of Wunderman UK. He had held the same position with Publicis UK in London before joining Wunderman. He graduated from Hallam University and continued his studies at the "School of Communication Arts". He has won over 40 international prizes for creativity and effectiveness, including D&AD, Cannes Lions, Creative Circle, DTAA and the DMA Grand Prix. Jon Williams created the most highly rated advertisement in the UK in 2003. He has been a member of the international jury of the New Yorker advertising festival, as well as at Cannes Lions. Jon Williams

is a member of the D&AD and the "Royal Society for the Arts". After more than 14 years in advertising, his work covers the full spectrum of media, from television to direct mails.

Chapter 1: Principles

Jürgen Hesse, Manfred Krafft and Kay Peters

Borderless direct marketing?
Status quo, trends and outlook

Overview

- This text is the first to define the characteristics of international direct marketing, from cross-border efforts to campaigns for customers of foreign origin.
- It includes the first-ever rough estimate of the volume of international direct marketing.
- The appropriate decision criteria for choosing international direct marketing, and the procedures proven to work backed by practical and scientific articles, are also detailed in this guide.
- The text identifies which key controlling and organizational aspects are required for successful international direct marketing.

1   Introduction

Direct marketing has developed rapidly over the past few decades. In all major industrial nations, it is now a key component of the entire marketing mix (DMA 2004a). With the increasing globalization of world trade, international direct marketing has increased in performance and relevance. Akhter (1996) assumes that, at the time of his study, 37% of all US mail-order companies were involved internationally, and that another 20% were aiming to do so shortly. He regards Lands' End and LL Bean as the pioneers, offering their products in 170 and 146 countries respectively, all around the world. An analysis of the the international ECHO awards CD-ROM (DMA 2005) includes at least nine international direct marketing campaigns, of which five are B2C- and another four B2B-campaigns from North America and Europe. All of them are hugely successful, representing approximately 10% of all documented award campaigns. Fowler (2003) estimates the volume of direct marketing to be worth approximately US \$20 billion annually in Asia alone. Schultz (1994) identifies also changing social and technological conditions as the driving forces behind this. The development of direct marketing databases (Topol and Sherman 1994), the worldwide spread of reliable payment methods (credit cards, electronic fund transfers), and the development of global shipping companies such as Deutsche Post, DHL, FedEx and UPS have all made the world a bit smaller. At the same time, regionally integrated economic areas with similar urban lifestyles are developing in America, Europe and Asia (Akhter 1996). Under these conditions, international direct marketing is a valuable tool, especially for the international expansion of small and medium-sized enterprises (Dallmer 2002). Spiller and Campell (1994) show in their study that 84% of all small companies in Canada, the USA and Mexico now use international direct marketing to win and keep customers. The increasing spread of international direct marketing is a logical consequence of the special advantages this tool can offer businesses (Iyer and Hill 1996). In marketing, the trend towards cross-media and interactive communication with individual customers encourages direct marketing. This likewise benefits the subsegment of international direct marketing (Rosenfield 1994, Schultz 1994).

   Although national direct marketing still claims by far the largest share of expenditure, international direct marketing is becoming an important option for businesses (Topol and Sherman 1994). The growth of international direct marketing is mainly driven by two developments: classic cross-border direct marketing by businesses, and global marketing campaigns by multinational corporations, often with national implementation and/or adaptation. Only a few studies address the volume of international direct marketing, relying either on statistics from postal companies or on customs and trade statistics. Both forms of statistics underestimate the scope of international direct marketing substantially: neither approach takes into account the cross-border effect of the individual national implementation components of international campaigns, nor can these approaches clearly define their reach. On the other hand, postal statistics are actually distorted by national campaigns, many of which are mailed from abroad for cost reasons. For example, for a while several German businesses sent their business correspondence from the Netherlands.* Overall, it can be assumed that the extent of international direct marketing has been underestimated considerably. The fact is that, irrespective of the underlying definition of international direct marketing, the challenges are similar, from the definition of the strategic target group and the analysis of its potential, to the operational implementation of the campaign and its fulfillment on the ground.

Despite the rising economic significance of international direct marketing, the scientific and practice-oriented literature offers only a few contributions to the field of international direct marketing. Most of the knowledge about this interesting topic has, thus far, mostly been exchanged at special conference tracks and trade fairs, e.g., at the DMA conference 2006 and the 4th European Dialog Day in November 2006. Thus it can be said that a systematic review of the current knowledge is required. This article is intended to help filling this gap and provide beginners and experienced professionals alike with a comprehensive overview of the subject.

The article begins with the definition of international direct marketing, its advantages, and a brief overview of its development in the last few years. The criteria which usually underlie a management decision regarding entry into international direct marketing are then compiled from the literature. In certain cases, a conscious, well thought-out decision against entry can be the right decision. However, for when it does make sense to implement an international direct marketing campaign, this article provides the reader with tried and trusted practical examples. These model procedures have strategic and operational elements which, in direct marketing practice, are implemented iteratively. Particularly important are simultaneous controlling and adequate organization of the entire process. Difficulties and challenges can arise at every stage, including during the supporting activities of control and organization. How these issues can be adressed is discussed in the following sections.

2   Definition and demarcation

The basis for a common understanding of international direct marketing is a consistent definition and demarcation of the term. First one has to define exactly what the term direct marketing refers to. Various definitions exist, and three are presented here briefly.

Direct marketing was first understood by Gerardi (1966) as simply a communication tool: "Direct marketing directly conveys a written, reproduced or printed advertisement to a select number of recipients, and is therefore tied to the post office or a private dispatch organization." Further exponents of this classification are Bird (1990), Batra (1990), Roberts and Berger (1999), and Stone and Jacobs

---

* Additional postage is now charged on such mailings based on German and European court rulings that they constitute remailings.

(2001). Dallmer (1997) expands the term to include the function of direct marketing as a distribution tool: "Direct marketing covers all market activities which use single-level (more direct) communication and/or direct distribution or dispatching to address particular target groups individually. Direct marketing also covers those market-oriented activities which use multi-level communication to ensure direct, individual contact." Elsner (2003) and Holland (2004) also adopt this view. Meffert uses the broadest definition (2002), even defining direct marketing as a management concept: "Direct marketing is holistically defined as a specific development of the marketing concept, which, with the help of modern information and communication technologies, places individualized customer relationships at the center of business activities (in the sense of a genuine dialog using the efficient personalization of all marketing parameters)." Bruns (1998) and Löffler and Scherfke (2000) also take this view. This definition to a large extent overlaps with classic customer-relationship management concepts. From a pragmatic standpoint, it appears very broad.

In this article, direct marketing will be understood as a tool for both communication and distribution. This definition is used below as a basis to define and demarcate international direct marketing.

In principle, transactions which are carried out across national borders can be regarded as international activities in a narrow sense. Here, a cross-border activity is defined in the spatial context first, and refers to a single activity. Such a narrow definition excludes preliminary or follow-up activities which are not themselves cross-border in nature. This certainly does not serve our purpose here. Preliminary and follow-up activities should accordingly be added to the list of international activities. We should also consider if, in multi-cultural societies like the United States or many European countries (Swiss Post 2006), this cross-border characteristic can be an adequate criterion for delimitation over the long term. By extension, an activity could have a de facto "international" character in the long term if it is addressed to a (sufficiently large) minority of foreign origin, e.g., the population of Latin American origin in the United States or the large Turkish minority in Germany. The definition of international direct marketing is the result of combining the definition of direct marketing and the definitions of international activities.

International direct marketing in a narrow sense

International direct marketing in a narrow sense includes only those market activities which use single-level (more direct) communication and/or direct distribution or dispatching for the purpose of individually addressing particular target groups abroad, and which happen to be cross-border in nature. International direct marketing in the narrowest sense also covers those market-oriented and cross-border activities which use multi-level communication to create direct, individual, cross-border contact.

International direct marketing in a broader sense

International direct marketing in a broader sense includes all market activities which use single-level (more direct) communication and/or direct distribution or dispatching for the purpose of individually addressing particular target groups abroad. International direct marketing in a broader sense also covers those market-oriented and cross-border activities which use multi-level communication to create direct, individual contact with target groups abroad.

International direct marketing in the broadest sense

Aside from the activities specified above, international direct marketing in the broadest sense includes all market activities which use single-level (more direct) communication and/or direct distribution or dispatching for the purpose of individually addressing particular target groups of foreign origin. International direct marketing in the broadest sense also covers those market-oriented activities which use multi-level communication to create direct, individual contact with target groups of foreign origin.

The difference between the definitions is obvious. The narrow definition covers only those activities which are themselves cross-border in nature. An example could be the sending of direct mails abroad, or searching for addresses using a foreign broker. The broader definition includes all preliminary and follow-up activities, whether they are implemented locally at home or abroad. The broadest definition is not tied to any fixed geographical base and focuses on the foreign origins of the target group. Thus direct mail campaigns directed at ethnic minorities in the home country also come under this expanded definition of international direct marketing. This makes sense, as the processes for these "international" mailings are the same and many of the basic conditions are similar. Hengst (2000) has already stressed that countries can have different, heterogeneous target groups. We can grasp this in the context of a case study, which highlights an example of a mailing sent to Turkish citizens in Germany (see the article on "Segment-specific ethnomarketing"). This clearly shows that the broadest definition of international direct marketing is the most appropriate for our purposes and will serve as the basis for our comments below.

3   Objectives and advantages of international direct marketing

Direct marketing was long equated solely with reaching specific sales goals. This impression, originally widespread, has substantially changed over the last decade. Thanks to the effectiveness of individual customer dialog via mailings, telecommunications and electronic media, today direct marketing is used to achieve all essential marketing goals. This is shown in an empirical investigation conducted in 2002 by the German Direct Marketing Federation (Gerdes 2002, p. 50). From the decision-maker's point of view, the main objectives of direct marketing are as follows:

- Acquiring new customers
- Building customer loyalty
- Improving customer service
- Reacquiring lost customers
- Sales of products and services
- Branding and brand management

The sequence of these intended objectives is also informative. The customer is located at the center of this communication, from the start of the relationship, through ongoing support, to winning back the customer (see also Robert and Berger 1999, p. 10). This hierarchy of objectives can probably also be transferred to international direct marketing, since many of the direct marketing decision-makers surveyed were also responsible for international direct marketing in their respective companies.

The advantages of direct marketing in achieving these objectives are obvious and can be summarized in three words: reportability, measurability and individuality (see also Spiller and Baier 2005, p. 9). This applies to both national and international direct marketing. Altogether there are six main success factors where the use of (international) direct and/or dialog marketing is especially valuable (see Holland 2004, p. 12):

1. Reacting to market trends
   (market niches; individualization; developments in information technology)
2. Dominance of customer orientation
   (customer loyalty; individual customer relationships)
3. Increasing effectiveness
   (customization; generating more interest)
4. Need for flexibility
   (internationalization, even for small budgets; flexible employment)
5. Accuracy in targeting objectives
   (reduced losses due to selectivity; rising costs for other communication and sales force)
6. Implementation of controlling
   (measurement of effectiveness; calculation of profit; testability)

Employing direct marketing is rewarding for many marketing management objectives. Here are some examples of such objectives (see Holland 2004, p. 20; Stone, Bond and Blake 2003, p. 44; Spiller and Baier 2005, p. 22):

- Acquiring customers:
  - Generating interest and conversion of prospective customers
  - Acquiring new customers
  - "Recommend-a-friend" advertising campaigns
- Achieving customer loyalty:
  - Customer activation and care
  - Collecting customer data
  - Promoting club activities
- Winning back customers:
  - Profiling, targeting
  - Individual customer retention offers
- Sales:
  - Direct sales
  - Testing product variations and innovations
  - Actions such as special offers and discounts
  - Up- and cross-selling
- Invitations
  - To trade fairs and events
  - Generating in-store traffic
- Classical communication:
  - Increasing awareness and promoting image
  - Exchange of information
- Other objectives:
  - Supporting the sales force
  - Gaining and cross-linking of enterprise-relevant data

Finally, the benefit of direct marketing should be seen from the customer perspective. These benefits relate to both national and international direct marketing.

Source: Meffert (2002), pp. 11-12

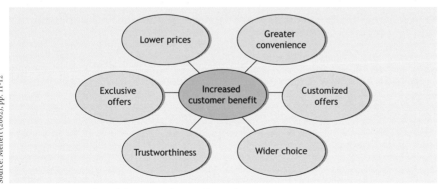

Figure 1-1: Benefits of direct marketing from the customer perspective

In the opinion of numerous authors, the satisfaction of individual needs is regarded as a central utility for the customer. This can be achieved either by exclusive offers targeted at a particular customer segment or, ideally, customized offers to individuals. Increased customer utility can also be generated by lower prices, wider choice and increased convenience, all of which may not be available through local retailers.

If a durable customer relationship can be achieved by targeted, professional direct marketing, then customer confidence also increases. Fig. 1-1 visually illustrates the dependence of customer utility on the above factors.

> ■ International direct marketing campaigns pursue three central objectives: the creation and management of customer relationships, the sale of goods and services, and branding and brand leadership. These objectives are the same as for national direct and dialog marketing campaigns.
> ■ International direct marketing offers three fundamental advantages: reportability, measurability and individuality.
> ■ International direct marketing is particularly valuable in support of six elementary success factors: reaction time, customer orientation, effectiveness, flexibility, targeting accuracy and controlling.

Figure 1-2: The advantages and objectives of international direct marketing

4   Development of international direct marketing

To our knowledge, no reliable statistics are available on the historical development of international direct marketing prior to the mid-1990s. The main reason for this is probably that, for a long time, neither state-owned post offices nor national direct marketing federations paid any particular attention to this area. One possible reason is that the field had a relatively small economic significance in relation to domestic direct marketing at this time. However, by the mid-1990s, when the first scientific studies on international direct marketing appeared, this was no longer the case. If we assume a typical diffusion development for international direct marketing, then we can infer that the first substantial development of international direct marketing began in the mid-1980s. The results of the first scientific studies support this, e.g., Padmanabhan (1990). In his study, he surveyed 140 European and US companies belonging to the American Direct Marketing Association (DMA). The findings reveal that, when targeting international markets, European companies tend to use direct marketing more than US companies, and consequently also have more experience and/or make better use of this tool. The fact that a study was conducted and that it received such a high response rate from the 640 companies surveyed, confirms that this tool was already in widespread use and of increasing interest by 1990.

By the mid-1990s, international direct marketing was already the subject of numerous studies (see the bibliography to this article). Topol and Sherman (1994) report disproportionate growth for international direct marketing as compared with national direct marketing, which was at the time the fastest-growing advertising medium in many countries (DMA 2004a). Other contemporary scientific studies support this. Spiller and Campbell (1994) report that 84% of small and medium-sized enterprises (SMEs) in the USA used international direct marketing. These figures were 94% in Canada and 75% in Mexico respectively (based on 180 SMEs). This unexpectedly high proportion is almost certainly due in part to the introduction of the North American Free Trade Agreement (NAFTA). The same scenario could also apply to the European integration process. Akhter (1996) reports that 37% of all US mail-order companies had established international programs overseas, and that another 20% wanted to introduce such programs soon. Some large mail-order companies, e.g. LL Bean and Lands' End, were already present in over 140 countries, without actually having a local presence. The latest international postal usage survey also indicates continuing growth in international direct marketing (DMA 2006). Iyer and Hill (1996) were able to confirm Padmanabhan's results (1990). Therefore it can be assumed that the US results, when transferred to Europe, are even higher.

Direct marketing expenditures (in millions of euros)										
Country	1992	1993	1994	1995	1996	1997	1998	1999	2000	2001
Austria				1,020	1,175	1,346	1,409	1,489	1,580	1,589
Belgium						917	656	660	718	727
Czech Rep.								151	192	230
Denmark	385	427	452	554	585	463	475	515	932	997
Finland	336	330	343	372	399	423	444	467	493	501
France	3,639	4,139	5,115	5,355	5,868	6,039	6,526	6,786	7,224	7,357
Germany	6,846	7,373	6,954	8,181	9,101	10,124	11,657	12,271	13,140	12,900
Great Britain	1,348	1,932	2,708	2,847	3,731	5,509	5,978	7,145	7,612	9,007
Greece				5					57	85
Hungary								134	152	187
Ireland	23	801	90	100	113	124	20	64	71	78
Italy	1,239	1,704	1,782	1,926	2,062	1,443	1,865	1,969	2,641	2,689
Netherlands	1,535	1,676	1,897	2,124	2,287	2,487	3,999	4,481	4,296	4,364
Poland									514	638
Portugal	13	19	23	26	30	35	38	42	54	59
Slovakia								10	14	47
Spain	66	1,657	1,742	1,844	1,973	2,151	2,415	2,825	3,163	3,196
Sweden	524	523	545	577	622	663	671	763	901	868
Switzerland									764	815

Source: FEDMA 2002, pp. 19

Figure 1-3: Comparative development of direct marketing expenditure in Europe

Each of these studies reveals only part of the story of the development of international direct marketing over this period without providing any actual indications of volume. The first quantitative references appear in the Statistical Fact Books of the DMA in the US, and in selected studies conducted by the Federation of Euro-

Direct marketing expenditure (in millions of US dollars)						
Country	2002	2003	2004	2007	98-03**	03-07**
USA*	144,494	151,985	160,952	191,155	4.4%	5.9%
Japan	71,729	75,851	80,140	97,287	2.2%	6.4%
Germany	27,941	30,586	33,375	41,393	4.7%	7.9%
Great Britain	18,322	19,955	21,493	26,275	5.2 %	7.1%
France	16,982	18,425	19,827	23,379	4.0%	6.1%
Italy	14,288	15,585	16,786	20,474	4.4%	7.1%
Canada	7,164	7,735	8,229	9,669	6.9%	5.7%
Taiwan	5,819	6,893	8,134	13,862	15.3%	19.1%
Netherlands	6,022	6,549	7,074	8,625	5.4%	7.1%
South Korea	4,931	5,728	6,518	9,681	23.7%	14.0%
Spain	4,994	5,458	5,953	7,438	5.4%	8.1%
Australia	4,788	5,323	5,797	7,371	8.4%	8.5%
Switzerland	4,925	5,060	5,188	5,576	-0.1%	2.5%
Belgium	4,407	4,814	5,210	6,402	4.4%	7.4%
Sweden	3,968	4,360	4,767	5,954	7.0%	8.1%
Hong Kong	3,265	3,821	4,484	6,751	2.8%	15.3%
Austria	2,927	3,174	3,414	4,128	4.9%	6.8%
Norway	2,646	2,817	2,957	3,409	9.9%	4.9%
Finland	2,365	2,617	2,872	3,617	7.7%	8.4%
Denmark	2,237	2,443	2,642	3,210	5.8%	7.1%
Ireland	2,054	2,392	2,748	3,915	14.5%	13.1%
Mexico	1,782	1,941	2,151	2,782	11.9%	9.4%
Argentina	1,151	1,256	1,364	1,707	0.6%	8.0%
Brazil	1,019	1,154	1,296	1,753	5.8%	11.0%
Portugal	606	673	745	955	6.6%	9.2%
Greece	565	630	706	910	7.2%	9.6%
New Zealand	521	551	578	725	4.0%	7.1%
Malaysia	452	536	638	992	12.5%	16.6%
South Africa	399	413	432	526	7.1%	6.3%
Thailand	156	173	187	245	6.6%	9.1%
Philippines	59	68	78	114	15.1%	13.9%
Total	362,978	388,966	416,735	510,280		

* USA based on DMA (2004a), p. 11 and p. 15

** DMA forecast (2004a)

Source: DMA 2004a, p. S. 218.

Figure 1-4: Comparative development of direct marketing expenditure worldwide

pean Direct Marketing (FEDMA). These studies provide an excellent overview of the development of direct marketing as a whole across various countries (see Figs. 1-3 and 1-4). It appears that, since 1990, direct marketing has not developed in the same way in all European countries (FEDMA 2002, 2005a). However, direct marketing seems to have grown strongly worldwide, particularly in Asia (DMA 2004a). A comparison of the direct marketing volumes given in each of these two studies highlights differences in the underlying definition of direct marketing. The DMA definition is substantially wider than the relatively narrow interpretation used in the FEDMA survey.

The differences between countries are exposed even more clearly when comparing direct marketing expenditure with that for traditional advertising media (see Fig. 1-5). It is apparent that, by 1998, direct marketing expenditure in the Netherlands already exceeded expenditure on traditional advertising. This trend can also be seen in many other large northern European countries, e.g., Germany, France, Denmark and Austria, as such outlays approached 80% of the amount spent for traditional advertising. By 2003, investment in direct marketing in Germany exceeded investment in traditional advertisement (ZAW 2004, Deutsche Post AG 2004b) for the first time. The data for the United States paints a similar picture (DMA 2004a).

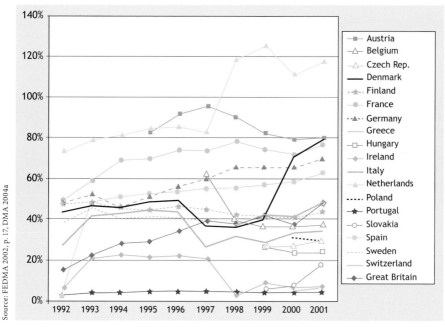

Figure 1-5: Proportion of direct marketing expenditure (as % of traditional advertising)

The DMA study (2004a) further highlights the wide differences in mailing volumes and per capita expenditure on direct marketing around the world (see Fig.

Expenditure on direct marketing (in US dollars per capita)				
Country	**2002**	**2003**	**2004**	**2007**
USA*	501	522	547	630
Japan	564	596	629	762
Germany	339	370	403	497
Great Britain	309	338	361	437
France	285	308	330	384
Italy	248	270	291	355
Canada	228	244	258	295
Taiwan	260	306	359	602
Netherlands	373	403	433	518
South Korea	104	119	135	197
Spain	122	133	144	178
Australia	244	267	288	352
Switzerland	676	688	700	735
Belgium	426	464	499	605
Sweden	445	487	531	656
Hong Kong	481	558	649	953
Austria	364	394	423	508
Norway	583	617	645	731
Finland	455	502	550	689
Denmark	416	453	488	586
Ireland	524	601	680	928
Mexico	18	19	21	26
Argentina	32	34	37	45
Brazil	6	7	7	9
Portugal	60	66	73	93
Greece	53	59	66	84
New Zealand	132	138	142	171
Malaysia	19	22	25	37
South Africa	9	9	9	11
Thailand	3	3	3	4
Philippines	1	1	1	1

Source: DMA (2004), p. 213

* USA based on DMA (2004a), p. 11 and p. 15

Figure 1-6: Comparative direct marketing expenditure per capita

1-6). The relevant reference values for the USA, Japan and Switzerland show that direct marketing still has considerable potential in many countries (DMA 2004a). Despite significantly higher direct marketing expenditure per capita, response rates in the USA still make such investment economically viable. The DMA's Response Rate Report (2004b) shows that the average response rates are approximately 10% for existing customers and 2.5% for new customers.

The absolute expenditures on direct marketing provided above can be used as base values to produce a rough estimate of the volume growth in international

Source: DMA 2004a, p. 213

Share of sales from international mailings (in %) (only 100 companies)	Origin of enterprises		
	All	US	Non-US
No share of sales	25%	33%	12%
1-25%	14%	14%	12%
26-50%	15%	21%	12%
51-75%	8%	5%	12%
76-100%	37%	26%	52%
Total (surveyed)	48%	38%	62%
Total (sales-weighted)	45%	36%	59%

Example: 26% of all US mail-order companies have a share of sales of 76-100% abroad, while in Europe 52% of all mail-order companies achieve this.

Figure 1-7: Proportion of mail-order company sales from international campaigns, 2003

direct marketing. In addition, the DMA survey (2004a) can be used to ascertain the share of sales due to international direct marketing as a proportion of gross sales by mail-order companies in 2003. Fig. 1-7 shows the main conclusions.

A direct comparison of European and US companies confirms the trend seen in the two previous studies, namely that European mail-order companies derive a substantially larger proportion of their sales from international direct marketing. If the results are weighted using the median of the share of sales, the average resulting proportion of sales due to international direct marketing is 45.1% for those mail-order companies surveyed. If we accepted that the resources used by mail-order companies can be transposed to national and international direct marketing, this would represent an amazingly high proportion. We can definitely assume that the composition of the sample significantly inflates this value. Nevertheless, it does not seem unrealistic to estimate that expenditure on international direct marketing accounted for about 10% of the entire direct marketing expenditure made in industrial nations in 2003. Based on the studies carried out so far, it is highly probable that this proportion will continue to grow disproportionately faster than the rise in direct marketing expenditure, even if this applies only to cross-border trade under the narrowest of international direct marketing definitions. Therefore, we can assume that international direct marketing already represents an important subsegment whose importance continues to grow. Fig. 1-8 gives a rough, conservative estimate of the volume of international direct marketing from 2002 to 2007. Based on this estimate, the volume of international direct marketing should more than double, from approximately $33 billion in 2002 to around $71.4 billion in 2007. In our opinion, the volume of international direct marketing will shift increasingly in favor of interactive online media, and this is borne out by the expectations of internationally active direct marketing marketeers (DMA 2004a). This is due to the cost advantage, timeliness and flexibility of this communication medium. Direct mail, however, will remain the dominant medium for some time to come.

Expenditure on international direct marketing (in millions of US dollars)**				
Country	2002	2003	2004	2007
USA*	13,004	15,199	17,705	26,762
Japan	6,456	7,585	8,815	13,620
Germany	2,515	3,059	3,671	5,795
Great Britain	1,649	1,996	2,364	3,679
France	1,528	1,843	2,181	3,273
Italy	1,286	1,559	1,846	2,866
Canada	645	774	905	1,354
Taiwan	524	689	895	1,941
Netherlands	542	655	778	1,208
South Korea	444	573	717	1,355
Spain	449	546	655	1,041
Australia	431	532	638	1,032
Switzerland	443	506	571	781
Belgium	397	481	573	896
Sweden	357	436	524	834
Hong Kong	294	382	493	945
Austria	263	317	376	578
Norway	238	282	325	477
Finland	213	262	316	506
Denmark	201	244	291	449
Ireland	185	239	302	548
Mexico	160	194	237	389
Argentina	104	126	150	239
Brazil	92	115	143	245
Portugal	55	67	82	134
Greece	51	63	78	127
New Zealand	47	55	64	102
Malaysia	41	54	70	139
South Africa	36	41	48	74
Thailand	14	17	21	34
Philippines	5	7	9	16
Total	**32,668**	**38,897**	**45,841**	**71,439**

Assumption: 9%, 10%, 11%, 14% proportion of international direct marketing

* USA based on DMA (2004), p. 11 and 15, ** Source: own estimate

Figure 1-8: Estimates of international direct marketing volume

5   Decision criteria for entry

The management decision to embark upon international direct marketing is of major consequence and thus of a strategic nature. The criteria on which such decisions are made are comparable with those used for the evaluation of new markets. The decision to pursue international direct marketing is often subordinate to the decision on how to canvass the new market, and this in turn depends on a number of factors (Anderson and Coughlan 1987). However, Spiller and Campbell (1994) show in their study that the decision by a company to export goods and services is usually followed immediately by the launch of an international direct marketing campaign. This section focusses on the pros and cons of developing the market by means of international direct marketing.

The criteria for the fundamental decision to develop new markets and to pursue appropriate marketing strategies will be discussed here only briefly (see inter alia, Szymanski, Bharadwaj and Varadarajan 1993; Jain 1989 and the relevant bibliographies for more information on this topic). Basically, the company itself must ensure that the venture is placed on adequate footing. This means, for example, that company resources should not already be fully employed in the domestic market (Hengst 2000). In fact, entry into international direct marketing needs substantial resources within the company itself (McDonald 1998 inter alia). Apart from the financial investment, the demands on management resources should not be underestimated. The successful development of a new foreign market depends in particular on the extent to which highly qualified personnel are employed on the project (Neumann and Nagel 2000). Since conditions within foreign markets are frequently in flux, companies need the commitment of experienced staff who are ready to make prompt adjustments to marketing and product programs where necessary. Simply replicating the home market approach can often result in rapid failure (Neumann and Nagel 2000). Even if the first step is successful enough without adaptation, it has to be assumed that the foreign competition will be able to react. In this case, it may not just be competition in the targeted foreign market that is intensified: foreign competitors may now decide to enter the company's own home market. Even if the foreign competitor does not make money it may be enough to sufficiently weaken the position of the new competitor through such an action (Akhter 1996). Apart from experience in (national) direct marketing, good positioning in the home market and availability of resources, a certain willingness to take risks and an openness to international influences are further attributes that companies intending to enter international markets will need (McDonald 1998, Topol and Sherman 1994 inter alia).

However, even with the complexity caused by the new situation, the associated investment and risk, a decision to enter new markets can also provide outstanding prospects (Hengst 2000). This applies above all to the basic goal of any company, i.e., the making of higher profits. The potential for higher profits can be improved both by increasing sales and cutting costs - a benefit of greater economies of scale (Akhter 1996). Likewise, internationalization presents a company with new strategic options. Entry into international markets can keep (potential) competitors busy far from the company's own home market, thereby creating barriers to entry of competitors into domestic markets (Akhter 1996).

International direct marketing is a special form of market development.[1] It is characterized by the fact that the company is directly addressing its potential customers in the foreign market. Alternatively, the company can turn to intermediaries for assistance (Akhter 1996), with the adavantage that it simply needs to send its goods to the foreign market and negotiate the conditions. In this case, the foreign target groups and local circumstances are, apart from any minor product adaptations, of only indirect concern. This strategy contains several disadvantages. For instance, there is no direct feedback from the target groups, and therefore the ultimate cause of any problems is often not properly recognized – was it the product design, the price or the launch campaign? In addition, using intermediaries requires significant upfront investment, often substantially cutting into the profit margin for the company (Akhter 1996).

In many cases, international direct marketing therefore represents a cost-effective option with many advantages for the company (Iyer and Hill 1996). Direct contact with the target group also offers the company comparably fast feedback. Any problems in the marketing mix - i.e., from the product to the price all the way to the promotional campaign - can be identified and fixed at short notice. Effective progress monitoring through the use of tests enables the company to use new information rapidly and, by extension, thus moderating associated risks more effectively. Generally, risks can be limited effectively by controlling the scope of market entry. International direct marketing's fast, simple implementation also makes it a cheap form of internationalization and particularly attractive to small and medium-sized enterprises (Iyer and Hill 1996, Albers and Gelb 1991). In the long term, the potential acquisition of regular customers offers a substantial source of growth and shareholder value for the company.

International direct marketing, according to a study by Topol and Sherman (1994), is usually employed by companies which are more innovative and more willing to take risks than others. This is due to significantly higher confidence in their own abilities. The high number of small and medium-sized enterprises in the USA, Canada and Mexico, which, according to the study by Spiller and Campbell (1994) referred to in section 3, already use international direct marketing, puts this statement into perspective. International direct marketing generally seems to be regarded as a popular tool for opening up and maintaining international markets, irrespective of company size or sector. Its benefits can be leveraged by any sound business.

Finally, it can be stated that international direct marketing represents a comparatively simple, quick-to-implement and cost-effective alternative for entering

---

[1] As an alternative, market development can take the form of exports, licensing, joint ventures, contract manufacturing, direct investments or management contracting (Spiller and Baier 2005, p. 378). None of these forms of market entry, however, exclude the use of international direct marketing.

and maintaining international markets (Iyer and Hill 1996). In combination with an effective risk control, it offers an especially attractive strategic option for small and medium-sized enterprises (Spiller and Campbell 1994, Albers and Gelb 1991). The following section describes in detail the classical procedure for implementing international direct marketing.

▨ The employment of international direct marketing is often associated with a general decision to develop new foreign markets.

▨ The company itself should be well established in its home market and possess the necessary additional resources.

▨ Despite the financial investment, the necessary employment of highly qualified personnel to this task should not be neglected.

▨ Entry into the new market usually meets with local competition, which may decide to retaliate and enter the company's home market.

▨ Nevertheless, international direct marketing generally offers outstanding prospects with many advantages in its implementation compared to alternative market entry strategies.

▨ The advantages of international direct marketing are in particular due to the ease and speed of implementation, its relatively low cost and its manageable risk exposure.

Figure 1-9: Decision criteria for the use of international direct marketing

6   How to proceed

An iterative process follows the decision to enter international markets using direct marketing instruments. This is presented here in sequential order: it has been analyzed in different ways in numerous studies and articles. The concepts, processes and principles are therefore, with certain exceptions, the same as those used in general and/or national direct marketing (McDonald 1998). This has resulted in an established model that is used to provide the framework for this section (see Fig. 1-10).

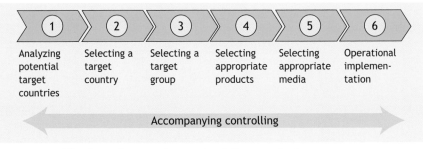

Figure 1-10: The classical steps in international direct marketing

These individual steps are described in more detail below, where the main insights of the relevant international publications on these topics are compiled, commented on and placed in the overall context.

6.1 Selecting the target country

Before embarking upon international direct marketing, companies need to analyze each of the target countries and select one of these. The simultaneous selection of several countries has proven to be impractical, even though doing so would allow the enterprise to spread its risk. Differences in the general conditions and between target groups across countries often increase the complexity so much that the resources for successful multinational entry are no longer sufficient (McDonald 1998, Hengst 2000 inter alia). Yorgey (1999a) uses the example of Rodale Press to demonstrate that entering markets in different countries sequentially can be a worthwhile alternative to entering several markets simultaneously. Fig. 1-11 shows the standard list of criteria for selecting a target country (see also McDonald 1998). Padmanabhan (1990) states that US-american and European companies (and possibly others) use similar criteria for the selection of a target country. The most important criteria are described here in greater detail (see also Spiller and Baier 2005, p. 376).

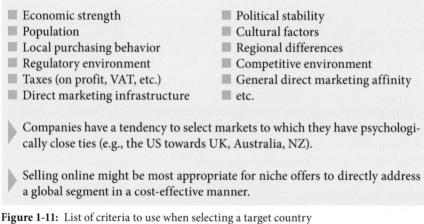

- Economic strength
- Population
- Local purchasing behavior
- Regulatory environment
- Taxes (on profit, VAT, etc.)
- Direct marketing infrastructure
- Political stability
- Cultural factors
- Regional differences
- Competitive environment
- General direct marketing affinity
- etc.

▶ Companies have a tendency to select markets to which they have psychologically close ties (e.g., the US towards UK, Australia, NZ).

▶ Selling online might be most appropriate for niche offers to directly address a global segment in a cost-effective manner.

Figure 1-11: List of criteria to use when selecting a target country

For a final decision each of the country-selection criteria listed above is weighted differently according to the characteristics of the product involved, e.g., its features and its usage situations. For instance, certain goods like necessities and discount products depend less on robust economic circumstances (McDonald 1998, Hengst 2000 inter alia). The size and structure of the population are often another critical factor. This is especially important when the product must be adapted according to local usage or to the average purchasing power of the target group (McDonald 1998 inter alia). The expected return on investment and the associated risks involved in entering the market can be more easily justified if the market is of a suitable size and/or offers large potential. It should be noted that, in many countries, the use of average values for the whole population can be misleading and thus lead to false conclusions. In many countries, regional differences between population centers and rural areas are often substantially greater than in Germany or France. Even large countries such as Brazil, which have acceptable average economic values, are good examples of this, as are countries such as Poland and Hungary (see also Neumann and Nagel 2000). Also the purchasing behavior of consumers differs not only between countries, but there may exist great heterogeneity within certain countries (Hengst 2000). Purchasing behavior is often historically and culturally conditioned. Close preliminary examination is therefore important (see also Rawwas et al. 1996, Gehrt and Shim 1998) and market research studies as well as the company's own tests can help in this regard. The test results will quickly indicate the appropriate level of investment for the product, price and promotional campaign (see also Neumann and Nagel 2000, 2007 for an explanation of the tool used by Deutsche Post). These are all important criteria for the selection of target countries. Investment requirements can increase substantially, especially when there is already intensive competition in the prospective target country.

In most cases, it can be assumed that the country is politically stable. Otherwise, investment in international direct marketing is often quite straightforward to manage. Political stability is of more importance with regard to the regulatory environment for direct marketing in the target country, e.g., privacy regulation (McDonald 1998 inter alia). While guidelines in the European Union and the United States are usually stable, this cannot be assumed as a matter of course in Eastern Europe, Asia and Latin America (FEDMA 2004c). But even within Europe there are numerous differences in the detail of regulation that require closer study (see the article "The Robinson Lists for Effective Direct Marketing").

Finally, the direct marketing experience and affinity, as well as the available infrastructure should all play a substantial role in the selection of a target country. Select studies provide key figures and comparisons for many countries, e.g., The Direct Marketing Monitor International, published annually since 2003 (Deutsche Post AG 2003, 2004, 2005, 2006 see final chapter, Swiss Post 2005), or the annotated descriptions of Neumann and Nagel (2000). Greater experience of direct marketing on the part of consumers usually indicates the presence of a better infrastructure (Akhter 1988). This is also apparent from the international comparison of 16 countries by Rosenfield (1994). Consequently, in many countries there is already a solid support structure for list material, list broking, agencies, lettershops and distribution all the way up to returns management. Companies can and should make use of these when implementing their direct marketing campaigns (McDonald 1998; Hengst 2000; Akhter 1988; inter alia). The general affinity towards direct marketing among the population requires independent assessment. Decisions cannot necessarily be made based on the average direct marketing experience of the population or on the infrastructure. In some large countries, for example, there are only a relatively small number of target groups with an affinity for direct marketing, which, owing to the size of the total population, may nonetheless be sufficiently large to justify a substantial infrastructure (McDonald 1999). Closer consideration should similarly also be given to the evolution of the indigenous direct marketing industry: which product categories are currently available via the direct marketing, how many foreign goods and service providers are already active in the market, etc.

Previous studies have shown that, when embarking upon international direct marketing, the majority of companies select countries with which they feel a certain psychological affinity. For example, US companies tend to start by targeting Canada and the UK, Australia or New Zealand. German companies, however, give first preference to Austria and Switzerland. A common language is often just one indicator of the cultural and historical proximity of countries (Iyer and Hill 1996; Hengst 2000).

Experience in international markets reveals an array of generalizations about individual regions or countries. In the eyes of US business, for example, European Union markets appear quite attractive, but at the same time fiercely contested. China and India have less competition, but companies have to devote considerable time and money in order to successfully enter these markets (McDonald 1998, Hengst 2000 inter alia). According to McDonald (1999), the main reason for this is that the direct marketing industry is still relatively young in these two countries, which are also very large and heterogeneous in their structures. In both countries, economic development has so far focused almost exclusively on metropolitan areas, and yet addressable segments of over 100 million prospective direct marketing customers have emerged in each country. The greatest obstacle remains the inadequate infrastructure for direct marketing that exists in many countries (Hengst 2000). In Latin America, the Brazilian market attracts the special attention of American direct marketeers. Households in Brazil already receive an average of up to ten mailings per month, although the availability of name lists is limited. The postal system is nevertheless regarded as adequate when compared to China, India or Russia (McDonald 1999). McDonald (1999) sees medium-term potential for successful direct marketing in all of these countries, especially if applied selectively and with local adaptations. Hengst (2000) also recommends that enterprises consider Japan, South Korea, Taiwan and Hong Kong as potential target countries in Asia, as well as Australia and New Zealand.

In parallel with the selection of a country and market entry by means of classic direct marketing, the internet is also being used more and more frequently as a universal distribution channel (Lester 2002, Mehta, Grewal and Sivadas 1996). This can be particularly worthwhile if the international target group is homogeneous. Levitt (1983) was the first to consider this in depth. A well-known example is the online retailer Amazon, which began to offer the option of international delivery soon after start-up. Yet even for this first step in the internationalization of a company, the individual stages of the process have to be well thought-out. As with classic direct marketing, this applies to such things as taxes, laws, payment collection and distribution procedures. Each element within the process has to be adapted and coordinated with respect to the target countries, so as to guarantee, insofar as possible, the success of the international direct marketing campaign. In this way, the selection of the foreign target group goes hand-in-hand with the selection of the target country. This applies similarly to international direct marketing in its broadest sense. Here, the foreign target group is the first priority as well. However, an analysis of the country of origin of the foreign target group will also give a good idea on how to approach the foreign target group in one's own country.

6.2 The foreign target group

After selecting the target country, companies have to specify the target group and produce an operational description. In practice, the first step is usually to focus on a domestic target group that has proved to be a good starting point in the past. Detailed profiles are usually available for a company's own regular customers based on many years of experience in the home market. Consequently, such groups are often the starting point for selecting addresses in the target market (e.g., Yorgey 1999b; Neumann and Nagel 2000).

Nevertheless, companies that focus on familiar profiles without undertaking a thorough investigation risk encountering some nasty surprises. It is well known in marketing research circles, for example, that socio-demographic criteria per se cannot reliably predict the purchasing attitudes of individual consumers (see also Gehrt and Shim 1998). The differences between the purchasing attitudes and behavior of consumers in different countries have already been addressed several times in scientific studies (Hengst 2000; Deutsche Post 2003, 2004a; Deutsche Post 2006, Swiss Post 2006). Especially the recent study produced by Deutsche Post (2006) gives some interesting insights into consumer attitudes towards direct marketing by product category across 24 major countries. For many countries, however, it is nearly impossible to gain access to the additional information required to produce a sound analysis (Soricello 1996). In this case, it makes sense for companies to undertake their own market research, although this involves additional costs.

The reasons for using mail-order by consumers differ substantially from country to country. In France, the emphasis is on the relaxed shopping atmosphere associated with catalog shopping, while in the USA, "convenience" is the dominant theme (Gehrt and Shim 1998). Milne, Beckman and Taubman (1996) use an investigation into the attitudes of Argentine consumers to show how consumer attitudes towards direct marketing differ systematically between Argentina and the United States. According to Rawwas, Strutton and Johnson (1996), this also applies to US and Australian consumers, while Lee (2004), highlights certain differences between consumer attitudes in Taiwan and the USA. In a comparison of German and US target groups, moreover, McDonald (1994) demonstrates that, with regards to direct marketing, even purchasing decision processes can differ depending on the cultural context. This means that, in many cases, the product benefits being communicated and even the form of advertising have to be adapted quite substantially in order to sell the same product portfolio to foreign target groups. Since this implies additional costs, it may be necessary to re-examine the selected target country when determining the target group. It therefore appears that the ideal process should be seen purely as a guide, since a different sequence and emphasis may be required depending on the circumstances.

In sum, companies should draw on the traditional marketing criteria when analyzing and determining target groups. However, particular attention has to be paid to the complex differences between countries. Despite numerous studies, there are often only regular tests and the company's own market research that are truly effective (Soricello 1996, Neumann and Nagel 2000). Domestic customer profiles, however unpredictable, have proven to be a good starting point. The specific data gathered in this respect by companies with international direct marketing experience confirms this. According to the study conducted by Topol and Sherman (1994), only 6% of all companies actually enter a new foreign market with a completely new strategy, and only 9% of the companies surveyed leave their strategy completely unchanged. The vast majority (72%) of all the companies surveyed adapted their successful domestic market strategies to the relevant target country.

- Customer profiles from the domestic market are usually a starting point for companies seeking to define a foreign target group.
- The general direct marketing experience of consumers in a particular market represents a good indicator of the prospects for direct marketing campaigns in that market.
- In many countries, there is only limited access to well-founded descriptions of the target group.
- The shopping behavior of consumers differs between countries.
- The company's own tests and market research are the best tools for adapting a domestic customer profile to the target market.
- 72% of all companies that use international direct marketing substantially adapt their proven domestic strategy, while only 6% develop a completely new strategy and only 9% leave their strategy unchanged.

Figure 1-12: Determining foreign target groups

6.3 Selecting suitable products

At the same time as selecting the target group, companies have also to specify a suitable product or product range. Hardly any company will decide to develop a foreign market using its full product program and service range (Neumann and Nagel 2000).

Management is often in a quandary when faced with the selection of a product and/or product range. On the one hand, the product program should be attractive to the foreign target group, with the largest possible range of products and services contained in the first offer. On the other hand, risk has to be contained. This latter consideration usually predominates. So, when marketing abroad, companies choose products from their portfolio which require little explanation and have low service needs. Additionally, because of the associated costs, products with lower return ratios are seen as more desirable, as are products cheap enough to justifiably be left with the customer in case of complaints (Iyer and Hill 1996).

Selecting such products is therefore mostly dominated by risk minimization. The simple structure of the products should also ensure that the target group receives the best possible first impression of the provider of the goods or services, thereby transferring the product image as successfully as possible from the home market. However, selecting such products also has a crucial disadvantage: competition for these products is often relatively high in the target country, and it is consequently difficult for the new provider to differentiate its offer. In this case, it is often necessary to ensure a substantial price advantage for simple product variants to provide the customer with a sufficient benefit.

One alternative is the adaptation of one's own products. This involves some costs, but also offers substantial possibilities. For instance, it is thereby easier to take local customer needs and potential purchasing power into account. Yorgey (1999a) uses the example of a worldwide encyclopedia of traditional household goods with a medical use to demonstrate that this method can be very successful. Of US origin, the encyclopedia was initially accepted only very hesitantly by the European market, as none of the remedies used was of local origin. However, by incorporating European home remedies, the company was able to persuade many customers in the target countries to view the encyclopedia as a local product. In fact, these remedies used in foreign countries have now also been incorporated into new editions of the US version.

When considering the selection of products, companies have to take into account the legal requirements. In addition to the needs of the target group and the competitive offerings, this includes such matters as warranties and product safety regulations. An examination by relevant local institutions or lawyers is recommended in order to avoid subsequent lawsuits or compulsory product returns.

6.4 Selecting suitable media

The selection of the target group and the product forms the basis for the selection of a suitable direct marketing platform. Now, many countries offer the same portfolio of direct marketing media: addressed and unaddressed direct mail, both door-to-door and household distributions, group advertising media, advertisements with coupons, inserts, radio and TV advertisements as well as telemarketing. Lester (2003a) recommends the parallel use of the internet as a direct marketing and communication tool. In their study, Spiller and Campbell (1994) show that many small enterprises also regard their sales force as a direct marketing medium.

Companies might, for the sake of convenience, be tempted to employ the same media across all markets. However, this can often prove to be dangerous. Iyer and Hill (1996) and Topol and Sherman (1994) each demonstrate this in their studies:

US companies usually prefer catalogs and direct mail as an entry medium (43% and 41% respectively of the 233 companies surveyed), much as they do in their home markets. However, it is worthwhile examining the advertising environment in the target market more closely. For one thing, the media in the target country may be subject to regulations which differ from those of the domestic market (Hengst 2000). For instance, specific products may be excluded from certain media or the use of certain media may not be permitted for the acquisition of new customers. Tempest illustrates this point by citing legislation currently in force in Denmark (see "Robinson Lists for Effective Direct Marketing").

More important, however, is the fact that media in different countries are used differently by the consumers (McDonald 1998, Light and Somasundaram 1994 inter alia). While in Italy it may be normal to use a newspaper as the medium for a certain product, in Germany the same product is typically marketed via direct mailings. The selection of suitable media should therefore be guided by the typical use to which particular media are put in the country in question. Also, basic attitudes about individual media - as well as attitudes about use - can vary significantly across different countries. Light and Somasundaram (1994), for example, examine the attitudes of young people to different direct marketing media in the USA, Canada, Hong Kong and India. Their findings show that the people in each country associate different characteristics with the media in question, and emphasize different uses for them. A consumer survey by Durvasula, Akhter and Bamossy (1996) produced similar results – albeit with slight variations – in the USA, the Netherlands and Singapore. Typical usage scenarios should therefore be considered before selecting a particular type of media, while the final marketing campaign should be adapted to the chosen medium. The validity of this approach has been proven by running multiple simultaneous test campaigns across various media (Soricello 1996). An evaluation of these experiments led to highly unexpected results in certain cases.

- Analyze the local advertising environment in the target country.
- Establish media mix according to intended use and product environment.
- Adapt campaign and media mix to local usage.
- Conduct test campaigns using individual media types (e.g., test mailings and test advertisements).
- Integrate electronic media: adapt website to the target country and use it as an inexpensive communication and response channel.

▶ Media usage differs strongly in cultural and historical terms in individual countries.

▶ Successful domestic campaigns usually need to be adapted to the target country if their success is to repeated.

Figure 1-13: Selection of direct marketing media abroad

6.5 Operational implementation

Processing operational details usually takes up the most time. The points addressed above provide the framework for action. Iterative steps are usually taken, during which even prior decisions need to be re-examined on the basis of new insights drawn from operational implementation. These insights may relate to any one of the following operational aspects: address lists, necessary payment options, local implementation of communication and marketing messages, operational implementation of local direct marketing strategies, and fulfillment aspects. Fig. 1-14 gives a summary of the topics.

- **Lists**
  (addresses, systems, samples,
  nixies/duplicates, list type
  [response vs. compiled])
- **Typical payment options**
  (currencies, purchasing power,
  payment terms and types)
- **Local communication and
  adaptation of the marketing message**
  (local addressing and response,
  translation and copy-writers)

- **Possible product adaptation**
  (to local purchasing power
  and preferences)
- **Operative implementation
  of adjustment**
  (institutions, suppression files)
- **Lettershop**
- **Fulfillment**
  (orders, storage, shipping,
  customs and taxes, return
  handling, non-deliverables,
  distribution options for the
  customer)

▶ Regular testing of all aspects has proven its worth.

▶ Local support is highly recommended, whether from local advisers or from a well-represented international service provider.

Figure 1-14: Summary on operational aspects

Addresses

The customer profile of the target group, as defined above, forms the basis for selecting lists of addresses for a foreign target market. It is a major challenge to convert the target group profile into an address list. In fact, Lester (1999) asserts that attaining an address list that is up to date and qualified constitutes 40% of the success of an international direct marketing campaign. It follows that numerous articles in the professional press already tackled the procedure for procuring suitable addresses for foreign target markets. All articles maintain that the pros and cons of potential foreign markets are often viewed from a "domestic" perspective. The articles nevertheless provide substantial insights.

In fact, the domestic profile can only ever serve as a starting point in the search for any addresses search (e.g., Yorgey 1999b). All articles stress that these profiles should only be an initial starting point, and offer examples to back this up: Hornikel (2004) emphasizes that even the most accurate definition of the domestic purchasing power are very difficult to transpose from one market to another. For instance, a person deemed reasonably affluent in Germany would, in certain Eastern European countries, belong to a very small, privileged group. Another example relates to the textile industry, where a product sold in Germany to a female target group of around 50 years of age would, in France, be sold to a target group approximately ten years older. The study of shopping behavior by Rawwas, Strutton and Johnson (1996) shows that consumer attitudes can also differ substantially. This is even the case when – from a European point of view – two groups appear relatively similar: Australian and US consumers, for example. Such differences can have a considerable impact on the structure of the campaign.

The domestic profile can therefore only be an initial starting point for any address search. Before the profile can be adapted successfully to the target market, the company has to overcome several additional challenges. For instance, in many countries there are less address providers available than in Germany, France, the USA or the UK. This applies both to the B2B and B2C markets. A further problem is that, in many countries, several of the lists available are derived from the same source (Lester 1999a). In most countries, this is due to a direct marketing infrastructure that is less than ideal. According to a current study by Swiss Post (2004), within Europe, the UK, Germany, France, Switzerland and the Netherlands are the only countries with a sufficiently high density of address providers. Southwards and eastwards, this density dissipates strongly and address searches become more difficult. According to its own account, Deutsche Post AG is one of the largest B2B address providers resident in every significant market (Deutsche Post 2004, p. 14, 2005a, 2005b). Covering 53 countries around the globe, Millar (2003) may provide a valuable resource for managers seeking local expert services.

The challenges however relate not only to the availability of addresses, but in particular to their quality and testability (McDonald 1998, Hengst 2000, Spiller and Baier 2005, p. 380, *inter alia*). International direct marketing studies prove that testing is usually possible, at least for database addresses. Samples are gladly provided in nearly all countries. The problem in many countries becomes particularly acute where mail-order buyer lists and/or response lists are concerned. Since a company cannot usually examine such lists on its own, only experienced and respectable list brokers or contacts in the industry can be of service here. Lester (1999a) and other authors have developed a list of questions which may be helpful in evaluating foreign address lists:

1. Is a selection according to active customers possible?
2. How have these addresses been acquired (advertising, etc.)?
3. In which frequency are addresses updated and mailed to?
4. Is there a compensation for returns?
5. What is the number of regular list users?
6. Is there a compensation for nixies/internal duplicates?

As a rule, mail-order buyer lists have proven to be the better choice abroad. The decision on whether to purchase or rent a list can also be quite different because of lower purchase prices in certain countries except for Germany, where rental is the norm (see also Yorgey 1999a).

As a consequence, almost all authors state that the use of local list brokers is usually a worthwhile investment and a key to success (Lester 1999a). With their assistance, local adaptations of domestic customer profiles can also usually be achieved quickly and professionally.

Typical payment options

Local price structures and local methods of payment often present an unexpected challenge (Hengst 2000). US mail-order companies in particular were used to starting with just one payment option: an identical amount in US dollars irrespective of the country, payable in advance via a widely acceptable credit card (Iyer and Hill 1996).

This however causes irritation among prospective customers in many countries. First of all, in many places credit cards are not as widespread as in the United States or Western Europe. Even in Germany, credit cards were still relatively uncommon at the start of the 1990s. Secondly, order values in US dollars place an additional limitation on the potential target group, especially in countries with low average incomes or foreign exchange controls. As many products are already manufactured in India or China, an adapted and still profitable pricing reflecting local purchasing power is becoming more and more viable (McDonald 1998 *inter alia*). Systematic price tests can be of assistance in this case (Lester 2003a). Contrary to US companies, those in the European Union are already much more likely to adapt their approach to local conditions (Iyer and Hill 1996). The implementation of a local pricing concept should also take into account possible fluctuations in the exchange rate. Exchange rate cover is recommended if necessary (McDonald 1998 *inter alia*).

The typical payment methods also differ widely between countries (Hengst 2000, Lester 2001a). For instance, in Germany, unlike many other countries, payment is frequently by direct debit following receipt of the goods. It is therefore useful for companies to have a local account, as customers are reluctant to transfer money abroad. Such an approach, however, also requires a prior credit check of potential recipients (Yorgey 1999b). UK and French providers are rarely prepared to do this, as in these countries it is usual to attach a check to the order (Lester 2001a). Local customs regarding payment by installments can also vary. In Germany, the minimum amount considered acceptable for such a payment method is often substantially higher than in other countries (Yorgey 1999a). German mail-order companies have to adjust to this in the context of international direct marketing. The problems with foreign currencies have largely been solved, at least with regards to intra-European goods and services. Unfortunately, this standardization has created a new problem. In new target countries, the website for the market is often modified at the same time as the offer (Lester 2003a). If the price and the payment methods for this market are now indicated in euros, customers in the home market or in other target countries may become aware of this. In this case, the decision to adjust prices according to purchasing power and offer different payment methods to different markets may have an unintended strategic boomerang effect.

Locally adapted forms of communication and address

The communication strategy developed for the domestic market is generally refined to become quite successful over time, and is therefore normally taken as a starting point when formulating a suitable advertising message for foreign target markets (Yorgey 1999a inter alia). However, it should be remembered that messages and forms of direct marketing which have proven successful in the domestic market are often the results of major efforts, and similar efforts are required in foreign target markets. When addressing the local customer, it is essential to take account of local customs (McDonald 1998, Soricello 1996 inter alia). The marketing message may have to be completely revised depending on the cultural environment and the attitudes of consumers (Soricello 1996). A professional translation of a tried-and-tested domestic message by local copywriters will not usually be sufficient. Instead, companies are urged to seek professional local support when designing a new campaign for a foreign market (McDonald 1998, Neumann and Nagel 2000, Soricello 1996, Yorgey 1999a and 1999b inter alia, see the article "International Dialog for the Successful Acquisition of New Customers"). Soricello (1996) cites the Far East as an example, where personally addressed mailings containing a picture of the director of the company and a personal recommendation have proven successful. The success of this approach is due to the basic pattern of purchasing behavior in Asia, where people rely strongly on recommendations from acquaintances. Therefore, they wish to ensure that the product meets their standards. The study by Iyer and Hill (1996) shows that this form of recommendation is much more widely used by EU companies than by their US competitors. However, there are only a few examples of such marketing delivering satisfactory results in Europe and the USA.

Apart from adapting the marketing message, Lester (2001a) also points out that the usual purchase incentives can differ strongly between countries. In France, for example, sweepstakes are widely used, even though these have proven less effective in other countries.

The provision of a local contact address for all key media is the final step in localizing forms of address (McDonald 1998, Hengst 2000, Yorgey 1999b *inter alia*). According to numerous studies, this works well because it builds confidence with the potential customers and makes it easier for them to make contact. Simply using call diversion or a local PO box is insufficient, however, unless at least one of the company's employees can communicate adequately in the language of the relevant country. However, this problem can usually be overcome easily with local assistance, provided the direct marketing infrastructure is good enough (e.g., Yorgey 1999b). Here again, Millar (2003) provides a good starting point for managers seeking local expert advice or help with implementation issues.

Local product adaptations

As already mentioned - in the context of product selection and the strategic selection of countries and segments - it may be worthwhile adapting the product for the target country. The reasons for this may lie in the different preferences of the target customers, their purchasing power and readiness to pay, the company's desire to minimize costs and risks, or differences in the regulatory framework (*inter alia* McDonald 1998, Yorgey 1999a).

Operational implementation of direct marketing adaptations

Local adaptations are not only a strategic cost factor when selecting a target country. The details have also to be implemented at an operational level, and differ according to the country involved. Tempest (see the article "The Robinson Lists for Effective Direct Marketing") and the FEDMA studies (FEDMA 2004a, 2004b, 2004c, 2005b) give a good overview of the relevant direct marketing regulations. These regulations govern two areas: suppression files and advertising authorities.

The Robinson list usually corresponds to the nationally adapted and maintained suppression files. Consumers can register on such lists if they do not want to receive mailings from advertisers, for example. Despite European guidelines, the particular arrangements and regulations differ substantially across countries (Hengst 2000 *inter alia*, also see the article "The Robinson Lists for Effective Direct Marketing").

There are also significant differences in the national regulatory arrangements governing the advertising industry (*inter alia* Hengst 2000). For example, in the UK, each advertising mailing has to be approved by the ASA (Advertising Standards Authority). Without its agreement, a company runs the risk of receiving a warning (Yorgey 1999a, see article "International Dialog for the Successful Acquisition of New Customers"). Such differences in legal regulations make it particularly advisable for a company to seek professional support. Worldwide mail service providers (e.g., Deutsche Post 2004, p. 6) and local lawyers can be of assistance in this regard (e.g., compare Millar (2003) for a listing of local providers across 51 countries). The cost is usually negligible compared to the potential damage.

Lettershops

Several studies on international direct marketing recommend the use of a local lettershop. For one thing, a local lettershop can handle all the individual steps in the process, while at the same time injecting its local expertise. This begins with a final review of the text and layout (e.g., Yorgey 1999b), since national differences extend to such matters as paper and envelope formats, among other things.

A final check of the local address format is also important as, even if the address data is correct, a large proportion of mail may otherwise be lost (Soricello 1996; Swiss Post 2004, Spiller and Baier 2005, p. 286 ff.). Neumann and Nagel (2000) and particularly Lester (2003c) mention the importance of ensuring that the address is correctly formatted in order to systematically reduce the proportion of non-deliverables from the outset. It is also important to bear in mind that address elements are positioned differently in each country. In some countries - for example, Switzerland - the address formats may even differ across regions (Swiss Post 2005). In the medium term, companies engaging in international direct marketing should set their software to a general address format.[2]

In addition to the usual local checks of the suppression files, the lettershop should also conduct a final review of the gender-specific form of address on the basis of first names in order to avoid irritating the recipient by addressing them incorrectly. It is hardly possible for the company sending the mailing to ensure this without assistance (see also the example given by Yorgey 1999a). Local printing is therefore a worthwhile alternative (Neumann and Nagel 2000).

For certain media, the form of the medium affects postage costs and local delivery methods. Local knowledge is also very useful for significantly reducing costs in this regard. An alternative is to work with an international service provider (major agencies, e.g., Publicis and/or BBDO or Deutsche Post AG) or to draw on the experience of local postal businesses (Neumann and Nagel 2000). Millar (2003) provides an exhaustive listing of local lettershops across 51 countries.

Fulfillment

Fulfillment is commonly broken down into the following steps of the process workflow:

- Order management
- Storage
- Shipping
- Customs and taxes
- Non-deliverables
- Returns
- Delivery options for the customer

Each step in the fulfillment process presents companies with a range of options. In terms of order management, for example, the choice of response channels (telephone, fax, mail, internet) has far-reaching consequences. While response channels such as the internet, fax and mail can be handled by the firm itself, telephone call centers require a much greater knowledge of the relevant language and may require the services of another company. This may also be necessary for follow-up order enquiries made via non-verbal response channels, although in this case such follow-up enquiries can be collected and outsourced in batches. In the case of

---

[2] Lester (2003c) recommends at least five lines, each with 40 characters. One line is assigned to the recipient's name, two to the street name, and one each to the town or city, the ZIP or postal code, the state/region/province, and the country. The address database should store this data in separate fields. Neumann and Nagel (2000) and the Austrian post office (2005) offer some examples and identify appropriate software.

services in foreign languages, it is usually recommended that companies establish strong links with local partners during the first tests, and only then outsource order management to them completely (McDonald 1998, Hengst 2000 inter alia).

Local storage should be based on expected sales volume. At the beginning, local storage is seldom worthwhile. However, the selection of an appropriate option depends heavily on the product or product range offered (Lester 2003b). With relatively low-priced products, international forwarding costs can quickly come to represent a disproportional part of the order value. Ultimately, local purchasing power and local competition also play a crucial role in determining how the customer evaluates the product. Costly and lengthy customs inspections may be another reason to favor local storage. While this is no longer of any importance in the European internal market or North America, it may be a significant factor in Eastern European and non-European countries, in which case it is often cheaper to ship a large single load through customs and then dispatch the goods locally (Lester 2003b, Yorgey 1999b). The decision regarding the type of storage therefore depends not only on storage costs but also on an examination of the overall process. Similar considerations apply to the shipping of goods. In this case, it is recommended that - at least at the beginning - several companies can be commissioned to make partial deliveries, so that a comparison can be made of these partners (see also Lester 2001a). The selection of a shipping partner should also take into account whether the partner uses local subcontractors and how many links there are in the distribution chain. This can result in costly enquiries when problems arise, increasing the probability that the deliveries will be lost (Lester 2003b).

With regard to local taxes, it should be remembered that, in addition to value added tax, other taxes may also be levied, e.g., business and profits. Most international logistics firms provide appropriate services in such cases, but these additional costs must be taken into account when calculating the price for the local customer. It is usually worth consulting a specialist lawyer and a tax expert to clarify these aspects. Chambers of foreign trade will also gladly provide help (Neumann and Nagel 2000).

Returns and non-deliverables are a normal part of business for direct marketing firms. For international direct marketers, however, these can rapidly become a problem depending on the storage and distribution companies that have been selected (Lester 2003b). If fulfillment is handled entirely from the domestic market, returns and non-deliverables are often sent back to the overseas address of the sender at considerable expense. The customer faces high barriers for returns (in terms of effort, expense, customs forms, etc.) and these are indeed already apparent when responding to the mail or catalog. In many countries, depending on the postal service, non-deliverables are not returned to the sender overseas, and may then be lost. Even if the money is received in advance from the customer, it is the start of additional, painstaking work. Difficulties with the customer, with the mail-order provider involved and possibly with the customs authorities are highly likely, generating additional cost for everyone involved. Because of this, many authors recommend using at least a local address or a local partner to take care of such matters in a professional manner (see also Hengst 2000, Lester 2003b).

Finally, international fulfillment requires that customers should, as far as possible, be able to determine the type of distribution according to their own individual needs. The company should at least plan its business development to show which options it needs and/or wants to be completed at what time. The minimum requirements should be aligned with local customs and the target segment. This covers, for instance, the type of transport insurance, the speed of delivery (24 hours, 48 hours, etc.) and the options regarding local delivery times (Lester 2003b). If the company selects established service providers in the target country, it can be confident that local customs will be observed. Millar (2003) provides a valuable source for managers that search for professional local assistance.

In global terms, operational planning and implementation are by far the biggest elements in the overall planning and decision-making process for international direct marketing. The biggest challenges in this respect relate to questions of detail that affect both customers and companies . Even with a drastically reduced initial effort, e.g., with the company exercising full control from its home market, the need for a local service quickly follows the first orders. Lester (2001b) clearly illustrates this using the example of the success of US mail-order companies in Japan. For this very reason, many experts recommend seeking assistance from international service providers or local professionals. The related investment is usually quickly recovered in terms of money saved elsewhere.

7   Controlling

The entry and ongoing support phases of international direct marketing should be accompanied by good controlling. In this context, controlling contains the entire planning, continual progress monitoring, analysis of deviations from the plan, and subsequent countermeasures taken within the team (Holland 2004 *inter alia*). In general, controlling of international direct marketing is closely related to controlling for domestic direct marketing. Proven processes can usually be transferred directly with minor adjustments.

- Production of a plan
- Ultimate objectives (both short- and long-term)
- Definition of processes and responsibilities
- Evaluation of tests and regular campaigns
- Regular adjustments according to the results
- Establishment and use of an early warning system

Figure 1-15: The controlling process for international direct marketing

Companies should pay particular attention when entering new markets. The controlling processes should regularly incorporate new insights regarding the foreign market and the target group. Many authors recommend that companies first define their short- and long-term objectives for international direct marketing (Neumann and Nagel 2001 inter alia). A two- to five-year marketing plan that adequately documents how and when objectives are achieved has been shown to work well in practice (McDonald 1998 inter alia). This plan should also document the internal and external processes and clearly specify responsibilities. It is then the job of the management and controlling staff to check continually that the plan is being adhered to, and if necessary, to make prompt suggestions for improvement. What makes controlling particularly difficult in an international direct marketing context is the fact that reliable benchmarks are not easy to come by, especially when data from the domestic market is not directly comparable. In addition, cross-border cooperation often makes it much more complicated to control planned or agreed processes adequately. Consequently, there is often a delay before the company's headquarter is able to analyze errors that occur in the foreign market.

It is therefore helpful to conduct regular tests and evaluations of normal international campaigns (Neumann and Nagel 2001). Many companies - at least in the initial phase - operate on many process levels with several service providers, such as agencies, mail-order companies or fulfillment partners, in order to produce reference values. The resulting insights can be used to modify the plan in an accurate and timely manner and to bring about the necessary decisions.

8   Organization of processes

The above sections describe the strategic and operational subprocesses of international direct marketing and present the most important insights in each case. They show that a complex process underpins both the organization of entry strategies and its ongoing maintenance. This highly innovative project and its related processes therefore require a professional organization to coordinate the tasks, subprocesses, responsibilities and active participants.

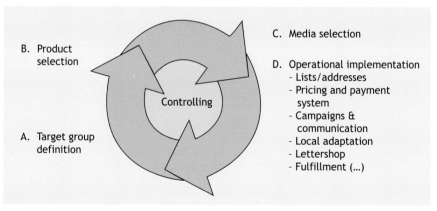

Figure 1-16: The total process in overview

In view of the importance of entering international markets, it is advisable for the responsibility for such a project to reside at the highest leadership level, since such ventures tend to be highly innovative, complex and important for the company. Entry into new markets requires high-quality personnel and significant financial resources from the company to ensure success. Operational process coordination for international direct marketing can, depending on the size of the company and the nature of its resources, be positioned at a lower level, e.g., with a manager for the foreign market concerned. It should however be ensured that this post is fully dedicated to the development of the new market. Assigning market development as an additional task to an existing position has been proven not to work (Neumann and Nagel 2000).

As in the domestic market (see also Dallmer 2002; Holland 2004), in recent years there has been an emergence of international direct marketing process specialists. Specifically, this applies to the organization and implementation of the classic elements in the process. Each country has its own set of agencies, list providers and brokers, lettershops and fulfillment providers. Therefore, the person in charge within the company should - at least in principle and to some extent – be able to organize the cross-border process in a similar fashion to the domestic direct marketing process. The small but significant difference lies in the matter of cross-border organization, which usually involves a lack of local experience, or some cultural and linguistic barriers. It can make international direct marketing much more difficult for a stand-alone organization, and greatly increase the risk of such a venture. This risk can be partially reduced through the use of local service providers in either the domestic or foreign market who specialize in international direct marketing. An example would be local list brokers specializing in consultancy work for foreign companies entering the US, or in consultancy work for US companies moving into foreign markets.

Due to the ongoing consolidation within certain sections of the direct marketing value chain, some service providers are already operating at an international level. The experience and presence of these providers can be used to great advantage by firms looking to expand their international direct marketing business and seeking support in designing and implementing an entry strategy. Some of these international service providers already explicitly offer the same type of experience and skills available from independent service providers. The box below gives some examples of this:

- International market research: GfK, Nielsen, etc.
- Direct marketing agencies: Ogilvy One, Proximity, Publicis, Wunderman, etc.
- International list management: Deutsche Post, Swiss Post, etc.
- International payments: DHL, FedEx, UPS, MasterCard, VISA, etc.
- Fulfillment/delivery: DHL, FedEx, UPS, etc.

Figure 1-17: Examples of international process specialists and their offers

In addition, new international products and services are currently being developed for managing the entire process workflow that underpins international direct marketing. Firms plan to offer an one-stop solution for all services, from target market analysis through to returns-handling policy and dealing with claims. These "meta-specialists" rely on other specialists for the partial provision of services, but are responsible for and coordinate the entire process themselves. The arrival of such specialists on the scene indicates the potential value associated with international direct marketing, particularly the value attached to the coordination function. providers currently offering this form of "meta-services" include DHL Global Mail, Swiss Post and the Austrian post (Österreichische Post 2006) office among others. According to numerous authors, companies have benefited from using specialist advisers and service providers, both for entry into international direct marketing and for the ongoing support of such ventures (McDonald 1998 inter alia).

9   Summary

International direct marketing has developed rapidly in recent years. In practice, it has increasingly moved away from the narrow definition of an individual cross-border direct marketing activity. Today, the process is usually implemented, to varying degrees, by specialists from both sides of the border. Experience in international direct marketing also helps enterprises to run domestic campaigns for target groups of foreign origin. What is more, international direct marketing has, to a certain extent, begun to move away from a narrow spatial definition. In some respects, the development of international direct marketing therefore mirrors the increasing globalization of many societies. At approximately US $46 billion, international direct marketing is now a major acitivity, and one that continues to grow exponentially.

Yet the implementation of international direct marketing in terms of its individual sub-processes - from target country analysis through operational returns handling - is increasingly a local business. The international consolidation of the value chain into distinct subareas has produced multinational players to which companies can turn when seeking to launch their own international direct marketing campaigns. In this way they can profitably combine their confidence in well-known domestic providers with the use of local experience abroad to systematically reduce their own risk. This also applies to providers that offer a coordination function by managing the entire process of international direct marketing. The companies themselves can learn from using these providers, and at the same time reduce their risk. Despite all its complexity, international direct marketing remains a relatively simple, quick and cost-effective tool for entering new markets successfully.

10 Bibliography

Albers, N., B.D. Gelb. 1991. International Direct Marketing Efforts: Are they Useful to Small Businesses in Establishing Consistent Patterns of Exporting? Journal of Direct Marketing 5(4) 29–38.

Akhter, S.H. 1988. Direct Marketing Infrastructure: An Indicator of Direct Marketing Potential in Foreign Markets. Journal of Direct Marketing 2(Winter) 13–27.

Akhter, S.H. 1996.:International Direct Marketing: Export Value Chain, Transaction Cost, and the Triad. Journal of Direct Marketing 10(2) 13–23.

Anderson, E., A.T. Coughlan. 1987. International Market Entry and Expansion via Independent or Integrated Channels of Distribution. Journal of Marketing 51(January) 71–82.

Batra, R. 1990. The New Direct Marketing: How to Implement a Profit-Driven Database Marketing Strategy. David Shepard Association, Dow Jones-Irwin, Homewood, Ill.

Bird, D. 1990. Praxis-Handbuch Direktmarketing. Verlag Moderne Industrie, Landsberg/Lech.

Bruns, J. 1998. Direktmarketing. Ludwigshafen, Kiehl.

Dallmer, H. 1997. Das System des Direct Marketing – Entwicklung und Zukunftsperspektiven. Dallmer, H., ed. Handbuch Direct Marketing. 7th edition. Wiesbaden, Gabler, 3–20.

Dallmer, H. 2002. Direct Marketing im Wandel. Zeitschrift für Betriebswirtschaft, ZfB-Ergänzungsheft 1(2002) 1–19.

Deutsche Post AG. 2004. Competence Center Global Mail. Presentation at the DIMA 2004, Düsseldorf.

Deutsche Post AG. 2003. Marketingfakten International 2003 – Neue Märkte. Neue Chancen. Bonn.

Deutsche Post AG. 2004a. Marketingfakten International 2004 – Neue Märkte. Neue Chancen. Bonn.

Deutsche Post AG. 2004b. Direktmarketing Deutschland 2004. Bonn.

Deutsche Post AG. 2005a. Dialog-Marketing 2005. Bonn.

Deutsche Post AG. 2006. Direct Marketing Monitor International 2006. Bonn.

DHL Global Mail. 2005. Direktmarketing-Scout. Bonn.

DMA. 2004a. Statistical Fact Book 2004. New York, N.Y., USA.

DMA. 2004b. The DMA Response Rate Report 2004. New York, N.Y., USA.

DMA. 2005. 2005 DMA International Echo Awards CD-ROM, New York, N.Y., USA.

DMA. 2006. Statistical Fact Book 2006. New York, N.Y., USA.

Durvasula, S., S.H. Akhter, G.J. Bamossy. 1996. A Cross-National Comparison of Consumers' Attitudes Toward Direct Marketing and Purchase Intentions. Discussion Paper No. TI96-36/6. Tinbergen Institute, Amsterdam.

Elsner, R. 2003. Optimiertes Direkt- und Database-Marketing unter Einsatz mehrstufiger dynamischer Modelle. DUV, Wiesbaden.

FEDMA. 2002. 2002 Survey on Direct and Interactive Marketing Activities. Brussels, Belgium.

FEDMA. 2004a. FEDMA List Council Fact Pack 2004. Brussels, Belgium.

FEDMA 2004b. Legal Fact Pack 2004. Brussels, Belgium.

FEDMA. 2004c. The Global Guide to Robinson Lists/Preference Services. Brussels, Belgium.

FEDMA. 2005a. 2003 Survey on Direct and Interactive Marketing activities in Europe. Brussels, Belgium.

FEDMA. 2005b. The Global Guide to Robinson Lists/Preference Services. Revised Version, Brussels, Belgium.

Fowler, G.A. 2003. Junk Mailers Discover Asia is Close to Heaven. The Wall Street Journal 3/5 B.1 & 2.

Gerdes, J. 2002. Macht sich Dialogmarketing bezahlt? – So macht sich Dialogmarketing bezahlt! Siegfried Vögele Institut, Bonn and Königstein, Germany.

Gehrt, K.C., S. Shim. 1998. A Shopping Orientation Segmentation of French Consumers: Implications for Catalog Marketing. Journal of interactive Marketing 12(4) 34–46.

Gerardi, A., H. Hoke. 1966. Einführung in die Direktwerbung. cited in How to think about direct mail. Hoke, H. Fachverlag Gerardi KG, Pforzheim.

Hengst, R. 2000. Plotting Your Global Strategy. Direct Marketing 63(4) 52–57.

Holland, H. 2004. Direktmarketing. 2nd edition, Vahlen, Munich, Germany.

Hornikel, S. 2004. Internationale Adressbeschaffung. Direkt Marketing No. 10 18–21.

Iyer, R.T., J.S. Hill. 1996. International Direct Marketing Strategies: a US-European comparison. European Journal of Marketing 30(3) 65–83.

Jain, S.C. 1989. Standardization of International Marketing Strategy: Some Research Hypotheses. Journal of Marketing 53 (January) 70–79.

Lee, M. 2004. Attitudes Towards Direct Marketing, Privacy, Environment, and Trust: Taiwan vs. U.S. International Journal of Consumer Marketing (IJCM) 14(1) 1–18.

Lester, L.Y. 1999. European List Experience: List Strategies That Worked for Three U.S. Direct Mailers. Target Marketing Edition dated March 1, 1999.

Lester, L.Y. 2001a. Case Study – Marketing into France. Target Marketing Edition dated May 1, 2001.

Lester, L.Y. 2001b. U.S. Cataloger Marketing in Japan – Far From Over. Target Marketing Edition dated June 1, 2001.

Lester, L.Y. 2002. A World of Opportunity. Target Marketing Edition of November 1, 2002.

Lester, L.Y. 2003a. 7 Ways to Uncover Big Opportunities in Global Markets. Target Marketing Edition dated August 1, 2003.

Lester, L.Y. 2003b. Overseas Delivery. Target Marketing Edition dated September 1, 2003.

Lester, L.Y. 2003c. Get Down With Global Data. Target Marketing Edition dated November 1, 2003.

Levitt, T. 1983. The Globalization of Markets. Harvard Business Review 61(May-June) 92–102.

Light, D., T.H. Somasundaram. 1994. International Direct Marketing Strategy: A Comparison with Alternative Media. Journal of Direct Marketing 8(1) 71–78.

Löffler, H., A. Scherfke. 2000. Direkt-Marketing: Instrumente, Ausführung und neue Konzepte. Cornelsen, Berlin, Germany.

McDonald, W.J. 1994. Developing International Direct Marketing Strategies with a Consumer Decision-Making Content Analysis. Journal of Direct Marketing 8(4) 18–27.

McDonald, W.J. 1998. Five steps to international success. Direct Marketing 61(7) 32–36.

McDonald, W.J. 1999. International Direct Marketing in a Rapidly Changing World. Direct Marketing 61(11) 44–47.

Meffert, H. 2002. Direct Marketing und marktorientierte Unternehmensführung. Dallmer, H. ed. Das Handbuch Direktmarketing & More 8th edition. Gabler, Wiesbaden, Germany.

Mehta, R., R. Grewal, E. Sivadas. 1996. International Direct Marketing on the Internet: Do Internet Users Form a Global Segment? Journal of Direct Marketing, 10(1) 45–58.

Millar, R. 2003. Directory of international direct and interactive marketing. 7th edition, Kogan Page, London and Sterling, VA, UK & USA.

Milne, G.R., J. Beckman, M.L. Taubman. 1996. Consumer Attitudes toward Privacy and Direct Marketing in Argentina. Journal of Direct Marketing 10(1) 22–29.

Neumann, U., T. Nagel. 2000. Neue Märkte – neue Kunden, mit Direktmarketing Europa erschließen. Beck-Wirtschaftsberater, dtv, Munich, Germany.

Neumann, U., T. Nagel. 2001. Professionelles Direktmarketing. 1st. edition. Beck-Wirtschaftsberater, dtv, Munich, Germany.

Neumann, U., T. Nagel. 2007. Professionelles Direktmarketing. 2nd. edition. Beck-Wirtschaftsberater, dtv, Munich, Germany.

o.V. 2000. International Direct Marketing, B to B. No. 85, Edition 19, Nov. 20, 2000.

Österreichische Post. 2005. Euro. Pass, Vienna, Austria.

Österreichische Post. 2006. Osteuropa im Fokus, 2nd edition, Vienna, Austria.

Padmanabhan, R.T. 1990. An Exploratory Study of U.S. and European International Direct Marketing Strategies. PhD Thesis, University of Alabama, USA.

Rawwas, M.Y.A., D. Strutton, L.W. Johnson. 1996. An Exploratory Investigation of the Ethical Values of American and Australian Consumers: Direct Marketing Implications. Journal of Direct Marketing 10(4) 52-63.

Roberts, M.L., P.D. Berger. 1999. Direct Marketing Management. 2nd edition. Prentice Hall, Upper Saddle River, New York, USA.

Rosenfield, J.R. 1994. Direct Marketing Worldwide. Journal of Direct Marketing 8(1) 79–82.

Schultz, D.E. 1994. When the World Got Smaller. Journal of Direct Marketing 8(1) 5–6.

Schweizerische Post. 2004. International Adress-Guide – Privat- und Firmenadressen aus 20 Ländern. 2nd edition. Bern, Switzerland.

Soricello, S. 1996. Going Direct into Overseas Markets. Direct Marketing 58(11) 52–54.

Spiller, L.D., A.J. Campbell. 1994. The Use of International Direct Marketing by Small Businesses in Canada, Mexico, and the United States. Journal of Direct Marketing 8(1) 7–16.

Spiller, L.D., M. Baier. 2005. Contemporary Direct Marketing. Pearson Prentice Hall, Upper Saddle River, New Jersey, USA.

Stone, B., R. Jacobs. 2001. Successful Direct Marketing Methods. 7th edition. McGraw-Hill, Chicago, Illinois [i.a.], USA.

Stone, M., A. Bond, E. Blake. 2003. The Definitive Guide to Direct and Interactive Marketing. FT Prentice Hall, Harlow et al., UK.

Swiss Post. 2005. Direct-Marketing-Pass Schweiz. 2nd edition, Sep. 2005, Bern, Switzerland.

Swiss Post. 2006. Direct-Marketing-Pass Europe. 1st edition, Oct. 2006, Bern, Switzerland.

Szymanski, D.M., S.G. Bharadwaj, P.R. Varadarajan. 1993. Standardization versus Adaptation of International Marketing Strategy: An Empirical Investigation. Journal of Marketing 57 (October) 1-17.

Topol, M., E. Sherman. 1994. Trends and Challenges of Expanding Internationally via Direct Marketing. Journal of Direct Marketing 8(1) 32–43.

Yorgey, L. 1999a. Rodale Press: A Market-by-Market Approach Helped This Publisher Build Its Direct Marketing Business Overseas. Target Marketing Edition dated June 1, 1999.

Yorgey, L. 1999b.. International by Design: Peruvian Connection Adds Germany to Its Global Mix and Expands. Target Marketing Edition dated Nov 1, 1999.

ZAW. 2004. Werbung in Deutschland 2003. Zentralverband der deutschen Werbewirtschaft, Bonn.

Kay Peters

Checklist for your international direct marketing

2

1 Planning

Determining the goals
- Prospecting / customer acquisition
- Customer retention
- Sales / up- & cross-selling
- Brand communications / generating or enhancing image
- Testing (e.g., target group response)

Remarks:

Analyzing & selecting the target country
- General economic & cultural factors
- Local market:
  - ☐ Local purchasing behavior
  - ☐ Local offers / competition
  - ☐ Regional differences
- Taxes / duties / customs
- General direct marketing affinity:
  - ☐ consumer experience / usage / size of DM / products
- General direct marketing infrastructure:
  - ☐ Adress lists & broker / local DM agencies / lettershops / logistics & fulfillment

Remarks:

Defining & identifying the target group, nationally and abroad
▨ Relationship structure type (B2B, B2C)
▨ Customer profile transfer from home / other market
▨ Potential positioning / USP for the target group / market?
▨ Segmenting market according to:
  ☐ Geographical criteria
  ☐ Sociodemographic criteria
  ☐ Behavior-related criteria
  ☐ Psychographic criteria
▨ Identification of target group:
  ☐ Selection criteria / address qualification
  ☐ Type of list / broker

Remarks:

Determining the budget
▨ Campaign
  ☐ Adapt design / creation
  ☐ Organize international production
  ☐ Media adaptation and local distribution
  ☐ Adapt response incentives
▨ Response management and fulfillment
  ☐ International response management
  ☐ International fulfillment / order / return management
  ☐ Production of fulfillment material
  ☐ Selection of international service provider(s)

Remarks:

Determining the timing
▨ Date of campaign launch?
▨ Date of briefing deadline?
▨ Timing for generating layout / copy / final proofs / editing / lithography
▨ Amount of time for production?
▨ Feedback & review by international / local experts?

Selecting advertising materials /channels
▨ Adapt media mix to target country
(adapt the media mix to local structures with regard
to consumers and competitors)

☐ Mailing   ☐ Fax
☐ Info flyer   ☐ DRTV (Direct Response TV)
☐ Print media insert   ☐ DRR (Direct Response Radio)
☐ Response ad   ☐ Brochure
☐ Coupon   ☐ Bulk mail
☐ Email marketing   ☐ Telephone marketing
☐ Web marketing

Remarks:

Determining offer (product /service)

▨ Product / service (core / additional benefits)
- ☐ Take local competitors into account
- ☐ Local product demands / expectations

▨ Price
- ☐ Adjust to suit local market
    - ☐ Carry out comparison with competition
    - ☐ Keep local currency purchasing power in mind
- ☐ Local payment methods / practices

▨ Distribution channels
- ☐ Channels preferred by foreign customer (mail order direct purchase)?
- ☐ Access to local retail / middlemen necessary?

▨ Contents of the communication
- ☐ Does the product / service involve high consultation/ explanation requirements?
- ☐ Claim
- ☐ Statement, tonality
- ☐ Adequately tailored to target country?

▨ Layout / design
- ☐ Observe CI /CD rules
- ☐ Adapt the imagery used
- ☐ Evaluate clarity of layout / design

▨ Determine international service providers
- ☐ Local / international advertising agency
- ☐ Professional translators
- ☐ Local / international address broker
- ☐ Local / international printers / production

▨ Local regulation requirements
- ☐ Check with local DMA (privacy / products & services / media)
- ☐ Check with specialist / consultant / lawyer

Remarks:

2 Execution

Keeping international requirements in mind
- Foreign requirements for advertising materials
  - ☐ CD guidelines followed?
  - ☐ Attention-grabbing?
  - ☐ Target group addressed / personalized (copy tone images)?
  - ☐ Message (benefits) clearly communicated?
  - ☐ Image rights purchased (licensed / public domain)?
- Foreign requirements for the response element
  - ☐ Call to action clearly worded?
  - ☐ Easy to use?
  - ☐ Technical and postal provisions fulfilled (postage-optimized shipping type)?
  - ☐ Where applicable, campaign coding to measure success?
  - ☐ Were personalization options used (pre-printed address field)?
  - ☐ Data protection statement included?
  - ☐ Customer signature /other legal regulations?

Remarks:

3 Measuring success

Evaluating the campaign
- Response management
  - ☐ Define criteria for success (with service providers)
  - ☐ Define and organize response evaluation process
  - ☐ CPI /CPO
- Use lessons learned for future campaigns
  - ☐ Communicate successes / failures to the relevant people
    - ☐ Employees in-house
    - ☐ Participating service providers
- Update database
  - ☐ Qualification (where useful, change / supplement existing customer info and / or add potential new customers)
  - ☐ Contact history
- Assessment of the entire campaign

Chapter 2:
Best practice

Introduction to Chapter 2

So much for the theory: how can the challenges be tackled in practice? The first chapter covered the rapid growth and increasing significance of international direct marketing. Some practical examples now follow that will demonstrate the broad applicability of these concepts.

The success of the campaigns illustrated here is an indication of the importance of international direct marketing, as are the examples of ECHO award winning campaigns referred to before (DMA 2005). This applies to cross-border marketing, as seen in the DHL Global Mail campaign and, to promotional customer dialog in the new, up-and-coming Eastern European markets, as in the case of Acxiom. It also applies to ethnomarketing and the example illustrated in the Hewlett-Packard campaign.

In order to present the widest possible variety, the individual examples were selected according the following factors: geographical criteria, transferability to other countries and differences regarding both procedures and target groups. As the book is primarily aimed at newcomers to international direct marketing, the focus is on gaining new customers rather than maintaining customer relationships. With cross-media campaigns increasing in importance, the selection also includes the use of as many different media as possible. Finally, the case studies reflect the different definitions of international direct marketing.

These examples also show that regional expertise is crucial to the success of cross-border campaigns. For a foreign company to be seen as a professional service provider and accepted as an alternative to current local market players, its message has to match closely not just the occupational, but also the cultural and social requirements of the recipients. Using the example of an international campaign by DHL Global Mail, Rosegret Nave describes the procedure for the parallel recruitment of new customers in 14 countries in Asia, Europe and North America. This multi-stage B2B campaign notably includes direct mail and advertisements in technical periodicals. The article describes a classic international direct marketing campaign.

The case of Acxiom offers a practical explanation of what makes the use of new statistical methods so successful: the search for previously unknown patterns in the relationships between products and their consumers. Auke van den Hout and Kay Peters describe these unusual ways to gain new customers. The Polish internet bank Inteligo appointed the international services provider Acxiom for this purpose. The addresses corresponding to the proven, classical customer profile had been exhausted. Together with Acxiom, the team abandoned the widely used, traditional methodology in favor of a new procedure based on innovative statistical methods that would identify prospective new customers. The case study is very informative, and definitely not just for the banking industry.

Thomas Nagel focuses on the acquisition of new customers in foreign markets. How are target countries selected? Which target groups should be addressed? Using what tools? Which experiences should be drawn upon? Thomas Nagel has tapped into his many decades of practical experience in writing this article. His recommendations are illustrated with examples from various European countries. He also suggests which form of media is appropriate depending on the country, product or target group.

Foreign markets are not necessarily located miles and miles away from the advertiser. Even in the advertiser's home market there are target groups that can only be addressed profitably using an international form of communication. Diane Rinas deals with ethnomarketing as a special case of international direct marketing: a target group of foreign origin in the German domestic market. She demonstrates how closely the requirements and processes of ethnomarketing resemble those of international direct marketing. As in international direct marketing, the media used, i.e., direct mail, TV and print, to name just three, have to be adapted to the historical and cultural background of the target group.

A certain degree of lateral thinking is sometimes required when marketing to avant-gardistic metropolitan target groups in international markets. The Hewlett-Packard campaign described in this book exemplifies this type of innovative dialog communication. The success of this campaign is essentially due to a radical shift away from mass marketing and towards an approach that caters to the personal experiences of the metropolitan target group. This in turn prompts them to rediscover original brand values. The authors, Jon Williams and Thomas Curwen, highlight these new perspectives. Even in the printer market, which is a mature and relatively static international market, close-knit communities can be recruited as future international trendsetters for an "mature", but revived brand.

But how does one reach a target group which is extremely critical of all standard advertising forms and messages worldwide? Together with Hewlett-Packard, Publicis found a surprisingly innovative solution. The media used are as avant-garde as the target group and give a good idea of how direct marketing media may be employed in the future. The campaign also shows that nowadays rapid globalization is the norm in close metropolitan communities. Thus after a debut in London and a subsequent rollout in Europe, the campaign soon became global by viral word-of-mouth - without previous intention. Clearly, the interaction of classic direct marketing tools with newer ways of addressing customers holds enormous potential for the future.

In cross-border terms, the most important goal for direct marketing today is to ensure that consumers remain good and loyal customers. After all, both sides will gain if advertisers use this direct approach to advertising in a responsible manner. The Robinson/Preference Services are at the heart of this responsible approach.

Alastair Tempest focuses on national differences in the legal framework governing media such as direct mail, telephone, fax, and email, while also referring to specific elements of the other case studies. His article shows the urgency of inter-national harmonization, which is still non-existent, even in the European Union. This heterogeneity makes the article a valuable resource in day-to-day use, especially as it refers to individual local solutions. It also leads into the third chapter of this book, which contains additional up-to-date facts for the implementation of international direct marketing campaigns.

In general, mailings are still the primary tool for direct marketing worldwide, even though internet-based tools are growing exponentially, both in volume and potential media experience for consumers. In many countries, mailings are regarded by recipients as an indication that the sender thinks highly of them. Therefore, mailings are often a core element of any direct marketing strategy. They stimulate interest, offer the opportunity to include additional materials and provide, above all, a tangible experience.

Author Content	Nave	van den Hout/ Peters	Nagel	Rinas	Williams/ Curwen	Tempest
Regional emphasis	14 countries in Asia, Europe and the USA	Poland	General	Turkish target group (Germany)	UK (France, worldwide)	Worldwide
Type	B2B	B2C	B2B/B2C	B2C (B2B)	B2C	B2C/B2C
IDM* aspect	Regional expansion	Local expansion with international service provider	Country selection and entry	Ethno-marketing as local IDM*	International use of avant-garde BTL** media	Worldwide legal comparison
Customer life cycle	New customers	New customers	New customers	New and existing customers	New customers	New and existing customers
Media	Mail, press ads, internet	Mail	All response-media	Mail, TV, press ads	BTL** media	Mail, Fax Phone, email
Single-/ multi-stage-campaign	Multi-stage	Single stage	Not relevant	Multi-stage	Multi-stage	Not relevant

*   *IDM: international direct marketing*
** *BTL: below the line*

Rosegret Nave

Global planning to pinpoint local targets

How DHL Global Mail* introduced an integrated direct marketing campaign in 14 countries

Overview

- Direct marketing is a proven and efficient tool for developing new markets. Its flexibility offers global companies unique opportunities to simultaneously address customers in different national target markets.
- The specific requirements for international direct marketing campaigns are described, as determined by their content or business aspects.
- Intensive cooperation between global planners and experts in the individual target markets has proven to be necessary for the success of the campaign.

---

* As was already mentioned in the foreword, Deutsche Post World Net Group companies offer products and services abroad under the brand name "DHL Global Mail" in the name and on behalf of Deutsche Post AG. Subsidiaries of the Deutsche Post World Net Group are collectively referred to below as DHL Global Mail.

1   Using multinational direct marketing to seize the opportunities presented by globalization

Since the 1980s, and in some cases earlier, companies with worldwide operations have been acting according to the principle "Think Globally – Act Locally". Accordingly, they have been developing central strategies for products and services whose success knew neither limits nor borders. They would then market, distribute, and even produce these products in customized versions for local markets. This approach has been used internationally with great success by car manufacturers and the large food and furniture chains, for example.

For various reasons, the principle "Think Globally – Act Locally" has so far seen less application in the area of marketing communications. On the one hand, most globally active companies have spent the past few years focusing on their core competencies. Because of this, they have not really invested in marketing structures in all of their potential target markets. On the other hand - and this is undoubtedly more important - "Think Globally - Act Locally" alone cannot take proper account of the requirements of either the content or business aspects of successful international campaigns without integrated, professional support teams.

Content-related and logistic challenges

The key business challenges are mainly the large organizational and logistical efforts of international campaigns. "Act Locally", for example, means that all tasks have to be locally planned, calculated and implemented in each country, from address management and correct dispatch to any and all follow-up actions.

Regarding the content of direct marketing, a campaign whose central message is designed globally without local adaptation can hardly be expected to succeed. The awareness and acceptance of globally designed messages by local target groups is depending on their values, attitudes and expectations, which in turn are influenced by their cultural, religious, ethnic or social backgrounds.

Global Mail Business is a DHL Global Mail product that addresses these challenges: it takes the local requirements of international direct marketing into account. The USP lies in its convenience for customers – Global Mail Business opens up all of the relevant markets for companies, while remaining remarkably simple and convenient to use. It also ensures the smooth and reliable dispatch of business mail to all destinations, from individual campaigns and confidential documents to business mail in all its forms. An international direct marketing campaign for the introduction of this product in 14 countries is the focus of this case study.

Despite having an USP that was suited to its own target markets, it was obvious during the project planning phase that, in order to maximize its impact, a direct marketing campaign for this product would have to meet the following requirements:

- A uniformly received local message
- The right local media mix
- Addressed to relevant local target groups
- Coverage of different markets
- Messages have to use images, words and emotions that are relevant to the particular region/culture
- As efficiently as possible

It is impossible to take proper account of all local target groups by transmitting a single centrally conceived message – "Think Globally" – directly to individual markets. Besides, only implementing "Act Locally" with 14 different teams without using scale effects on the international level would be remarkably inefficient, too: teams in every target market would have to identify small numbers of addresses in comparison to the overall campaign, so as to ensure problem-free production and dispatch. This would also neglect any prospect of positioning DHL Global Mail by establishing a uniform core advertising message worldwide in relation to companies, products or services.

Figure 2-1-1: Direct mailings

Create Globally – Think Locally – Act Globally

Yet reversing and expanding the aforementioned principle to "Create Globally – Think Locally – Act Globally" seems to promise greater success, as the core statement and emotional attitude reflect the self-image and objectives of DHL Global Mail. This framework is then locally adapted as necessary by incorporating the knowledge and experience of the teams in the individual markets. Finally, the planning and realization of the direct marketing campaign is organized, directed, implemented and evaluated by an international team.

DHL Global Mail has now shown, using its own example as a worldwide leader in the provision of one-stop B2B communication solutions that this is actually a practicable and successful approach. Thus a direct marketing campaign for "Global Mail Business" - a turnkey solution for international mail dispatch - was designed and implemented in 14 countries in Europe and the Asia-Pacific area. The campaign achieved the desired result, namely a measurable increase in both the name recognition and product sales of DHL Global Mail.

2   Positioning against local competitors with worldwide competencies and a clear USP

A vital prerequisite for the design of a global direct marketing campaign is the knowledge of the situation – in particular the competitive position – in the individual target markets. It is only worth entering a market if the quality, price or convenience of local competitors can be beaten.

The main competitors of DHL Global Mail in each market were the local postal companies. Due to their long-standing monopolies and their resulting character as "national businesses", they have a very high degree of name recognition and usually enjoy a high degree of confidence. Along with the fact that customers are often unaware of alternative providers, the local postal companies are usually the first choice for companies seeking a partner to handle cross-border marketing activities.

International competence for mail solutions
First of all, DHL Global Mail was able to counter the historical high profile and presence of local competitors with the global reputation of the DHL brand. This reputation has been build through DHL Global Mail's worldwide mail solutions network, offering direct connections to more than 200 countries through 17 offices on four continents.

The product Global Mail Business also offers - in terms of its features and value for money delivered - a proposition superior to the competition in almost every respect. Global Mail Business offers customers an all-in-one solution for all services related to the dispatch of international mail, from the collection of business mail, sorting and franking, to returns of non-deliverables and the sending of follow-ups.

Positioning and sales promotion as objectives
In light of this competitive landscape, the objectives of the direct marketing campaign were obvious: to position the brand DHL Global Mail as a global and highly competent alternative for international mail solutions with decision-makers and staff responsible for these solutions in selected businesses. Ultimately, the strategy would translate into a significant increase in sales of the Global Mail Business product.

Figure 2-1-2: Direct mailing

The interaction between headquarters and regional experts, as described above, ensured that the knowledge and resources of various teams were deployed and integrated into the overall concept already during the campaign design phase. Un-

Figure 2-1-3: Asian mailings

der the leadership of DHL Global Mail's central marketing department in Bonn, Germany, a lead agency was given responsibility for the basic concept in terms of content and form, incorporating the existing corporate design.

Marketing and sales experts from each of the target markets were also included; if necessary, they could draw on advice for the local adaptation of the campaign from agencies with direct marketing skills in each of the respective countries. Teams therefore consisted of both headquarters staff and staff from the respective regions, working together to produce common solutions that would work in all target markets. Each team "translated" the basic concept into a local version for their region, while ensuring a common understanding of the specific objectives across individual markets.

The teams were able to use the full range of direct marketing tools in the design phase. It is a fact that campaigns that integrate different coordinated media are more successful than one-dimensional approaches using a single medium, as this usually guarantees only one type of customer contact. The accessibility and communication behavior of the defined target groups were decisive in the final local selection of tools.

3   Integrating local know-how into global campaign planning to address local market conditions

The start of the design phase of course included the definition of the target groups. This meant identifying those groups of people responsible for making strategic decisions on the employment of new service providers, or those whose daily business entails working with these partners. In this case, these were mainly shipping and logistics managers and direct marketers.

Defining core target groups

In this way, three core target groups were initially defined: senior managers, purchasing managers and mail room managers. It was clear in the definition phase that the different relationships of each of these three groups to the mail business would require them to be addressed differently. Depending on the size of the business and on the differences in business cultures, these target groups might also be expanded to include secretaries and office managers. As direct users of the service, they do not only have personal contact with the staff and products of DHL Global Mail. Their proximity to decision-makers also assigns them the role of opinion leaders and agents of influence for word-of-mouth networking. This target group, too, had to be addressed in an appropriate, i.e., individual manner.

Specifying target markets

Defining the target markets was the second step in project planning. As this was a campaign for a product to be sold via the global DHL network, no special preparatory work was necessary: Global Mail Business could in principle be marketed in any country in which DHL was represented. Finally, countries were selected according to their economic importance providing a sufficiently large number of internationally oriented companies. The focus was thus on Austria, Switzerland, Belgium, Luxembourg, France, the Netherlands, Denmark, Sweden, Singapore, Thailand, Taiwan, Japan, Australia and New Zealand.

Identifying addressees with target companies

Once the companies and the types of employees to be contacted in each country had been identified, the next task was to identify the individual addressees and their contact information. In view of the international resources of DHL Global Mail – in terms of technology as well as with address lists and additional research capabilities – the complexity of this task would only appear to hold a special challenge for the project planners. It is nevertheless a core competence of the business and a necessary requirement for providers of international mail solutions.

Indeed, DHL Global Mail was able to perform the work procedures rapidly, efficiently and to a very high standard, despite having to filter companies from 14 different countries according to segment and size so that the contact data of the various target subgroups could then be researched. This clearly demonstrated the major advantage that DHL Global Mail enjoys with regard to the "Act Globally" principle, an advantage that was found to be important.

Figure 2-1-4: US mailing

As one of the few companies with comprehensive experience in the field of international address management, DHL Global Mail was able to put this principle into practice. This task could therefore be mastered quickly, reliably and at an acceptable cost. There are of course numerous other service providers specializing in comparable services who could also have been considered as partners for cross-border direct marketing: however, in each individual case care should be taken to determine whether these service providers also have the requisite know-how for each individual target market.

Creating the central message

Regarding the next question – which core statement should be used to introduce the product to potential customers in all countries – it was first necessary to encapsulate the product characteristics in a word imagery, which in turn had to be understood by recipients in all countries while having exclusively positive associations. The lead agency responsible for this central task integrated DHL staff from the various countries early on to ensure these objectives could be met.

The result of this guided creation process was the phrase "The first time". This slogan ostensibly refers to the fact that the comparatively recent Global Mail Business product was new to the vast majority of addressees, and that the aim of the direct marketing campaign was to encourage them to try it out; it also covertly plays on the positive connotations that most people associate with this expression, i.e., the beginning of a pleasing or desirable relationship.

Integrating local competencies

By selecting key visuals that were emotionally charged but at the same time rather modest in terms of imagery used, care was taken to ensure that there were no ambiguities or direct sexual allusions which can be a particular problem in countries with large Muslim or puritanically-minded populations. In each country "merely" a pair of female eyes was to be shown - friendly, romantic and promising, but not aggressive, familiar, or presumptuous.

The decisive factor in selecting the message and its visual representation was the unanimous view of the DHL Global Mail staff from the various target countries that both elements could, with appropriate customization, work well in all countries, and that no cultural or religious feelings would be upset.

Figure 2-1-5: Flemish mailing

Compiling a local media mix for three functional levels of content

Following the decision regarding the basic outline of the campaign, the international teams worked out which local media mix would achieve the greatest possible success, i.e., which direct marketing tools should be used at what time and with what function.

Figure 2-1-7: Danish website

Figure 2-1-6: Danish advertisement

The idea was that the overall campaign should address three levels in terms of content:

- The emotional level, stimulating a positive interest with the addressees though the adapted core message and it's adapted visual representation.
- The proof level, in which the product promise is credibly substantiated.
- The action level, which provokes a response to the campaign from the recipients and allows them to experience the product.

The core element of the campaign was a mailing that covered all three levels. The advantage of using such an approach is that it minimizes scatter losses, since it allows addressing members of the target groups individually. With appropriate preparation, mailings also ensure a high-quality, exclusive introduction to the brand. In the example described, the mailing was a flat parcel featuring a female face which invited recipients to open it with the slogan "Let yourself be seduced" and, once opened, addressed the person individually depending on its target group association. It contained:

- a personalized cover letter with basic information outlining the reasons for the campaign – an individual introduction to the recipient depending on its function within the company.
- a carefully arranged fold-out section, with testimonials from satisfied local users printed on the flaps. These satisfied customers not only described the advantages of the product, but also appealed to readers to try the service for "the first time" – this lends the product promise strong credibility.
- a sweepstake located inside the fold-out section with which participants were progressively led to the correct solution via the sales arguments. This was performed in such a way that the recipients were not only induced to act, but were once again exposed to the product advantages.

As single mailings always run the risk of not attracting sufficient notice, additional media exposure was used to increase the overall awareness of the campaign:

- At the same time as the mailings were sent out, advertisements were placed in trade publications in the respective countries and banners were booked on local, frequently visited websites. The advertisements and banners both featured the same local testimonials.
- In a follow-up mailing, prospective customers were supplied with a starter kit containing a brochure that enabled them to try out the product for "the first time" without making further inquiries.
- Those target recipients who had not responded to the campaign up to this point were then contacted using telephone marketing.
- Detailed product information was made easily accessible on the DHL Global Mail websites.

Gradual rollout permits timely readjustments

As this was a new methodology for addressing a target population of customers across 14 countries, it was decided to implement the rollout process gradually, i.e., not in all countries at once. This enabled timely readjustments on the basis of the initial experiences, if necessary. However, owing to the careful preparation, this was not in fact needed.

After it had been determined, using the above processes,

- which target groups were to be addressed,
- in which countries,
- with what message,
- in which form,
- with which media,

the next step was the local adaptation of the messages and visuals. It was primarily the task of the local agencies to adapt the design and text, tailoring them on the one hand to local expectations and attitudes, and on the other to each of the different target subgroups.

Figure 2-1-8: Country-specific campaign adaptation

Converting text and visuals into local code

Both ad copy and visualization were consistently adapted to each of the target markets: the copy was written in the respective national language, with multilingualism also taken into account in countries like Belgium and Switzerland. Localization of the copy was not just an exercise in translation though. In fact, it was more a matter of the idea of conveying the tone and message of the campaign in the relevant language and word images by getting the messages across in a sensitive fashion.

This very delicate task was made considerably easier thanks to the fact that experts from the various countries had been involved with the project at a very early phase, namely during the selection of the slogan and the visuals: this ensured that the required adaptation would not be offensive due to its content or cultural aspects.

Although the key visual of a "female pair of eyes" was not expected to be misinterpreted in any of the target countries, the image did vary across countries nevertheless: Japanese customers were welcomed by Asian eyes, Swedes by blue eyes and French people by a dark-haired woman with brown eyes. In contrast to the translation of texts into the respective national languages, which had to ensure that the material remained both comprehensible and catchy, here it was simply a matter of introducing the new product by using a familiar "native" perspective.

Finally, the prizes for the sweepstake introduced in the central mailing were also adapted to reflect typical national expectations and customs. While Germans were encouraged to participate by the offer of a handheld text scanner, the Japanese, who are generally well equipped with technology, were offered a teddy bear, which at the time of the campaign stood right at the top of their wish list.

To ensure that production of the individual media was both efficient and faithful to the corporate design, materials for the European target markets were centrally produced in Germany, and for Asian markets in Singapore. This achieved uniformly high quality standards on the one hand, while on the other hand, it prevented unnecessary expenditure and delays which are quite common when dealing with parallel production across 14 countries.

4   The campaign achieves its core objectives: clear brand positioning and an increase in sales

For DHL Global Mail, the multinational direct marketing campaign for the Global Mail Business product serves as a template for future campaigns. Nevertheless, to make sure that such campaigns could be run in parallel with current business, the planning and realization of the project formed an integral component of daily operations. The documentation shows that the selected organizational structure – including the early and continuing integration of experts from each of the target countries – functioned in an exemplary manner. Above all, the target groups noticed the campaign and the defined objectives were achieved.

Full achievement of campaign core objectives

It became clear at an early stage that, with accompanying media employment, mailings would stimulate a very high level of interest and produce a high degree of brand awareness. This assessment stemmed from the responses to the subsequent telephone marketing: staff assigned to this consistently reported that no preliminary description was necessary for the actual discussion or sales talk, as the call recipients immediately remembered the name of the company, the product and – not least – the slogan.

The second positive result of the campaign was related to this: the response rate was between 5% in Austria and 27% in France, with up to one-third of total responses generated by the follow-up telephone marketing, which in many cases also led to new contracts.

In this way the first of the two core objectives of the project was achieved, i.e., a noticeable and significant increase in sales of the Global Mail Business product. Although a detailed economic analysis was not part of the project, even a cursory overview of the subsequent business development shows an additional increase in revenue in the seven-figure Euro range for the target countries.

The other lasting benefit of the campaign was that it clearly strengthened the positioning of DHL Global Mail as a first-class international provider of postal services in all the key markets, and especially with key customers. This was particularly pleasing as it promises great things in terms of future business development, as well as indicating that the second core objective had also been achieved.

An internal evaluation showed not only a perceptible increase brand awareness, but also that customers "learned" to make the association of DHL Global Mail with "high performance" and "resourceful" in the international mail business. This means that not only were new customers recruited directly, but that leads were also created with potential customers who at the time of the campaign did not have any shipping-related decisions to take or who had not yet considered the possibilities of international direct marketing as part of the range of tools available to them.

Since the two core objectives were so clearly achieved, no further detailed evaluation of results was required, particularly as no real weak points were perceived. The only recognizable area for improvement that emerged was the fact that response rates differed so widely from country to country.

A wide range of factors, each of which would have to be studied individually, could underlie this, e.g., the quality and success of the relative competitive offers, fundamental fluctuations in response rates between countries, the quantitative significance of direct marketing in all 14 countries and/or the significance of international business for companies in these countries.

A successful solution for all sectors and locations

It can in any case be concluded from the development and implementation of the campaign that this approach can achieve a high degree of success in the marketing of products and services. Nor should it prove impossible to integrate other countries with additional characteristics – for example the Muslim world, the cultural patchwork of the Indian subcontinent or China with its Confucian influences. This is especially true if the service providers tasked with the mission are of a similar size, international structure and logistical competence to DHL Global Mail under the aegis of Deutsche Post World Net.

For international product and service providers, this means that new customer groups can be developed through the use of direct marketing campaigns aimed simultaneously at different national markets. And in view of the excellent prospects for success, the cost is considerably low. For the realization of such campaigns, companies can chose to use providers like DHL Global Mail, which offer blanket market coverage and qualified, sensitive staff who can tackle constructively all the challenges of the overall planning process. Alternatively, product or service providers can run international campaigns with the support of a number of national and/or specialized service providers. However in this case, care must be taken to ensure that these service providers (either individually or collectively) fully meet the requirements for international direct marketing.

DHL Global Mail is at any rate capable of guaranteeing its customers a very convenient, efficient, and above all successful method of simultaneously addressing their customers in all important markets. At this point, this is still a comparatively new practice, however, and anyone taking this step today can be sure to remain one step ahead of the competition.

5   Summary

■ Direct marketing campaigns run according to the action principle "Create Globally – Think Locally – Act Globally" are a welcome addition to the range of marketing tools tailored to companies with an international focus. These are companies that simultaneously market products and services in different target countries and want to take specific cultural, ethnical or religious attitudes into account.

■ Using mailings to address identified recipients with personalized core messages and visualizations leads to an increase in brand awareness. In addition, it strengthens the positioning in target markets and directly increases sales of the advertised products. The impact of the mailings is enhanced through supplementary advertising media and activities, which are coordinated with regard to their timing and content.

■ This model project allowed DHL Global Mail to prove that centrally planned direct marketing campaigns, tailored to different target markets and/or target groups, can work. It thus opens up a new way for all international companies to address diverse customer groups both individually and successfully. This is possible at a lower cost than distinct campaigns designed for individual countries.

As the core element of such campaigns, mailings can significantly increase the chances of success, provided that they take account of the different content levels which are tailored to the individual communication patterns of the particular target groups. Both, the message and visualization, have to gain the attention of the recipients immediately. Ideally, the mailing would be supported by supplementary measures such as tie-in advertisements in trade journals and follow-up actions.

Personal letters are evidently the medium of choice in gaining the attention of opinion leaders and decision-makers, irrespective of their location. By their very form, such communication shows that the advertiser has not only taken the specific requirements of the target group on board, but has also understood them.

Auke van den Hout, Kay Peters

A successful departure from the beaten track

Inteligo identifies new prospects for its services in Poland

2

Overview

- Poland, like the rest of the world, has witnessed rapid growth in online banking. Unlike traditional banks, internet banks depend solely on direct marketing to recruit and keep their customers.
- For Inteligo, a leading internet bank in Poland, seeking out promising prospects as new customers is a critical success factor. However, the bank had already exhausted the classical methods of address selection.
- Unconventional analyses led to the discovery of previously neglected relationships between products and customers, and thus identifying a new target group to be addressed.
- 30% of all those prospects addressed in the new target segment actually became new Inteligo customers.

1   The rapid worldwide expansion of internet banking

Until the beginning of the 1990s, anyone wanting to pay rent, set up a standing order or taking out a loan had no option but to visit a branch of a bank. Some 15 years ago, the first so-called "remote services" appeared in the USA and Western Europe before rapidly spreading worldwide. This was the inception of online banking. It was now possible for private customers to conduct their banking transactions from home. The spread of these services led to a fundamental change in the attitudes and behavior of bank retail customers. Financial services became more readily available, independent of time and distance, convenient as well as faster and cheaper (Fig. 2-2-1). Banks also saved substantial costs, since they needed fewer branches and staff. At the same, highly qualified staff was released from routine tasks in order to provide consultation for more complex and profitable products. This prepared the ground for online banking.

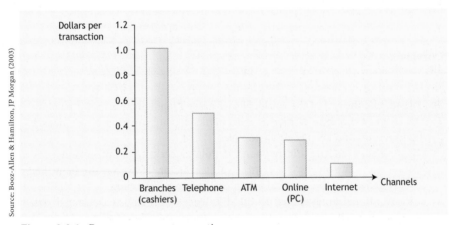

Figure 2-2-1: Process costs per transaction

The rapid expansion of the internet in many countries led to the emergence of pure online or direct banks, which saw no need for any branches whatsoever. Communication with customers was entirely by mail, telephone or internet. These new banks were particularly dependent on direct marketing to gain and keep customers. Under the pressure of this new competition, the traditional banks also launched successful online banking ventures. After a certain delay, this trend has now spread beyond the western industrialized nations. Fig. 2-2-2 shows the growth of online banking in 2002 and compares it with other services.

Online banking is most popular in the Scandinavian countries and Germany, followed by various OECD states, the Eastern European countries, Mexico and South Korea. In 2000, Poland belonged to a group of latecomers that nevertheless represent large potential markets.

Country	Actual GDP per capita in % (US= 100)	Mobile phones per 100 inhabitants	PCs per 100 inhabitants	Internet users as % of inhabitants	Bank customers using online banking (%)
Sweden	69	58	45.1	41	31
Finland	71	65	36.0	41	29
Germany	74	29	29.7	18	12
USA	100	31	51.1	27	6
Great Britain	70	46	30.3	21	6
Singapore	70	42	43.7	24	5
Australia	75	34	-	32	4
Mexico	25	8	4.4	2	4
Czech Republic	40	19	10.7	7	3
South Korea	49	50	18.2	23	3
Argentina	37	12	4.9	2	3
Braszil	21	9	3.6	2	3
Hong Kong	71	64	29.8	36	<2
China	11	3	1.2	1	<1
India	7	<1	0.3	<1	<1
Malaysia	24	14	6.9	7	<1
Poland	26	10	6.2	5	<1
Thailand	19	4	2.3	1	<1
Japan	79	45	-	21	-
South Africa	27	12	5.5	4	-
Nigeria	2	<1	-	<1	-

Sources: Claessens, Glaessner, Klingebiel (2002a, 2002b), Computimes New Strait Times (2002), Sept. 2002

Figure 2-2-2: Comparison of international e-banking development

Further growth has been rapid and will presumably continue. Fig. 2-2-3 shows that in 2000, only 6% of bank customers in the USA made use of the convenience of online banking, while in 2003, this figure had risen to approximately 25% of all households. Some 12% of all bills for private households were presented and settled entirely online. A similar development can be expected soon among the so-called latecomers.

Figure 2-2-4 supports this expectation. It shows that the growth of online banking was at first limited to the industrial nations. But while growth in these regions is now already stagnating in percentage terms, other regions are just beginning to grow. Customer numbers in Asia are climbing at 45% annually and in Eastern Europe and South America the annual pace of growth is a respectable 20%.

The emergence of online banking follows a similar pattern in every country. At first, simple services such as account management, transfers and standing orders prove popular. As customers gain more experience, they begin to demand more complex services online, such as loan information, share transactions or insurance, and these usually require a higher level of support.

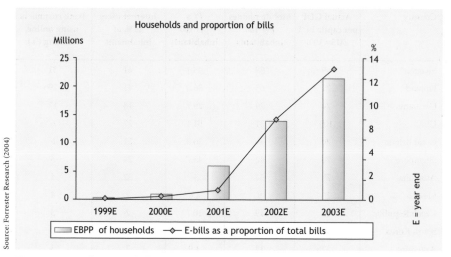

Source: Forrester Research (2004)

Figure 2-2-3: Electronic bill presentation & payment (EBPP): forecast for the USA

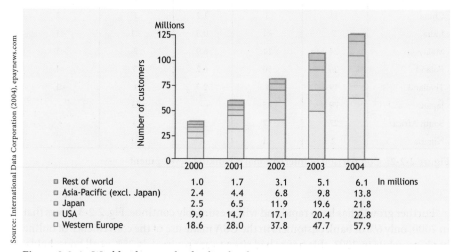

Source: International Data Corporation (2004), epaynews.com

Figure 2-2-4: Worldwide growth of online banking

The use of internet banking services differs in many countries according to customer segment. Nonetheless, international similarities in user structures can still be seen. Internet services are used most often by relatively high-income households, with the age of the head of the household playing only a minor role. Only in lower income groups are younger users more numerous.

These preliminary observations and illustrations show that online banking has achieved rapid growth worldwide. This has also helped to harmonize user structures and services across the globe.

Internet banks are the driving force of this new evolution. Having broken with the traditional bank structures, they are particularly dependent on direct marketing to gain and keep new customers. They often start by finding their customers using standard address selection methods. But this is becoming increasingly difficult, as untapped segments of particularly internet-savvy customers are becoming harder to find. Internet banks are thus more dependent on new methods and approaches of identifying prospects to open up additional customer segments. Poland's Inteligo is an entirely internet-based bank that had to face these challenges. By cooperating with the address and service provider Acxiom, Inteligo discovered new methods of gaining customers, paving the way for internet banks in other countries to follow suit.

2   Internet bank Inteligo strengthens its position in Poland

Fifteen years ago, markets such as Estonia, Hungary and Poland were behind the Iron Curtain, playing only a minor economic role for Western companies. That all changed with the end of communism and, since 2004, some of these former Eastern Bloc countries have already joined the European Union. Poland has by far the largest economy in the eastern part of this community of nations. According to a study by the IWH (Halle Institute for Economic Research) in Germany, Poland represents 23.5% of the economic output of the new EU member states. For many international and national companies, direct marketing appears to be the right tool for opening up the Polish market. Direct mailings and telephone marketing are the most popular means of advertising communication, as they are both well received by consumers. Because of this, 81% of all advertising enterprises in Poland use a number of different direct marketing tools.

With over 5,500 personnel worldwide, Acxiom is one of the largest providers in the customer data management market. It recognized the significance of the growing Polish market for advertising some years ago, and set up its subsidiary Acxiom Poland, in early 1998. By sending questionnaires sent to households throughout Poland, the company managed to create a database containing approved addresses of some two million Polish households within four years.

Rising consumption in Poland, combined with a budding real-estate sector, make the country particularly attractive to banks. Besides traditional banks, new providers are also fighting for a share of this growing market, including the internet bank Inteligo. Many were skeptical when the concept for Inteligo was first proposed, since market research at that time had shown that prospective customers had relatively little interest in online banking. However, those working on the project were encouraged by developments abroad. The Polish market exhibited signs of the same gap that new internet banks filled overseas. Traditional banks were offering products via standard sales and communication channels. The first market segment addressed by Inteligo using direct mailings was that of young internet users with a high level of education living in large cities. Inteligo launched the campaign using the claim "Don't spend your money on bank branches with fancy marble halls – Use Inteligo". The company pioneered the use of direct marketing in the Polish financial services sector, which has since become one of the largest users of direct marketing.

When Inteligo was launched, less than 1% of the population was aware of online banking. Nowadays, 90% of bank account holders know about this service, and at least 10% have used it at least once. What's more, the use of online banking in Poland is meanwhile no longer confined to the young: 48% of current users are 35-65 years old, 21% live in villages and 60% have no higher education (according to a study by ARC Rynek i Opnia). The latest research by GfK Polonia shows that 25% of all Poles over the age of 15 now use the internet, and 13% go online every day. They regard internet banking as a service that makes banking transactions simpler, faster and more convenient. The rapid growth of online banking customers confirms this. In the last year alone, Inteligo recorded 33% customer growth. At present, approximately 6.4 million people in Poland have access to online banking and, according to information from the Polish Bank Union, 4.9 million people use e-banking at least once a month.

As a pure online financial services provider with no "brick and mortar" branches, Inteligo is entirely dependent on direct marketing for communicating with its customers. In the space of two years, the bank rapidly developed a large base of regular customers through direct customer dialog, making particular use of the addresses provided by Acxiom Poland. The requisite addresses were selected according to criteria such as age, income, size of home, and the availability of an internet connection. The profiles of existing customer relationships were used as a basis for selecting prospect addresses. However, the datasets corresponding to previous selection criteria had been completely exhausted by the beginning of 2003. Because of its prior success with direct marketing campaigns, Inteligo wanted to reenlist the help of Acxiom and its address database.

It thus became necessary to define a new set of selection criteria for the identification prospective online banking customers. The use of a new statistical selection process and the avoidance of well-known, default profiles formed the starting point for this new approach.

3   The database as a goldmine

The selection criteria used for previous successful direct marketing campaigns focused strongly on the attributes of regular customers and their attitudes towards Inteligo products, as well as the relationship of this target group to the internet. This method of prospect address selection had proven successful for Inteligo in the past. However, even after intensive treatment of these potential Polish customers, new address material was necessary to develop the market further. But which criteria should be used to select these prospects? The answer was to identify target groups who would react in a similar, positive way to Inteligo's direct marketing -

by opening online accounts. This new group had to be filtered by Acxiom Poland from the existing volume of data.

Acxiom decided not to base its research on the profiles of regular customers and product information from Inteligo, but instead chose to start completely from scratch. This new data selection process would produce addresses which had not been considered in the past, as they did not fit into the standard selection pattern.

New patterns, structures and samples, corresponding as far as possible to those of online banking customers, now had to be uncovered in the data held by Acxiom Poland. Just like gold diggers, the address experts went looking for the hidden treasures in their databases. The idea was to identify new patterns of behavior among potential online banking customers in order to substantially increase the target audience for Inteligo advertising campaigns. This was also a test for Acxiom: was it really possible to generate new leads from a database which seemed to have been exhausted?

Synopsis

- The datasets in the Acxiom address database that conformed to Inteligo's regular customer profile had been completely exhausted.
- A new selection process and a move away from standard profiles expanded the address base for planned campaigns in an intelligent and promising manner.
- The aim of Inteligo and Acxiom was to match the outstanding number of new customers produced by previous campaigns.

4   The end of old profiling approaches

Acxiom Poland first decided on the use of modern statistical tools. Analysis was to focus on the lifestyle, desires and needs of previous Inteligo customers, avoiding any orientation towards standard selection criteria. A conscious decision was made to ignore content-specific data for this analysis, so as to prevent Inteligo or Acxiom from inadvertently corrupting the process by transferring incorrect assumptions about the profiles of potentially profitable customers. One basic assumption served as a guide: "Similar people behave in similar ways as far as how they lead their lives, their preferences and attitudes. Therefore, the people who most resemble the existing users of a certain product are the most promising customer leads for this product."

On this basis, Acxiom selected a group of long-standing online banking customers from its data. This group of addresses, just like Acxiom Poland's other addresses, was defined on the basis of approximately 1,500 different variables: lifestyle and sociodemographic data, media consumption, and consumer behavior in different vertical markets, including the financial services they used. By employing new data-mining techniques, Acxiom identified the particular characteristics of internet account holders. These critical characteristics formed the sample against which Acxiom Poland compared all the addresses. Apart from selection criteria like education, occupation, position, household incomes and/or purchasing power, hobbies and other behavior characteristics were also of major importance in the search for target groups who would prefer online banking. This process led to the breakdown of Acxiom Poland's data into numerous small segments. These all showed large similarities to internet account holders, but in differing ways. The potential interest of these segments in Inteligo's bank services also varied widely.

The best potential new customer segments discovered using this process all had one thing in common, and it astonished both Acxiom Poland and Inteligo. It turned out that the most attractive prospects for online banking often had no internet access at home. This meant that the new target groups identified did not correspond in major aspects to the ones previously addressed. The popularity of the internet among recipients of the advertising had been one of the most important characteristics in the selection of addresses – the advertiser was, after all, a purely internet-based bank.

In view of these surprising results, Inteligo and Acxiom Poland initially doubted the value of the new analysis and the associated address selection process. According to these findings, internet access - indispensable for an online account and the very element so closely linked with the core characteristics of the product to be marketed - seemed not to be relevant when selecting addresses of prospective customers. The new situation was discussed with Inteligo, and both parties decided that an advertising test with a limited number of recipients was the best way to judge the value of the new methodology.

Emphasis of this approach

- Analyses instead of hypotheses. The only assumption made was that similar people behave in similar ways as far as how they live their lives, their preferences and attitudes. Therefore, the people who most resemble the existing users of a certain product on these characteristics are the most promising new customer leads for this product.
- In the place of simple criteria based on information about products and customers, Acxiom Poland and Inteligo used modern statistical processes to select promising prospects.

5   New customers are good customers

The results of the test and of the subsequent campaign proved Acxiom Poland and Inteligo right. Both the new process and the move away from standard customer profiles when selecting prospects contributed to this success. On one hand, the new process is especially good at revealing similarities between the individual characteristics of users who do not fit the usual preconceptions of address brokers and advertisers. On the other hand, the success of such methods depends on those involved understanding the need to first distance themselves from standard customer profiles. Use of the new address database led to above-average results. About 30% of the recipients of the advertising became new customers, three times more than with addresses selected according to the previous standard criteria. This is even more significant if compared to the benchmark for a successful advertising campaign in Poland, since this figure was exceeded by a factor of almost twenty.

The most important results

■ Some 30% of the new target groups addressed registered as new customers, three times more than the previous response rate.
■ With the help of modern statistical processes, and by moving beyond standard customer profiles, it was possible to identify a large number of attractive prospects.

6   Summary

By means of customer analysis and the use of up-to-date statistical methods, it was possible to create a completely new profile for prospective Inteligo customers. This represents a strategic advantage, particularly in the face of increasing competition. Overseas internet banks will certainly not be the only ones wishing to profit from this knowledge. The example highlighted here suggests that other industries and businesses couls also benefit from similar approaches.

The success of the advertising campaign using new customer profiles also highlights the opportunities that are lost if a campaign is focused solely on standard customer profiles. It is impressive proof that in a dynamic industry like online banking, customer profiles can soon become outdated. People who appear unattractive in traditional marketing terms can turn out to be valuable new customers if new evaluation criteria are used. This continual search for new patterns is what makes the use of such modern methods so effective. And these patterns are found in the relationship not only between products and consumers, but also between users and non-users of a product. The insights produced by these investigations have implications far beyond address selection and advertising presentation: they may lead to a complete repositioning of a company, and to the adaptation of its products to a newly defined target group. It is therefore well worth comprehending these changes in direct marketing, so as to be able to strike out in new directions.

7   Bibliography

BAI (2003). Interest in Internet Banking by Segments.

Claessens, S., T. Glaessner und D. Klingebiel. 2002a. E-finance in emerging markets: Is leapfrogging possible? World Bank Financial Sector Discussion Paper, No. 4, June.

Claessens, S., T. Glaessner und D. Klingebiel. 2002b. E-finance: Reshaping the Financial Landscape Around the World. World Bank Financial Sector Discussion Paper, No. 7, September.

Computimes New Strait Times. 2002. September 2002.

Dannenberg, M, D. Kellner. 1998. The Bank of Tomorrow with Today's Technology. International Journal of Bank Marketing, February 1998, pp. 90–97.

Forrester Research. 2004. US EBPP Forecast.

Guru, B.K., B. Shanmugam, N. Alam, C.J. Perera. 2003. An Evaluation Of Internet Banking Sites in Islamic Countries. The Journal of Internet Banking and Commerce, Vol. 8, No. 2 (www.arraydev.com/commerce/JIBC/articles.htm).

International Data Cooperation. 2004. Growth in Internet Banking. epaynews.com.

JP Morgan Interviews. 2003. see BAI (2003).

Perumal, V., B. Shanmugam. 2004. Internet Banking: Boon or Bane? The Journal of Internet Banking and Commerce, Vol. 9, No. 3 (www.arraydev.com/commerce/JIBC/articles.htm).

Rhind, G. 2003. Never Underestimate the Importance of Local Culture. The Journal of Internet Banking and Commerce, Vol. 8, No. 1 (www.arraydev.com/commerce/JIBC/articles.htm).

Sahut, J.-M. 2003. On-line Brokerage in Europe: Actors & Strategies. The Journal of Internet Banking and Commerce, Vol. 8, No. 1 (www.arraydev.com/commerce/78JIBC/articles.htm).

Singhal, S. 2003. Internet Banking The Second Wave: A Banker's Guide to Internet Strategy in the Post Dotcom Era. Tata McGraw-Hill Publications.

Singh, B., P. Malhotra. 2004. Adoption of Internet Banking: An Empirical Investigation of Indian Banking Sector. The Journal of Internet Banking and Commerce, Vol. 9, No. 2 (www.arraydev.com/commerce/JIBC/articles.htm).

Vijayan, V.P., V. Perumal, B. Shanmugam. 2004. Waves Of Multimedia Banking Development. The Journal of Internet Banking and Commerce, Vol. 9, No. 3 (www.arraydev.com/commerce/JIBC/articles.htm).

Thomas Nagel

International dialog for successful acquisition of new customers

3

Overview

■ Internationalization offers both small and medium-sized companies count-less opportunities. Direct marketing is a good way to open up new markets overseas.

■ The risks of internationalization can be minimized by using direct market-ing. By explaining key strategic and operational issues, this article will dem-onstrate how these opportunities can be developed systematically.

■ In the context of the direct marketing strategy, the selection of the appropri-ate direct marketing media is of great importance. This will vary according to the target group, industry and product, and will also depend on the target country.

1   Market observation is the starting point

Particularly in these economically competitive times, it is important that compa-nies present themselves to the customer not as a sales organization, but as a solution provider for individual challenges. Directly addressing customers helps to build trust between companies and consumers. This is the basis for a durable customer relationship and it is precisely why more companies are employing direct market-ing. Moreover, a direct customer dialog offers extensive opportunities to measure the success of advertising efforts. This leads to increased effectiveness within the existing marketing budget.

Nonetheless, direct marketing professionals know how difficult and expensive it can be to successfully acquire and retain new customers in the long-term, even in a company's familiar domestic market. How much more difficult might it be to do this in unfamiliar overseas markets?

Yet the signs bode well for successful market development beyond national borders. The introduction of the euro in particular has made European markets more transparent for buyers and sellers, offering numerous opportunities for companies to operate across borders and tap into new customer segments. International direct marketing is therefore an appropriate tool for companies with such ambitions. However, it cannot be used in the same way across the board but should instead take careful account of the particular conditions in individual countries and industries. At the same time, it should be noted that the mix of direct marketing tools used can vary depending on the stage of the relationship with the customer.

In the case of advertising to the active customer, addressed mailings are the most commonly used direct marketing tool. This is because the relatively high response rate ensures that this approach is cost-effective. The response rate for mailings to active customers is usually significantly higher than that for mailings sent to indiscriminate addresses, i.e., prospective new customers.

When planning a mailing to active customers, companies can consult their databases and CRM systems and select at the touch of button which addresses are suitable for further mailing activities and which are not. In this respect, the most important selection criteria are the time of the last purchase/order, the order frequency and the order value/total order amount. These selection procedures are known as RFM (Recency/Frequency/Monetary Value) methods. Accordingly, more and more companies are using them to systematically select inactive former customers for reactivation mailings.

In most cases, this procedure is not suitable for acquiring new customers, however. The process is considerably more expensive than maintaining the existing customer base. Acquiring new customers is important for any company, but finding the right customers is even more important.

It is crucial that customer acquisition is done in the most efficient way. Active customer data can be used to build a profile of the ideal new customer. Such profiles encompass not only customer valuations based on transaction history, but also other criteria contained in the database. In addition to sociodemographic characteristics, geographical and psychographic factors are also of particularly importance. This includes information about values, attitudes and preferences, e.g., quality awareness, media preferences and price sensitivity. Equipped with these profiles of valuable target customers, advertisers can then search the various address sources for potential new leads.

Direct marketing activities aimed at acquiring new customers have to be constantly analyzed and refined. Many years' experience is required, along with the courage to keep trying out new ideas. Analytical aptitude is also necessary, as is the willingness to regularly question even the accepted wisdom accumulated over time. What is already a challenge in the national context becomes even more so when doing business across borders. International direct marketing is considerably more complex, due to differing competitive environments, languages, legal systems and cultures.

Even so, the potential risks are offset by the excellent opportunities for profitable new business. In particular, companies should consider international expansion when foreign companies begin to penetrate their domestic market and start accumulating market share. This article will draw on numerous specific practical examples to demonstrate how to exploit overseas opportunities while incurring only moderate risk.

Challenges of international expansion

■ Compared with the domestic market, differences in the sociodemographic factors are to some extent more acute.
■ Consumer values, attitudes and behavior often differ from those in familiar markets.
■ Due to differing competitive environments and mature market structures, foreign target groups may demonstrate different attitudes towards the usual marketing mix, e.g., use of different media, price sensitivity or quality awareness.
■ Companies have to take these differences into account if they are to be effective in acquiring new customers and retaining them in the long-term. It is important to establish a consistent image in the new market.

2   Fundamental issues regarding the international acquisition of new customers

Before entering a foreign market and planning direct marketing activities, a whole range of strategic and operational issues has to be clarified:

Which countries, based on geographical, demographic and economic conditions, should be considered "target countries"? Is there a genuine demand in that country for the products or services offered? In which segments? What is the extent of the demand? Will the product need to be modified or adapted? Will packaging modifications be sufficient, or will the name have to be changed as well, perhaps because it is difficult to pronounce or could be mistaken for another product? Is the product competitive in terms of quality, design and price? What are strengths and weaknesses of the competition? Can these weak points be exploited? Are there any special inspection requirements or safety regulations that have to be observed?

There are many questions to be answered. Some can probably be dealt with based on experience alone. For others, it may be necessary to seek professional advice. This advice may be obtained from sources as German and overseas trade associations, market research companies, address suppliers, and media agencies ready to do business with would-be advertisers. Many of these companies perform certain preliminary services free of charge. Among their number is DHL Global Mail, which actively supports companies intending to develop foreign markets by means of direct marketing. It is possible to book time with an experienced direct marketing manager by contacting DHL's competence center for international direct marketing. These and other providers develop turnkey solutions, from analysis and planning all the way to execution of direct marketing campaigns. Naturally this also includes evaluation of response and fulfillment.

Once the target country has been selected, consideration has to be given to the following questions regarding the acquisition of new customers:

Strategic and operational questions regarding implementation

Strategic questions:
- Can foreign target groups be identified on the basis of existing domestic target groups? Are there perhaps additional, different target groups?
- Will the consumer benefits be as attractive to consumers in the target country as they are to domestic customers?
- Can the same promotional and creative approaches be employed?

Operational questions:
- Does the advertising contravene foreign laws regarding competition?
- What data protection needs to be obeyed?
- What address will be given for orders and any potential returns?
- What methods of payment are available to new customers buying the goods abroad?
- Where can companies find the right translator for overseas promotions?

Can foreign target groups be deduced on the basis of domestic target groups?

If the target group definitions are simply transferred directly from the company's home country, considerable risks may be involved. There are significant differences in the sociodemographic factors, e.g., between Germany and other European countries, such as family status, number of children, buying power, home ownership, occupation, education, age distribution and the proportion of working women. In Germany, for example, one in every three households is a single household, whereas in Italy, it is one in every six, and in Spain just one in ten.

Values, consumer habits and attitudes to certain issues will continue to differ across Europe for a long time to come. Whereas in Germany, safety and prestige are a primary concern, in France, consumers are more concerned with comfort and convenience. When describing a product in France it is usual to emphasize or even exaggerate the benefits, sometimes in a humorous way. The technical details, on the other hand, are given less attention. German companies, however, are happy to weigh down texts with technical data. Such information would be sent out in France as part of a second mailing, after contact with the prospect has already been established.

Another area in which there are considerable differences is environmental protection. In Germany and the Scandinavian countries, environmental protection carries greater weight than in Spain, Portugal or Italy. For this reason, promoting a product as "environmentally friendly" would boost sales in Germany but may not work at all in Mediterranean countries. Likewise, a more suggestive design may go down well in some countries and less well in others.

Nevertheless, there are many aspects that are similar: youngsters in France suffer from acne and lovesickness to the same degree as youngsters in Germany. British women are as keen to make the housework easier by using modern household appliances as are women in Denmark. And Austrian men certainly love their cars as much as German men do.

Internationally active companies therefore try, wherever possible, to compete in as many countries as they can, using the same advertising. This reduces costs on the one hand and ensures a consistent image on the other.

There are also differences in how well direct marketing is accepted in different countries. Large countries, like Germany, France and the UK, lead the way in terms of expenditure on direct advertising and the number of mailings sent out. In contrast, Austria, the Netherlands and Switzerland are at the top of the table in terms of the number of mailings per capita. This almost certainly has something to do with how well direct marketing is received by people in those countries. But it also relates to the degree to which to this form of advertising has been developed and to the level of income. Considering that the buying power in the new EU member states is only about one eighth of that in Germany, it may be the case that, although people in these countries might find a product attractive, they often cannot afford it. These aspects should be taken into account.

And just as there are huge differences in buying power between countries, there can sometimes be a world of difference between regions within a country. Poland's capital city Warsaw, for example, stands out with an average purchasing power (disposable income per capita per year) of €4,888 per annum (the German average is €16,926). But at the same time, there are communities in the poorer regions of Poland, along its borders with the Ukraine and Belarus, where purchasing power is less than €1,500 per annum. Nevertheless, in the long-term, it is the new member states of the European Union that offer the greatest potential.

For advertisers, this means that it is important to assess not only average purchasing power but also purchasing power differentials within the country. This is one way to avoid some of the costly losses incurred due to non-selectivity during a direct marketing campaign.

Will the consumer benefits be as attractive to consumers in the target country as they are to domestic customers?

In this respect, consumer attitudes can make all the difference. Market research with the help of specialized institutes can ensure a high degree of certainty.

*Example: A foreign provider of goods wants to find out how European housewives re-
spond to a promotion for food products at a significantly reduced price. 1,200 women
who had experience with such promotions were surveyed in France, Germany, Great
Britain and Italy. French women found this kind of promotion "exciting" (77%),
whereas British women did not find it exciting at all. For them, such promotions are
clearly nothing new. Around 33% of German housewives were put off by something
about the offer, and 12% were of the opinion that "a low price indicates poor quality which can be dangerous we are talking about food". Among Italian women, only
about 12% expressed dislike, and hardly any made a connection between a lower
price and poor quality. Nonetheless, this remained the main reason for refusal in all
four countries. Opinions therefore differed significantly, as did the reasons underlying them. All in all, however, the reduced price offer was positively received by a
majority of the women.*

Can the promotional and creative approaches be employed?

It is well known that people react differently when it comes to matters of taste.
And this is true even within a single country. Advertising material is criticized as
harshly as literature or art, even though it is hardly taken as seriously. It is possible
to maintain that "if it is liked here, it will be liked elsewhere". With one proviso: if
something appears "typically German", it may be met with some reservation overseas. In respect of advertising designs, the fact that people's appearance differs can
play a significant role, especially if adverts or brochures feature people who are
meant to be typical of their target group. Thus, a fair-haired family pictured in a
north German environment would be seen by the advertising recipient in Sicily as
thoroughly "exotic". A German consumer would react in the same way to a Palermo
street scene featured in a mailing. In such cases, it is advisable to create a deliberate-
ly neutral environment, unless the intention is to emphasize the product's origin.

Does the advertising contravene foreign competition law?

Despite all the efforts towards harmonization within the EU, many countries still
retain their own competition law. Whereas in Germany the laws governing discounts and regulations for free samples have been relaxed, care has to be taken in
other countries when it comes to price reductions and gifts intended to stimulate
orders.

In France – where, incidentally, the law stipulates that advertising must be in
French – gifts intended to prompt a response or increase the order value are common. In the UK as well, discounting and competitions are frequently used as at-
tention-grabbers. Nonetheless, the ASA (Advertising Standard Authority) oversees
and regulates the industry in accordance with advertising standards. Advertising
must under no circumstances entice people into dependency or endanger children. Campaigns must be scrutinized and approved prior to launch. This applies
in particular to suggestive advertisements showing naked skin. In this case, the
campaign may be banned. In one instance of a multi-mailing involving several
postcards, each individual postcard, together with the order of the postcards, had
to be scrutinized and approved by the ASA. If the ASA withholds its approval, then

other ASA members, such as publishers and postal distribution organizations, can prohibit distribution or publication. In addition to the ASA, a fully qualified lawyer specializing in competition law should also be consulted.

In Germany, it is relatively easy for pressure groups or consumer protection associations to obtain an injunction against advertising companies that contravene the laws against unfair competition. In Austria, there are added complications in that not only the company, but also the executive can be personally sued by the Chamber of Labor. Depending on the offence and its severity, this can rapidly lead to a penalty of several thousand euros in damages. Furthermore, it is often the case that the guilty party must publicize the outcome in a national daily newspaper – at its own cost. This, too, can easily result in costs running into thousands of euros.

For these reasons, it is always recommended that all advertising material for overseas campaigns is scrutinized by a local legal specialist.

What data protection issues need to be considered?

Data protection is a major concern in Scandinavian countries in particular. This primarily affects the use of purchased addresses. Usually, the advertising company will receive information about data protection from its address supplier.

In the majority of European countries, citizens who do not wish to receive any direct marketing from companies can have their names placed on a Robinson List. Advertisers are able to check addresses against these lists. This reduces non-selectivity losses when sending out mailings and prevents legal complications. The article by Alastair Tempest later in the book discusses the significance of Robinson Lists and how they are used.

Austria has its own peculiarity: each and every reply card and coupon must offer mailing recipients the option to indicate that they do not wish to receive further advertising material, even from third parties. The reply card or coupon would probably display the following wording: "I am aware that I have the option to refuse further mailings, including from third parties." If the recipient crosses out this sentence and returns the card or coupon, then s/he should not receive any further mailings. Incidentally, the "cross-out rate" is usually below 5%.

Which address will be given for orders and any potential returns?

If a company has its head office overseas and the consumer is not familiar with the company, the reply address can act as a major obstacle to placing orders. The advert will be met with greater skepticism if the mailing comes from overseas. A local address is therefore recommended. This means that customers in Switzerland send their orders to a Swiss address and French customers send their orders to an address in France. The same goes for the address given for returns, used by customers wishing to exchange or return goods. In the long-term, only satisfied customers remain good and loyal buyers. Customer satisfaction is an important factor for sustaining any business, and so new customers should be given the option of sending returned goods to a local address. This builds trust and may well be rewarded with subsequent orders. Although a logistical challenge, this is an issue that should be addressed in the interests of customer convenience.

The same applies to telephone hotlines. Recipients who are happy to call an overseas telephone number in response to a mailing are hard to find. Even though the cost of making overseas calls is considerably lower than it used to be, many customers are still not prepared to make such calls. Perhaps this is not entirely based on the higher cost of calling abroad: it may also be due to the assumption that they will have to speak a foreign language. The answer is to offer simple, user-friendly customer service numbers, which can then be diverted to an overseas number.

What methods of payment are available to new customers buying goods overseas?

Payment for goods ordered is an important criterion during the planning phase. There are sometimes considerable differences in payment methods and habits between individual countries.

In France, more than 30% of all private individuals pay in advance by check. This means that payment is received before the merchandise is delivered. Another popular method of payment in France is the private charge card, used by almost 30% of French people.

The situation in the UK is similar, with customers usually paying by check or credit card.

In Germany, the norm is for goods to be delivered on open account. Payment by automatic debit transfer or credit card is less common. Cash on delivery is a rarely used method, and new customers who have not yet had dealings with the company do not favor it. Offering just this payment method in mailings may significantly reduce the response rate. In the case of merchandise delivered on open account, companies should bear in mind that some new customers will not settle up until a reminder has been sent. If they still do not pay, the payment request may have to be assigned to a collection service. All of this incurs costs and, at worst, losses should it prove impossible to collect payment. For this reason, companies operating in Germany are advised to check the address lists of Deutsche Post Direkt or Creditreform prior to delivering orders above a certain amount. Both companies provide data on the creditworthiness of customers. Companies have to pay a fee to check their lists, but it is usually worthwhile because regular checks can significantly reduce the risk of non-payment.

Where can companies find the right translator for overseas promotions?

The most important communication medium is language. Only those who master the language of others can gain an insight into their mentality. Unfortunately, language experts are few and far between. Someone who has only a reasonable grasp of the foreign language is unlikely to notice errors in an inadequate translation. And when complaints begin to arrive – particularly in the case of technical appliances – it is usually too late to do anything about it. The brochures and directions for use etc. have already been printed and the mailings sent out. The money invested is lost.

Of course, it is not always that serious. But it can nevertheless be annoying. Below is a simple example for a simple item: a shaving brush from Italy. English directions for using this item read:

IMPORTANT

Badger hair is the best that you can get for effectively soaping up your face. Thanks to its elasticity and fineness, you only need to gently message to get a rich foam. There is no need to continue with the brush over every surface that needs to be soaped, because this causes hairs to break and soon the brush will be useless. It is however necessary to reach inside the fibres of the brush to remove acids contained in the shaving cream that remain between the hairs.

Anyone having a quick read through this would probably miss the many small errors and would only query the last sentence. Of course, the reader would have a general idea of what was meant. However, the Italian company probably thinks that its text is quite wonderful – as it was in Italian.

Another sample is the following from a tourism brochure:
XXX is without doubt the land of idyllic nature, is rich in animals and plant types as well as snow and adventure, but is also distinct because of its tradition, as well as the ownership of its own artistic culture and its great cuisine. Few provinces like this can offer visitors so many and linked prospects, etc.

In both cases, it is obvious that English is not the translator's mother tongue. After all, a dictionary is of little use if the user, though meticulous, picks the least appropriate of the English expressions offered.

A more fluid translation would be as follows:
XXX is a land of idyllic nature, rich in animals and plants, snow and adventure. Of equal importance is its cultural inheritance, cuisine and other arts. Only a handful of provinces can offer visitors such varied landscapes that are so delightful to behold.

What the company advertiser needs, therefore, are not English translators, but native English speakers. Even so, it is important to choose carefully. A foreigner who has been living and working in an English-speaking country for some time usually has a good feel for the differences between the regions and their inhabitants. No doubt such a foreigner would be particularly valuable if s/he also had some knowledge of the company's industry or product. This means that a mail-order business specializing in all kinds of household appliances would be better selecting a female translator rather than a male. Simple, but often true.

It would of course be even better if the native speaker has some knowledge of advertising. Since advertising texts have to be as vivid as possible, catchphrases and slogans should stimulate interest by using humorous puns. But beware: what sounds good in English may not sound right in the foreign language if the translation is poor. The native speaker with a feel for the language will perhaps know another pun that renders the original concept just as well. A different pun may be better understood by the readers and may even be more enjoyable for them.

In particular, when a text is to be translated into several languages, it may be advantageous to work with a translation agency. This ensures that a standardized procedure is followed for all languages and that the work is carried out professionally. Furthermore, most translation agencies are equipped with the full range of data processing tools. This means that if the customer can supply the original in electronic form, the agency can retain the layout and simply type over the original text. More often than not, the procedure is performed with the same software as the advertiser uses. This solution may cost a bit more, but it saves a lot of money that would otherwise be spent on the foreign-language version. Above all, this solution shows at a glance whether there will be problems of space if the original layout is maintained, since text length can vary greatly between languages. In the case of a brochure in German, the foreign-language text may simply not fit however hard one tries, as English texts tend to be shorter than German ones. In contrast, Finnish texts are usually considerably lengthier because of the longer words used in that language. As a consequence, it may at times be necessary to shorten the text. This, too, is one of the demands placed on the translator.

When the proofs for a foreign-language text arrive, the advertiser should not simply give one of the staff the responsibility for making corrections. They may well think, "It's OK to just check the manuscript against the original. That can't be too difficult." But that job is difficult, even with an excellent knowledge of the foreign language. Hence, a native speaker should be consulted again, even though this may incur additional expenses. As a rule, the majority of translation agencies use native speakers – although it is worthwhile confirming this. Generally, however, translators remain anonymous. For technical texts, it is essential to ask for a translator with technical knowledge.

If translations are needed for several countries, it is imperative to ensure that each translation is derived from the original text. Thus, do not translate from German into English, then from English into French, and finally from French into Italian, simply based on the availability of translators. The final text will be barely recognizable.

In addition to the translation, some translation agencies also write an adaptation of the German advertising text on the proof. First of all, a native-speaking translator establishes a raw text, which is then formulated into promotional text by a native-speaking copywriter. The greater investment is worthwhile.

Example: A German slogan reads "Milch macht müde Männer munter". A literal, thorough and methodological translation of this gives "Milk makes tired men awake". The translation, completely lacking in pizzazz, definitely does not have the effect intended by its author. A good translator/copywriter would reproduce the alliteration in the English version: "Milk makes moody misters merry". This sounds at least as good as the original, if not funnier.

The upshot is that, the better and more original the advertising text, the more worthwhile it is to have a native-speaking advertising copywriter produce an adaptation.

Of course, German advertising for use in Austria does not need to be translated. Nevertheless, a bit of flair cannot do any harm. In promotional mailings, it is important that Austrians be addressed by their proper title. These are not restricted to "Professor" and "MD", but also include "Chartered Engineer" for example. Even the wife of a "Ph.D." should be addressed as "Mrs. Dr. Moser" - something completely unfamiliar to Germans.

There are even differences in the actual language used in Germany and Austria. A German supplier of bakery products offering "leckere Plätzchen" [tasty biscuits] in Austria, would probably choke on his biscuits if s/he knew that both "Plätzchen" [biscuits] and "lecker" [tasty] are clichés that should be avoided. While many Germans find some Austrian terms quaintly charming, this can be a source of irritation to Austrians.

Many words may at first glance appear identical in both languages, but can still lead to mutual misunderstandings. For example, a German "Stuhl" [chair] would be called a "Sessel" in Austria, whereas "Sessel" in Germany refers to an armchair (which is called a "Fauteil" in Austria). This is worth knowing if you are a furniture manufacturer. The same holds for many words if one compares European to Latin American Spanish.

Preparation for international expansion

- It is important to review the target groups in the new market, focusing not only on sociodemographic characteristics, but also on values and attitudes, including those regarding marketing tools.
- The product benefits for the consumer have to be reviewed as well as countries differ in how much importance their consumers attach to individual product features.
- The design of the advertising material has to be reviewed. Images considered "exotic" overseas should be avoided unless the company running the promotion intends to emphasize its origin.
- A local legal specialist should examine the advertising material in order to avoid expensive and unpleasant surprises. This applies in particular to data protection provisions in the country concerned.
- Prospective customers should be given a local address for orders and returns. This builds trust and increases response rates. It is also advisable to follow local customs and conventions with respect to payment methods.
- Engaging a professional translation agency with native-speaking copywriters is a worthwhile investment in the case of advertising copies and product instructions.

3   Selecting the direct marketing tools

Success is the result of careful planning and cost control.

Once the essential prerequisites for entering the new market have been met, the next job is to define an efficient strategy for acquiring new customers with the help of direct marketing. The direct marketing strategy and media planning describe the proposed advertising activities, the budget, controlling activities and use of the chosen direct marketing tools.

All in all, direct marketing strategy provides information about:

- the selection of effective direct marketing tools, be they mailings, ads with response elements, inserts, bound inserts, door-to-door mailing or coop advertising;
- the relevant volumes for the chosen advertising media, together with a precise timetable for the campaign;
- the budget;
- controlling measures for the proposed activities, including cost input;
- expected response rates, benchmarks (CpI and CpO) and break-even points;
- follow-up plans.

Companies that regularly use direct marketing with great success not only plan carefully in advance, but also evaluate progress after every stage of their campaigns. This form of analysis provides important information that can be used for assessing the efficiency of advertising. In order to conduct such analysis, companies have to collect data consistently, e.g., contact costs, response rates and order values. Efficient controlling is crucial to the success of any direct marketer.

Risk minimization is another imperative when entering a new overseas market. If a direct marketing concept is successful in the domestic market, then advertisers should only change what is textually, legally or logistically necessary, based on prior research in the new market. However, everything that has proved successful thus far will have to be tested in the new market after the necessary adaptations and amendments have been made. By changing as few parameters as possible, companies can better compare and analyze the pilot results.

Another way to minimize risk is to run the above tests using a variety of direct marketing tools. The tests should be as small as possible but large enough to obtain a satisfactory number of respondents. It is crucial that the advertiser obtains meaningful and valid numbers.

Addressed mailing: direct advertising medium no. 1
If, in the home country, addressed mailings to selected address lists produce a satisfactory response in terms of new customer acquisition, then research has to be done to see whether it is possible to lease sufficient numbers of addresses for the corresponding target group in the new market. This will determine whether there

are a sufficient number of potential addresses, what they cost and whether the list owners will give permission to use them. In parallel to this, it is necessary to assess what costs will be incurred not only for using the addresses, but also for further processing, producing the linguistically-adapted campaign, postage costs, etc. Only then can comparisons and decisions be made as to whether it would make sense to try to acquire new customers using addressed mailings.

A brief note about postage: due to postal regulations, the standard DIN formats with a weight of up to 20 grams or C4 for large letters are the dominant sizes used in Germany, while the standard size in France is C5. Provided the address is machine-readable, postage for items weighing up to 35 grams is only €0.26 in France. It is therefore a bit more difficult for French businesses to adapt to the German market than vice versa, as German companies operating in France are able to increase the size and weight of their mailings and still enjoy reasonable prices.

If an overview of all the cost is available, it should be compared with the corresponding cost structure in the domestic market. For proper planning and costing in the next step, information on other benchmarks from the domestic market will be needed, such as the average response rates and the rate of expenditure that is required for each new prospect or new customer. Direct marketers quantify these benchmarks as CpO and CpI values. CpO stands for Cost per Order. This is the amount of money that has to be spent to obtain the first order of a new customer. CpI stands for Cost per Interest and describes the expenditure required for each new prospect. If a two-stage approach is used – with an initial mailing to stimulate interest and then a follow-up to convert these prospects into customers – then the benchmarks should reflect this.

These values can then be used to calculate expenditure: the company may invest, for example, €10 for a new customer and the complete mailing campaign costs approximately €1 per mailing. If the target average marginal income per first order is set at €25, a response rate of 2.86% is required. If, however, the entire costs of acquiring new customers has to be recovered immediately because subsequent purchases are not likely, a response rate of 4% would be needed.

Based on the values calculated, companies need to determine whether the response rates they require from an addressed mailing are realistic. If the advertiser draws the conclusion that the response requirements will most likely not be met, then the contact costs of a personalized mailing for the acquisition of new customers would be considered too high. In this case, other direct marketing tools would have to be considered.

Door-to-door mailings, unaddressed mailings and self-mailers as inserts in magazines and newspapers

If it is not possible to obtain enough addresses in the new foreign market, or if the contact costs for a mailing are too high, then an economical alternative is needed to achieve the desired results. It would make sense to consider unaddressed promotional mailings that can be widely circulated via door-to-door distribution or as inserts in magazines and newspapers. These direct marketing tools allow for a considerable reduction in contact costs compared with addressed mailings.

With door-to-door distribution, advertisers can reach almost all households in the country. In most European countries, it is possible to select target groups according to precise "geographical criteria". In Belgium and some other countries, the selection can be made according to zip codes, residential districts or even on the individual streets. In Denmark, there is the added option of using average demographic figures, for example, data on age, sex and income. The situation is similar in the Netherlands, Norway and Sweden. In this context, it is somewhat surprising that there is such a high level of acceptance of unaddressed mailings. Many consumers do not regard door-to-door distribution as a second-class medium at all, seeing little difference between this instrument and an addressed mailing. For advertisers, this presents an attractive opportunity to save costs.

Costs for door-to-door distribution vary according to the size and weight of the advertising material, the number of recipients, the distribution frequency and the number of response elements. The higher the annual circulation and the more frequent the distribution, the greater the discount that can be obtained. The international reply card is a good solution for companies that distribute advertising material to households in new overseas markets and want to enable new customers to return their order cards free of charge to an overseas address. Just like the familiar national reply card, the international version makes it easier for the customer to reply to international correspondence.

Inserts are another interesting way to build address resources. Inserts are advertising materials that are not are inserted, or blown in, by machine without being fixed to the publication. Inserts annoy some people because they often fall out when the magazine is opened. But this could be the exact reason why inserts are so effective – an advertising medium that has to be picked up actively.

The number of media available for insert advertising is huge. In Germany, there are over 8,000 such media in the form of magazines, newspapers and journals. In this field, the German market with its relatively large population offers many advantages in this area over other markets. In addition to special interest magazines on practically every subject imaginable, available from kiosks or on subscription, there are also many magazines provided by associations and institutes, such as health insurance companies, insurance brokers, banks, trade unions and professional associations that can be used to reach particular target groups.

Circulation figures vary from a few thousand to more than 13 million, as with "Motorwelt", the magazine for members of the ADAC (German Automobile Club). This represents an enormous source of potential for new customers, and one that can be tapped into gradually. Many magazines offer the option of a partial circulation according to Nielsen regions or zip codes. Often the minimum quantity per placement is between 30,000 and 50,000 inserts. Alternatively, inserts can be allocated to the full circulation within a Nielsen region. A key deciding factor is the split between retail distribution and mail subscription delivery. It is important to bear in mind that a certain number of copies allocated to retail distribution will be returned as unsold on a 'sale or return' basis, whereas with subscription circulation by mail an advertiser is assured that all copies actually reach their intended recipients. That means that with a return rate on unsold retail circulation of 50%

only every other second insert will reach its intended recipient, thus substantially limiting the advertiser's response.

The cost of inserts usually depends on the weight. The usual weight limit is 25 grams in Europe. For promotional mailings below this weight limit, a thousand inserts will generally cost about €50 and €150. It is always worth discussing the terms and conditions with publishers, who will usually be prepared to negotiate with advertisers on the price for test runs. In France, inserts distributed in newspapers and magazines have to be sealed. For example, the advertisement has to have a sealed flap that can be reopened. Brochures of more than one page that cannot be sealed due to their design are often not accepted by the publishers, or are inserted into magazines at a relatively high price.

In addition to inserts that are tucked loosely into the medium, advertisers may opt for bound or bound-in inserts. These advertising media are firmly stapled into the publication. The advantage of the bound insert is that for subscription circulation by mail, in contrast to loose inserts, no additional postage is incurred. A disadvantage is that the response elements, such as perforated reply cards, have to be actively separated by consumers. To acquire prospective customers, mail-order companies often use bound-in postcard inserts made of two postcards firmly stapled into the magazine. While one of the two postcards is usually stapled into the front of the booklet and prompts the reader to request a free catalog, the second postcard is placed towards the back and is used by another mail-order company offering a different catalog. This form of advertising is relatively inexpensive in terms of contact costs, since the two companies share the costs for the bound inserts. Readers interested in the free catalog can detach the postcard and use it as a reply card, usually free of charge. For publications with print runs of more than a million, the cost is generally between €20 and €30 per thousand items, including printing and stapling.

When designing loose or bound inserts, an advertiser should be mindful of the size and total weight. The advertising media should be inexpensive to produce and not likely to cause any technical difficulties in terms of further processing. It is recommended to send the publishers an advance sample copy in order to obtain approval in terms of content and to identify any technical issues that might arise. If this is not done timely in advance, the publisher may not confirm the booking and will request that a sample copy be provided.

Direct response adverts: efficient and cost-effective

Direct response adverts are a widely used marketing tool in Germany and in the UK. Direct response adverts are adverts providing an explicit impulse for consumers to respond. In most cases, it is debatable whether the advert falls into this category. However, good and effective response adverts generally achieve an above-average response rate. Experienced direct marketing specialists know how such response adverts should be designed. In an effective direct response advert, even the headline will prompt action. The advert will contain an order element that is easy to fill in and will provide a clear and legible web address or hotline number for telephone orders. The choice of publication is also important for direct response adverts. Stern and Spiegel, two well-known German magazines, are certainly not the preferred media, for example. Other media, where entire advertising environment supports response adverts, are more suitable: Often these are magazines with high circulation issued by health insurance companies, charities or trade unions. These tend to use thinner paper than lifestyle magazines. High-quality special interest magazines are generally not considered fertile ground for direct response adverts. Readers are often reluctant to cut anything out of their precious magazine, even if it is only a coupon.

Readers of the advert should have a choice of how to order. Since every potential customer has his or her own preferred response method, offering a choice of order channels will result in higher response rates. In France, for example, more than 40% of private consumers typically place their order in writing, about 30% over the telephone and nearly 20% via the internet. Of course, this depends heavily on the sector and target group, as well as the product advertised.

The great advantage of direct response adverts is that the contact costs per thousand readers, in particular for magazines with very high circulation numbers, are very low. Direct response adverts are therefore worthwhile if the advertiser has a rough idea of the target group and for the purpose of new customer acquisition, only one specific selected product is offered at a time. Generally speaking, advertisers have to accept that there will be considerable losses due to non-selectivity with every advertising activity. But with direct response adverts it is still possible to achieve a low CpO, even with very low response rates, since the costs per thousand for a 1/1 four-color advertisement are also relatively low.

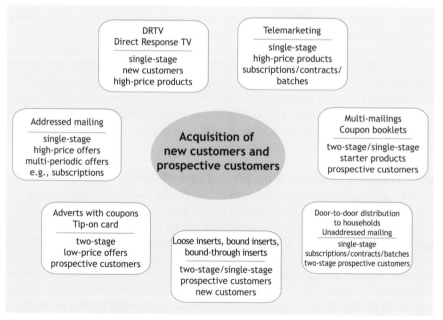

Figure 2-3-1: Direct marketing tools and their objectives

In the example given earlier, for an average marginal income of €25 per initial order and with contact costs of €1 per mailing, the company needed a response rate of 2.68% in order to obtain a CpO of €10 per new customer. A standard per-thousand price for a direct response advert appearing in a typical European medium would be €10 for a 1/1 four-color advert. This would result in a price of €10,000 for a print run of 1 million copies. In order to obtain a CpO of €10, precisely 286 orders would be needed. Nearly 300 orders would mean a response rate of 0.03%. In this connection, non-selectivity actually has its benefits. Acquiring approximately 300 new customers out of a million readers, who for the most part fall into the target group, is a realistic objective.

Some companies launch direct marketing campaigns aimed at acquiring new customers without doing any costing in advance. But only advertisers who accurately know their basic economic data, such as marginal income per order, response rates and costs, will know before the campaign even starts what response rate must be attained in order to achieve the CpO and CpI targets. If these figures do not appear realistic, then certain changes have to be made in the selection of tools and media.

Those who have little experience with direct response adverts should seek external assistance and engage a consultant with a proven track record. Such professionals will not only suggest appropriate media and be able to negotiate attractive terms and conditions for placing ads, they will also suggest locally successful graphic designs for direct response adverts. Only when important prerequisites are met is there a good chance to effectively and successfully acquire new customers via direct response adverts.

Generally, direct response adverts have to satisfy the following in order to be effective and successful: they should be striking, catching the reader's eye immediately and holding on to the reader's attention. The headline has to be formulated in such a way as to establish an instant connection with the reader, causing the reader to pause for a moment to look at the advert.

"Coop advertising": together we are stronger

Coop advertising is a very appealing way for acquiring new customers and as a result has become very popular in many European countries. The most commonly used forms of advertising are card packs and coupon books. Card packs are usually addressed mailings. They comprise numerous shrink-wrapped postcards containing offers from various companies. They are widely used in Holland and the UK in particular. Unaddressed coupon books, which are predominantly delivered door-to-door to private households throughout most of the country, are also accepted and popular in Scandinavia, the Benelux countries, France, the UK, Austria, Switzerland and Germany. Mail-order businesses consider them an efficient and cost-effective medium for acquiring new customers. Companies that have not yet had much experience with coupon books sometimes react with skepticism when this type of advertising material is proposed. To an outsider, it may indeed seem amazing that so many people react so well to this kind of coop advertising. Perhaps the reason for the good response rates is that the coupon book is designed in postcard format and, for the recipient, the postcard often acts as a "silent call" for action. Everyone knows from experience that one can order something with a postcard; one just needs to fill it in and send it off.

The most significant advantage of the coupon book is that, compared with other direct marketing tools, the cost-benefit ratio is practically unbeatable. Since several companies from various sectors join forces, the costs are split between the participants. With the coupon book, it is possible to reach far more private households than on average at a very low cost. At times, circulation can reach over ten million, so the cost per thousand contacts can be below €10. Furthermore, since it is a countrywide activity, almost every household can be reached, enabling the advertiser to achieve virtually total market coverage.

This can be a significant advantage when developing a new overseas market. With this particular coop direct marketing tool, it is possible to test the new market several times a year, usually in spring and winter, and to rapidly build up an impressive base of new customers.

Coupon books are generally used as part of a two-stage approach. In the first stage, the coupon is used to acquire prospective customers, and in the second stage a catalog or mailing is used to encourage these prospects to place their first order, turning them into new customers. Coupons can be used as on their own in the case of an item that needs little explanation and is inexpensive (under €20), e.g., collectible coins or cosmetic products. In this respect it is important that prospective customers realize just how beneficial this offer could be for them. If this is not the case, the consumer will undoubtedly continue leafing through the coupon book until an attractive offer is found. The wide range and abundance of different offers is another significant advantage that serves to keep the reader's attention.

Most of the consumer benefits on offer suggest to recipients that they will be able to save money. Coupons achieve good response rates only if the offer on the coupon is as attractive to the consumer as the other offers in the book. Analyses show that a customer does not send in all the coupons, but seeks out the two or three most appealing ones.

Alternatively, the coupon can be used for market research and generating contacts for the sales force. This medium is less useful if the target group is too small to warrant countrywide, door-to-door distribution.

Addressed, high-value multi-mailings can be useful for acquiring prospective customers in certain industries. This is especially true if a supplier within a particular industry wants to reach a clearly defined target group and is also looking for a value-oriented, brand-compatible advertising presence. This approach focuses on image-building as well as the efficient pursuit of new or prospective customers.

The upshot is that, in international direct marketing, multi-mailings and coupon books can play a significant role as efficient direct marketing tools for acquiring prospective new customers overseas.

Direct response TV: direct marketing on the television

To companies that have not yet used the direct response TV (DRTV) for acquiring new customers, it may seem an unsuitable tool for direct marketing. Yet the medium is becoming ever more attractive for companies thanks to the massive growth in digital television, the multitude of new channels and the innovative technologies for interactive purchasing. Last but not least, shopping channels like QVC and Home Shopping Europe, which have been experiencing a boom for years now, are demonstrating just what opportunities this medium offers.

A company entering a new market should therefore check the significance of this medium in the respective country, e.g., which channels may be suitable and find out how the costs are structured. DRTV ads are characterized in terms of content by the fact that the products on offer are always immediately available via the hotline displayed on screen. As a rule, these ads are not very spectacular and employ technically less complex technologies than ads for branded products. The visual and spoken sales pitch is at the forefront of the activity. The objective of production companies specializing in DRTV is to make the products as attractive as possible on the screen. Important elements for a good DRTV ad include a good voice-over or a credible presenter who can get across the advantages of the product and, most importantly, get the viewers to order. Accordingly, it is important to show a memorable telephone order number for as long as possible. The same applies for important information, which can also be emphasized using visual cues. DRTV ads are not usually shown during prime time, at least not on major TV stations with large audiences. On established stations, this type of ad is shown either early in the morning or, occasionally, in the afternoon or late evening. Smaller TV stations that only broadcast regionally and special interest TV channels also show DRTV ads during prime time, i.e., between 8 and 10 p.m. DRTV ads can be 30, 45, 60 or occasionally even 90 seconds long. The airtime has to be inexpensive if the costs per ad are to remain within budget. New TV stations that have not yet completely filled their advertising airtime may offer an entry-level CpO model with a fixed sum as the base price. This means a lower portion of ad placement costs is paid as a fixed sum, and the remainder is paid afterwards, based on actual orders.

In DRTV, everything depends on the product and the price. Individual CpO targets have to be set with the TV station's marketing firm, and this in turn depends on whether the company is offering coins, a CD collection or other products. As long as the DRTV ad is achieving good results, the TV station and the company running the campaign will be pleased, of course. However, with DRTV ads, it is important to bear in mind that the ad will often only generate an order response only when it has been repeated quite a few times. It takes some time for viewers to absorb the advantages of the product, memorize the telephone number and finally place their order.

Telemarketing: sales over the phone

In general, telemarketing is an important tool in direct marketing. However, in many countries it cannot be used as "active" outbound telemarketing without written consent from the private individuals receiving the calls. Telemarketing is therefore often not suitable for the direct acquisition of new customers. However, with the exception of Germany, consent is deemed to be given if a close customer relationship has already been established. Telemarketing is ideal for taking orders, especially in the B2C market.

Online activities for acquiring new customers

More and more consumers are placing their orders over the internet. This trend, which does not only apply to online mail-order companies, will become increasingly important and is expected to grow steadily.

However, online direct marketing tool will not be replacing traditional direct marketing tools any time soon. Email newsletters can only be sent to private individuals who have expressly given their consent. This means that only a relatively small proportion of the target group can be actively targeted via this medium in many countries. Furthermore, email, unlike traditional mailings, has the disadvantage that, due to a lack of time or care, it may be deleted without ever having been opened. Unsolicited traditional mailings coming through mailboxes, on the other hand, are somewhat less likely to be thrown out immediately. These mailings are usually put aside until the recipient has the time to deal with the written offers.

The upshot is that the internet and electronic media are currently a worthwhile addition to traditional direct marketing tools. With the web it is especially important that new customers receive their merchandise quickly. Traditional mail-order businesses therefore often have to optimize their logistics network in order to handle online orders and meet the associated customer expectations.

Appropriate selection of tools

- Accurate campaign and cost planning is the basis for the selection of appropriate direct marketing tools in any country.
- Addressed mailings are particularly suitable if the target group profile overseas is well known and the members of the target group can be identified effectively.
- Unaddressed mailings (door-to-door mailings, self-mailers and inserts) are, in view of their costs, alternatives worth considering.
- The impact of direct response adverts is usually underestimated. They represent a reasonable alternative for acquiring new customers in certain product categories.
- In many countries, coop advertisements using coupon books or card packs are very popular with consumers. Provided the right partner is selected, this tool provides a good alternative if the target group is wide and diffuse.

■ Direct response TV also enjoys varying levels of popularity in different countries. Depending on the target market, the target group and the product on offer, this tool is worthy of further consideration.

■ For legal reasons, it is not feasible to use telemarketing to acquire new customers in most countries. This is increasingly the case for the internet as well, with regard to emails and newsletters. If a company offers an online ordering option, it is essential to meet the customer's expectation that the products are delivered promptly.

4   Direct marketing is also effective overseas

There are numerous tried-and-tested direct marketing instruments that can be used efficiently in the acquisition of new customers overseas. First, however, suitable conditions have to be in place, market research performed and the relevant foreign market sufficiently analyzed. This is because there are many differences between domestic and overseas markets: the legal framework, data protection laws, payment habits as well as consumer attitudes. But above all it is the language that can cause problems. Advertising companies should therefore take special care to select the right translator. It is advisable to employ a native speaker who masters the subtleties of the foreign language.

Campaign and cost planning has to be undertaken at the start of any advertising activity, regardless of the direct marketing tool to be employed. The company should be well informed about the likely cost and associated response rates as well as on benchmark figures for the CpO and CpI. Advertising is an investment that needs to pay for itself. A fast return on investment is an essential criterion, particularly for small and medium-sized companies. Only truly effective advertising that achieves a substantial return will lead to economic success.

The precise direct marketing tools used depend largely on the target group and the product: What is the size of the target group? Is the product low- or high-priced? Does it need a single- or multi-stage approach? In this respect, it is important to ensure that people with local experience are involved in the planning and execution as early as possible. Most important of all, in most countries mail is regarded by recipients as a mark of respect on the part of the sender. Therefore mailings are often still a fundamental element of any direct marketing strategy.

If all these different aspects are taken into account, entry into overseas markets, even for small and medium-sized companies, will be crowned with success.

Diane Rinas

Segment-specific ethnomarketing

International direct marketing in domestic markets

4

Overview

■ The Turkish population in Germany represents an interesting target group that has barely been addressed as yet on a needs-oriented or consumer-specific basis. It is effectively a "market within a market".

■ Use of ethnomarketing could develop this potential. Doing so will allow for clear parallels to be drawn between intercultural marketing inside domestic markets and cross-border advertising campaigns.

■ Carefully planned market segmentation is essential to effectively address international target groups inside the domestic market. For this reason, the entire heterogeneous market is divided into several more homogeneous submarkets. This allows for specifically addressing each target group using direct marketing tools.

■ With the help of a case study it will be demonstrated how Deutsche Post developed a target group-oriented direct marketing solution for ethnomarketing in Germany.

1   Ethnic target groups: international segments within the domestic market

Brand-conscious, affluent and receptive to advertising messages: Turks living in Germany are a marvelous target group for businesses. In Germany alone, they spend €12.3 billion per year on consumer goods. Having decided to live their life in Germany, these people have long since abandoned their traditional saving habits. At around €2,000 per month, the income of the approximately 720,000 Turkish households in Germany does not differ significantly from the average financial position of households in Germany. This group is also relatively young on average as 70% of the Turks in Germany are between 15 and 49 years old. Yet up until recently, few advertisers have recognized this potential market. The result is that either ethnic marketing is not being used at all, or that there is little effort made to tailor marketing activities to different ethnic target groups.

The reader may well ask what ethnomarketing within domestic markets has to do with international direct marketing? The answer is that intercultural and cross-border advertising share some interesting parallels. By understanding the principles underlying the respective communication methods, it is possible to employ the same (direct) marketing tools to good effect in both ethnic and international direct marketing. In international campaigns, advertisers have to contend with numerous imponderable issues, which, for the most part, they are not used to dealing with in their own domestic markets. These include important economic, social and cultural differences between the target groups. Other significant challenges that have to be overcome in order to produce a successful advertising campaign include legal issues, foreign languages and the frequent lack of addresses. However, anyone who assumes that domestic markets are very homogeneous, in particular with respect to language and culture, is mistaken. Nowadays, societies such as those in Germany, the Netherlands and the USA comprise a colorful mix of the most diverse ethnic groups. With regard to culture, religion and language, these people in many cases live in a kind of subculture, although they still have close ties with the society in which they live. They therefore represent a very interesting group of potential consumers for the respective markets. Domestic advertising has to understand, consider and address the values, attitudes and behavior of these consumers, in the same way that international advertising does. This is often referred to as "intercultural marketing" or "ethnomarketing". Its importance in domestic markets should not be underestimated and it may contribute to building an intercultural and global marketing strategy. Ethnomarketing works like international marketing, but is implemented within the domestic market. Any company who manages to get different ethnic groups within their domestic market interested in their products and services will then be able to use the same tools to achieve the similar success internationally.

Naturally, there is the issue of how ethnic subsegmentation can be put to practical use. In a mature domestic market, how is it possible to identify and target ethnic groups of consumers based on their different needs? In this situation, it is useful for a company to split its prospective and actual customer base into ethnic subsegments, designing a differentiated offer to each of the ethnic subsegments and then communicating these in an adapted way that provides those subsegments with a tailored solution.

This is precisely what the concept of segment-oriented marketing – the subject of this article – strives to achieve. Providers of goods and services have to appreciate the heterogeneity and complexity of today's consumer market; their long-term survival depends on adapting their direct marketing activities and advertising dialog to suit the ever more differing needs of individual consumers. In order to harness the efficiency of one's marketing toolkit, it is essential to group together those consumers who react in a similar way to a set of activities of the company - the task at the heart of market segmentation.

This gives rise to the following key questions: how and with what degree of success or difficulty can the theoretical concept of market segmentation be applied to domestic, but international direct marketing business practices? Which segmentation criteria are of particular relevance to ethnomarketing and, with respect to the ethnic target segments, what is the best way to employ direct marketing tools? Does the concept of ethnic subsegmentation actually help companies to achieve their objectives better?

It is not within reach of this article to discuss and explain all details of market (sub)segmentation. Instead, an example will be used to demonstrate the extent to which an ethnic segment-specific concept contributes to successful (direct) marketing. The case study illustrates a basic and reliable path to a segment-oriented approach and highlights procedures that may be applied to other ethnic target groups.

Intercultural marketing is currently of increasing relevance due to the constant growth of consumers with foreign origins, particularly in the North American and European markets. In the German market alone, immigrants of non-German origin comprise 11.5% of the total population, representing significant buying power. The steady growth of these ethnic groups underlines the need to adopt special measures for addressing these target groups. The fundamental idea of intercultural marketing (used here as a synonym for ethnomarketing) originates from the USA. Since the 1970s, US marketers have been developing marketing concepts for specific ethnic minorities that take into account their cultural, linguistic and religious characteristics. In the USA, ethnic marketing especially for Afro-American and Latin American groups is of high importance. In Germany, for example, the notion of ethnomarketing does not focus exclusively on Turkish citizens as a target group as Eastern Europeans represent another important consumer group. However, with approximately 2.5m people, the Turks represent one of the largest and, at the same time, most appealing ethnic target groups in Germany. In particular, their preference for high-quality goods is of great interest, since they are willing to spend correspondingly on them. The group of Turkish origin in Germany is therefore an important target group for advertising. This holds equally for the B2C as well as B2B communication, as there are around 60,000 Turkish businesses in Germany. They are primarily found in the retail and mail-order industries, as well as in the

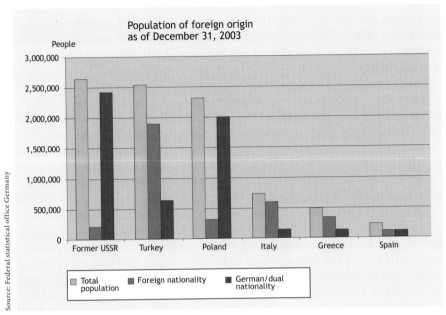

Figure 2-4-1: Population of foreign origin in Germany

services sector. Many companies consequently have much to gain by refining their B2B communication in order to target this group. It is therefore all the more surprising that most businesses have not yet recognized this potential, and significant product marketing opportunities have thus remained unexploited.

2   Ethnically subsegmented markets lead to commercial success

Anyone who sets sights on a particular "market within a market" must define this market precisely and distinguish it from the overall market. Such a target group could be the population of Latin American origin in the USA or that of Turkish origin in Germany. To achieve a sufficient and operationally employable market segmentation the overall, more heterogeneous market needs to be divided into a set of more homogeneous subsegments. Customer groups formed as a result of this market segmentation should be as homogeneous as possible within themselves, but very different when compared to other segments. This concept is based on the fact that consumers have diverse preferences, attitudes, expectations and patterns of perception. Hence the company is faced not with one heterogeneous and undifferentiated market, but with overall demand broken down into various segments that can be addressed with tailored marketing strategies according to their individual profiles.

In the context of an intercultural approach to marketing, this means that ethno-marketing can be considered a special form of segment-oriented approach to marketing. In this respect, marketing strategies and advertising campaigns are tailored towards the cultural backgrounds and preferences of ethnic segments. This ensures that the needs of these particular target groups are met more effectively. The present case study uses the following definition of intercultural market segmentation.

Intercultural market segmentation represents a marketing strategy that

- allows to identify profitable target groups by dividing the heterogeneous market into more homogeneous ethnic submarkets by using appropriate segmentation criteria, and by subsequently evaluating and selecting ethnic target segments for development; and

- targeting the selected ethnic segments by employing segment-specific marketing strategies (e.g., direct marketing), and thereby improving the marketing performance of the company.

In order to produce meaningful, homogeneous ethnic subsegments, the actual criteria chosen for the segmentation should include cultural and linguistic similarities as well as traditional segmentation criteria. The latter range of criteria comprise traditional geographic, demographic, socioeconomic and psychographic characteristics. The result is that these ethnic target groups can be addressed directly and its needs better satisfied.

Requirements for ethnic marketing

- A meaningful ethnic segmentation of the overall market and a subsequent identification as well as description of the ethnic target group (e.g., the Turkish population in Germany) are crucial success factors for ethnic marketing strategies.
- The appropriate selection of segmentation variables determines the success of the marketing strategy.
- Within the context of intercultural marketing, ethnic as well as traditional marketing variables are the primary variables by which markets are segmented.
- An operationally employable segment profile allows for accurately tailoring a company's offer, matching the needs of the ethnic target group.

3   The campaign: mailing solutions for Turkish target groups in Germany

Most companies are facing ever more intense competition, saturated markets and the need for improving long-term customer loyalty. Under such adverse market conditions, an ethnomarketing strategy may open the door to additional business. For many years now, Deutsche Post has been specifically addressing citizens of Turkish origin as a separate target group. These customers are very important for its business as they maintain close contacts with Turkey, and in so doing use mail and parcels to communicate.

In order to tap the segment of Turkish customers in Germany, the contents of the mailing campaigns are designed to address their specific needs. The campaign in question illustrates the advantages of mailings as a communication tool, using messages tailored to the target group to increase the volume of mail sent by this customer group. Thanks to ethnomarketing campaigns, the customers in this group have overwhelmingly chosen Deutsche Post as a partner for their personal communication requirements. After being addressed with advertising in their mother tongue and visual messages adapted to the needs and feelings of Turkish consumers, they feel accepted and taken seriously.

The objective of the campaign illustrated here is to encourage people of Turkish origin in Germany to develop a brand preference for Deutsche Post. Achievement of this would translate into a substantial image improvement and significant sales increase for Deutsche Post with regard to this particular target group. The target group chooses Deutsche Post, an internationally active company, as an important partner in helping it to maintain contact with friends and family overseas.

Intercultural direct marketing enables companies to achieve a multitude of objectives. The approach places the ethnic segment with all its private and business communication needs at the center of the company's marketing plan. With its intercultural activities, Deutsche Post is not only pursuing strategic, but also product-specific objectives: the company has identified the needs and preferences of the Turkish target group and used these to further improve and develop tailored product offers. This applies to both the business and private correspondence of the Turkish target group. This has significantly increased the potential for growth in an otherwise stagnant market, and has strengthened customer loyalty – important factors for gaining a sustainable competitive edge.

Any company seeking to implement ethnomarketing successfully has to define its objectives and desired position in the market. The initial step involves also the use of differentiating variables to come up with a good segmentation. These serve to identify and outline the distinguishing profiles of the ethnic segments. During this phase the corresponding growth opportunities associated with the new segmentation may become obvious. Based on these ethnic segments companies can decide on the attractiveness of each segment is for its business. Furthermore, it can also identify the additional demand as well as its competitive position with respect to the ethnic consumer segment being targeted. All segments under consideration may be visualized with a portfolio. The purpose of this is to separate the attractive from the unattractive segments and select the ethnic target groups the advertiser considers important. The next step involves the development of detailed descriptions of the selected ethnic groups. In so doing, consumer needs, preferences as well as challenges in addressing them should be carefully explored using traditional market research techniques. Then, on the basis of these results, the final step consists of creating tailored marketing strategies for the ethnic target groups. Following the implementation and rollout of the direct marketing campaign, it is strongly recommended to measure its success. The results should be used as feedback to help set new objectives and reassess the own market position. If the marketing strategy fails to meet the objectives, either the ethnic target group needs to be redefined or the marketing activities have to be refined.

Figure 2-4-2: 3D postcards tailored to suit the target group

Deutsche Post managed to fulfill these requirements in its ethnomarketing campaigns: first, market research tools were employed to analyze the particular preferences and individual characteristics of the largest target groups of foreign origin in Germany. For this task, highly specialized market research institutes (e.g., Data4U) were hired. Amongst the traditional, quantitative segmentation criteria, demographic and socioeconomic variables count as directly measurable personal characteristics. Demographic variables refer to general data regarding population statistics and are, to a certain extent, associated with sociological factors. Higher levels of segmentation were intentionally ignored as the resulting fragmentation would not have been economical with the subsegments being too sparsely populated. A team of experts from Deutsche Post then selected and described the relevant set of target groups. The most important ethnic segment selected is the group of private customers of Turkish origin living in Germany.

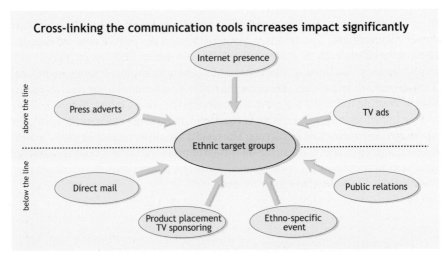

Figure 2-4-3: Communication appropriate for the target groups

For this ethnic segment the advertising campaign described below was developed and implemented.

The advertising campaign was launched to coincide with the New Year celebrations, when Turks traditionally send out greetings cards. The campaign supported this very family-focused and intimate form of maintaining contact. People of Turkish origin in Germany were offered tailored mail solutions by Deutsche Post that satisfied their need to communicate with friends and family in Turkey. The tailored message was addressed through various media to a large Turkish group that regularly uses mail to communicate. In order to gain the ethnic group's attention and to ensure the campaign was well received, it was supported by the hugely popular Turkish musicians Zerrin Özer and Yasar. Yet even with the use of testimonials, a thorough preliminary analysis was necessary in order to prevent any boomerang effect. Hence the impact of using the two Turkish stars was tested beforehand by way of market research. The market research revealed that both singers were valuable in terms of prominence and popularity. Zerrin Özer, for example, was known to 87.4% of those surveyed and liked by nearly 80%.

Within the context of intercultural marketing, Deutsche Post used a cross-media campaign. This means that different instruments were combined according to their respective strengths, and were cross-linked with other marketing instruments. This multichannel strategy ensured blanket coverage, thereby generating a high level of recognition.

Mailings

The core element of the advertising campaign was a personally addressed, bilingual mailing with a response element, which was sent out to 250,000 private Turkish households in Germany in mid-December. The people targeted were men and women between 20 and 60 years old. The mailing and the other advertising instruments used were all bilingual, dialog-oriented and in tune with Turkish attitudes.

Consultants of Turkish origin helped with the design, because something that may appear harmless for a German company may sometimes offend the sensitivities of ethnic groups. These consultants helped prevent this from happening.

The mailings consisted of a bilingual (Turkish/German) cover letter with a dialog element and an information brochure in Turkish, which contained detailed descriptions and pictures of the products. To make it easy and likely for customers to respond, a stamped and addressed reply envelope was also attached. Postcards containing sketched images of a bridge between Germany and Turkey were also included in order to stimulate the target group's interest in the mailing. For additional impact and to strengthen the likelihood of response, the mailings also contained a competition. Prizes for the winners included a car and dinner with the popular Turkish artists Kiraç and Funda Arar. In terms of content, the competition was used as the flagship element among all the cross-media advertising tools employed. This made it possible for the advertising recipients to establish a strong link between the individual instruments and the overall campaign.

There are important ethnic aspects to consider when designing a mailing. These include language and aesthetics, as well as the specific needs and values of ethnic target groups. Linguistic differences with the target group are only a secondary barrier, although market research show that the addressees prefer Turkish and bilingual messages. Many of the advertising recipients really appreciate being addressed in their mother tongue, as it generates a feeling of acceptance, understanding and trust. Anyone seeking to enter into an advertising dialog with consumers of Turkish origin should avoid the literal translation of German texts and the use of imagery from German campaigns. Turks like advertising to be more "flowery" and "warm". Most notably, their color preferences are often different from those of "average Germans"; red in different shades is particularly favored by the Turkish target group. Emotional themes and imagery from their country of origin depicting well-known Turkish landmarks are very effective. Deutsche Post's experience with the ethnomarketing campaigns carried out so far shows that special care has to be taken when selecting addresses for personalized mailings. Numerous address suppliers offer Turkish addresses that can be selected according to various criteria. Address quality is crucial to the success of direct marketing activities. It is of vital importance that the leased addresses have been regularly maintained and updated, and that the list contains only addresses of Turkish origin. Often dubious suppliers in the address trade offer datasets that have simply been lifted from telephone books according to phonetic criteria and therefore offer no guarantee that the addresses are actually of Turkish origin. A name that sounds Turkish does not necessarily originate from Turkey. Should an advertiser make such a blunder and write to Germans or people of other nationalities in Turkish, the result can often be irritation and even anger on the part of the advertising recipient. In order to ensure that the address list does not inadvertently contain Germans or people of other nationalities, all addresses should be individually checked by a native Turk.

TV ads

At the same time the mailings were dispatched, the campaign initiated TV ads on various Turkish stations. Cross-linked advertising was shown during prime time on the Turkish channels Kanal D, ATV, Flash TV, Kanal 7 and TRT. The adverts invited people to respond, and mentioned the prize draw. This ensured a smooth transition between traditional advertising instruments and direct marketing tools. The famous entertainers were also mentioned in the TV advertising. In terms of content, they were the common theme appearing across all advertising media. This ensured that the cross-media campaign achieved a high level of recognition and was crucial to its success.

Figure 2-4-4: Brochures and cover letters

Generally, television is of high value to Turks in Germany. The average Turkish citizen watches television for 203 minutes a day, which is 10 minutes longer than the average German citizen. Over 20 Turkish TV channels can be received in Germany. According to the Data4U 2003 survey (an analysis of Turkish advertising media), well over half (58%) of the people of Turkish origin in Germany predominantly or exclusively watch Turkish television channels, whereas not even a fifth (18%) predominantly or exclusively watches German channels. The remaining 22% watch both in equal measure. For these reasons, television is a good complement to mailings and other advertising media in an integrated campaign aimed at Turkish people living in Germany. Another advantage in this respect is that it is significantly cheaper to broadcast adverts on Turkish TV stations than on comparable German stations.

Press adverts

To complete its integrated communication campaign, Deutsche Post also placed picture ads with response forms. These complementary measures appeared in the high-circulation Turkish daily newspapers Hürriyet and Milliyet. In the context of cross-media campaigns, daily newspapers do not have the same value for Turks in Germany as TV. In the course of a week, only around half of the target group read a daily newspaper, and only about a quarter on any particular day. Those Turkish people that do read newspapers tend to prefer the Turkish paper Hürriyet. This title has a virtual monopoly in the market and, in addition, consistently enjoys the best image. According to our own research, press advertising in daily newspapers generates very few additional contacts – unless it is placed in Hürriyet.

Figure 2-4-5: Adverts in the Turkish media

Internet

Internet use is also rising steadily amongst the vast majority of Turkish people in Germany. This modern medium was therefore also incorporated in Deutsche Post's ethnomarketing campaigns. Users can download TV adverts and background information about Deutsche Post's solutions for special target groups from the company's website. The dialog idea was also integrated into the websites in order to bring the company closer to the customer.

Events

An event is an excellent attention-grabbing conclusion to a cross-media ethnomarketing campaign. In particular, it carries the company's intention to develop a closer relationship with its Turkish customers. After all, there is no form of dialog that is more direct than a face-to-face conversation. Such an event – a charity performance – closed the Deutsche Post campaign described here. This final campaign event, with entrance fees donated to charities (earthquake victims in Turkey and medical care for sick children), was broadcast on numerous Turkish television stations. Highlights of the program included the draw for the first ten prizes in the competition and a concert by the campaign supporters, Zerrin Özer and Yasar. Amongst the approximately 3,000 guests at this sold-out event were numerous high-ranking participants such as media representatives, representatives of the Turkish Consulate General, chairpersons of business associations and other personalities from the business world. This generated a high level of interest in the event with the Turkish press – a PR multiplier effect to round off the campaign.

Particular features of this line of approach

- In the ethnomarketing campaign, Deutsche Post employed a cross-media approach for addressing the Turkish target group.
- With respect to the linguistic and graphic design, the preferences of the Turkish target group were analyzed meticulously and the campaign drawn up accordingly.
- Popular celebrities provided testimonials to help convey the message to the Turkish target group.
- The use of mailings within the context of a cross-media campaign was particularly effective.

4   International expertise in practice

All in all, with the direct marketing campaign described here, Deutsche Post is underlining its competence as an international mail and logistics company that cares about what its customers need and offers appropriate solutions. The above-average response rate of 24% in last year's campaign shows that in this respect, things are moving in the right direction. The experience of recent years, however, has shown that in order to successfully run an ethnocampaign, one cannot simply adapt existing campaigns intended for German consumers. Literally translating mailings, advertisements and publicity spots is more than often not supporting that objectives will be met. Ethnomarketing is successful if it is part of a long-term strategy and if the campaign combines the use of different media. This approach ensures that prospective customers may be touched, for instance, on several occasions. These occasions, however, may differ from those applicable to German consumers. To send a Muslim a Christmas card would defeat the purpose of the communication. On the other hand, Ramadan, Eid, Valentine's Day and Mother's Day are all promising occasions for this target group.

Another insight from the ethnic campaigns is that these target groups with only isolated use of individual marketing tools are indeed hard to reach. A combination of activities is more effective for achieving the company's marketing policy objec-

Figure 2-4-6: Factors of success/intercultural marketing knowledge

tives in the long-term. In this respect, comparisons can be made with an orchestra, where all the musicians play in tune with one another to create a harmonious effect. In the same way, it is vital to employ an appropriate, integrated range of marketing tools in order to reach the target group effectively.

But what about meeting financial and product-specific objectives? There are often difficulties in quantifying the economic success of segmentation. More often than not, success is measured by means of quantitative and qualitative market research and/or by ascertaining customer satisfaction and customer loyalty. Continuous quantitative and qualitative market and media research are essential sources of information in gauging the success of the approach. After the campaign, international mail sales to the target group increased significantly (by approximately 18%) compared with the previous year (survey & analysis by GfK). This indicated that the advertising campaign has been highly effective on a moderate budget.

Qualitative market research also confirmed the good results for this intercultural direct marketing approach: 95.85% of the target group rated the TV ads as very good or good, 95% rated the press advertising as very positive and 96.3% rated the direct mail as very positive. 94.9% considered the overall advertising campaign a success (data4U survey, supplementary advertising research).

Based on the market research, Deutsche Post's campaign can be considered successful. The most effective elements of the campaign were the direct mailings and the TV ads, while the newspaper adverts, which only managed to generate a few additional new contacts, were seen more as complementary measures. The design of the advertisements also suited the target group's taste. Hence in each case, more than four-fifths of the target group rated the various publicity media, advertising mail, TV and press advertisements as positive. The target group's enthusiasm for the campaign was revealed in countless letters, some with dedications and pictures.

Key results

■ Thanks to market segmentation, and the more tailored target group message that can be created as a result, direct marketing generated an above-average response rate of 24%.
■ A cross-media campaign combining different marketing tools facilitates the long-term achievement of the company's brand policy objectives.
■ Continuous qualitative and quantitative market research as well as additional surveys provide both, the information needed for designing the campaign as well as the benchmarks for measuring the success of that campaign.
■ Deutsche Post managed to position itself in the eyes of the target group as a valuable partner for cross-border communication and achieved a high level of positive awareness, as well as an significant increase in sales.

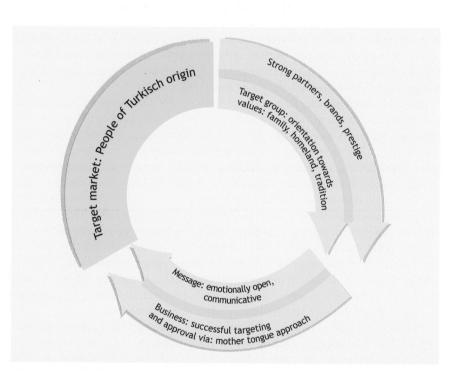

Figure 2-4-7: Turkish target groups

5   Summary

The starting point for the campaign described here was the fact that consumers both overseas and in domestic markets have different preferences, desires and needs. The approach of ethnic market segmentation allows companies to tailor its products and communication messages to attractive subsegments of the overall market, based on their specific cultural backgrounds and needs.

Differentiation of a company's product portfolio based on an intercultural marketing approach, for example, may bring about growth even in seemingly saturated markets. Direct marketing, and in particular direct mail, is an efficient instrument for addressing ethnic target groups. In the case of Deutsche Post's Turkish target groups in Germany the TV ads were of crucial importance, particularly for establishing awareness with the target group. Placing ads in the daily newspapers proved to be complimentary. Of course, what has to be considered is the fact that producing and broadcasting TV ads is usually expensive, so much so that in this particular case study, personalized mailings proved to be the most economic instrument for targeted the ethnic target group.

Jon Williams, Thomas Curwen

The HP HypeGallery

A carefully staged, event-oriented multimedia campaign

Overview

- Hewlett-Packard (HP) wants to reposition itself on a long-term basis in the global printer market. In order to do this, an affinity for the HP brand has to be developed first in the "iMac generation" or "graphics professional" target group, since this group acts as a pointer to the mass market of the future.
- The challenge: graphics professionals are considered to be particularly skeptical and mistrustful of large brands and advertising in general.
- An interactive campaign grew out of the "HypeGallery" – an exhibition created by the artists themselves, both online and in the real world. HP large format printers produced the prints. All works of art appeared on the campaign homepage, www.hypegallery.com.
- The integrated campaign produced by Publicis predominantly used avant-garde direct marketing media that were particularly popular with the target group.
- The media and target group resonance was enormous: since 2003, London's original "HypeGallery" had 9,000 visitors with works from 1,200 artists, 2004 in Paris had 32,500 visitors with 2,300 artists, 2005 had Moscow with 19,000 visitors and 1,700 works, Singapore with 12,000 visitors and 600 works and finally back to Europe: Milano. Amsterdam and Berlin were the HyPe cities of 2006. Meanwhile, more than 10 million hits were generated on the international website worldwide.

1   Reaching the trendsetters

Hewlett-Packard has had to face new challenges: despite constant technical improvements, printers are generally considered commodity products and have found their way into home offices. Many people acquire their printers as part of a complete system, or as a replacement for a defunct device. As market leader in this segment, Hewlett-Packard (HP) actually benefits from this attitude. However, it has had to recognize that its reputation as a technological leader in the industry was fading in the eyes of younger consumers. For the "iMac generation", i.e., for the consumer trendsetters of tomorrow, HP was no longer achieving the desired sales impact.

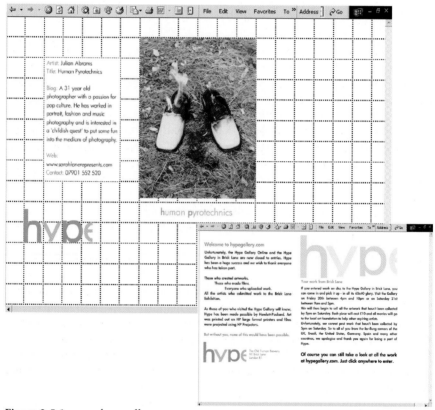

Figure 2-5-1: www.hypegallery.com

This target group had been somewhat neglected in marketing terms. Typically, HP advertising delivered a relatively rational message: the focus of the campaigns have actually been on the printer product, emphasizing new technical attributes, prices, or promises. Such an approach left this very skeptical target group cold, in the truest sense of the word: the HP brand was not emotionally charged, and therefore at a strategic disadvantage in comparison with a trendy brand such as Apple. With the help of image-based positioning, Apple had succeeded in winning both buyer confidence and market share.

Hewlett-Packard therefore commissioned the advertising agency Publicis to develop its new campaign. The goal was to implant the HP brand emotionally in the consciousness of the iMac generation, considered the trendsetters for the future mass market. The group is familiar with strong design aesthetics and at the same time has a distinct mistrust of all traditional advertising.

In order to reach the generation of iMac users and explain the advantages of HP printers, the campaign adopted an approach that was substantially different to traditional advertising. HP and Publicis had to communicate with the target group in an innovative way in order to give the HP brand a new lease on life. Printers became both an experience and an event. What could be more intimate than integrating HP printers into the process by which the ideas of this target group are incubated? The printer had recently been reduced to being the "last push of a button" at the end of the creative process. The goal was to change this through the help of an unorthodox live performance using the products.

The starting point of the campaign was the realization that creative types like to visualize their ideas and images on paper and present them to others. This was the potential strong link between the target audience and HP printers.

The planned performances that Publicis finally agreed on with HP took into account the influential role that the iMac generation will have on future markets, as each targeted individual can be expected to influence many others. The campaign therefore focused more on a change of mind in the target group and less on actual sales.

The nature of the mission

■ The objective of the campaign was to increase the relevance of the Hewlett-Packard printer brand to the iMac generation.

■ The challenge was that the target group was very mistrustful of big business and traditional advertising. This defensive attitude had to be overcome.

■ The starting point for the Publicis campaign rested on the idea that creative types like commit their ideas as well as images on paper and present them to others.

2   HypeGallery –
three steps to the hearts of the target group

Conventional methods of contact are of little use with target groups who not only ignore advertising, but are avowedly opposed to it. These approaches are also of little use with target groups that have very little time. For Publicis, this meant exploring new options. Classic PR and advertising normally appear in daily newspapers and on TV, but HP and Publicis had to arouse the curiosity of their target group using a new channel that would actually reach the target group and stimulate interest in HP printers. The starting point was the target group's need for self-expression, communication and peer recognition.

This was the origin of the "HypeGallery", an art exhibition by the design community in both the virtual and real worlds. "Hype" provides young artists with exactly what they need: a stage and forum for expressing themselves creatively and presenting the results to a wider public. "Hype" is essentially an open gallery space where artists can promote themselves for free. The campaign team decided on Brick Lane in the East End of London, a district inhabited by artists and students, as the location for this exhibition. The street lies at the heart of the design community in the British capital, with several groups of artists living and working nearby. They proved indispensable for the spreading the message of "Hype" within the community.

The one condition imposed on the artists was that the letters H and P had to appear in the title of their work, which could be either submitted by e-mail, uploaded to the website, or be brought on CD directly into the gallery on Brick Lane. There the work was printed out on large-format printers from HP and exhibited.

The exhibition grew rapidly to include more than 160 individual works. Precise timing was essential. The team had planned meticulously and designed the show in phases so as to make a positive first impression and ensure that it lasted for the duration of the exhibition, thereby encouraging the target group to create and submit their art.

Ultimately, www.hypegallery.com is intended to become the heart of a worldwide community and a valuable resource for the creative community in its search for new talents – all free of charge.

Figure 2-5-2: Fly poster and clean graffiti on the pavement

Figure 2-5-3: On target – infrared hypertags from a poster via SMS to a mobile phone

The creative part of the campaign can be divided into three phases:

- Phase I of the campaign centered around an "inspirations website". This was revitalized week after week with new works of art. The temporary content was to serve as a guide and inspiration for visitors, who were invited to register to help create a community database. Weekly "appetizers" were crucial in ensuring acceptance.
- Phase II was for uploading. Artists from all over the world could now send their works to the gallery. The contact details for the database were derived from visitor information obtained at the entrance to the gallery as well as from the registration on the website that had to be submitted online by all participants. Similar projects in Europe and around the world will expand the database further.
- Phase III, three weeks later, saw the works which had been uploaded via internet or brought into Brick Lane on CD appear on the website.

The target group only noticed the fact that HP was also part of the show when its works of art were printed out in glorious Technicolor on a large-format HP printer. The effect was tremendous. The comments heard and read by the campaign team from the crowds in the gallery encouraged their belief that this campaign would fundamentally change public perception of the HP brand.

Avant-garde communication for a special target group

To publicize the gallery idea, the campaign team used all traditional and innovative media and communication channels that were available: from clean (legal) graffiti, hypertags (small electronic labels), viral marketing and fly posting, to mail packets, press, radio, cinema, websites, online banners, JVTV (Astra TV) and postcards – all media were integrated into the campaign. And they were emphasized throughout the three phases in different ways.

www.hypegallery.com/Phase 1: mystery, tension and attention

The website (http://www.hypegallery.com) was critical in guiding the curiosity that had been awakened and in bringing the "Hype" experience to life. It not only described what "Hype" was, but also allowed for registration and uploading of art and films from all over the world. Thus an artist from Tokyo, for example, could exhibit his or her work in London. The website was created one month before the artists could upload their work.

The target group was "surrounded", both when working and studying:

- Publicis commissioned the well-known graffiti artist ("street brandalist") Moose to create legal "clean" graffiti that caused a buzz on websites favored by the worldwide designer community. A chatroom infiltration program supported this. The "HYPE" logo started appearing on pavements, walls, telephone boxes and studios in areas of London populated by art students. "HYPE" emerged mysteriously almost overnight. From just one letter on the steps and walls of the St. Martins and Goldsmiths art schools, clean graffiti produced a chain reaction, spreading the message outwards from the community site. In three months, it reached over 300 websites, message boards, forums and newsgroups used by the target group.
- Fly posters containing pictures and the website address appeared in prominent locations in the area, helping to attract further attention.
- Small-scale adverts in magazines with events listings, mimicking the publicity for art exhibitions and film posters, invited readers to submit their work to the "HypeGallery".
- Publicis put up a new type of poster with integrated infrared hypertags. These small electronic labels were designed to lure people into the gallery. Hypertags "scent" the type of mobile phone carried and "inject" calendar entries into the mobile phones of passers-by via SMS. At 4:30 in the afternoon, the day of the gallery opening, mobile phone alarms went off to remind people

of the opening. In keeping with the style of the entire campaign, this was the first time this type of technology was ever used in the public domain. The hypertags were placed at five strategic, particularly hip locations frequented by the target group. The posters resulted in 762 SMS interactions.

- Each individual SMS interaction cost £4.53. However, what was remarkable was the infectious nature of the digital information. Prompted by the element of surprise ("Look what I've got"), these text messages spread like wildfire between end consumers and/or their peers. The speed of the proliferation made it difficult to track.
- In addition, information packs were sent to colleges so that they could include "Hype" into their teaching programs. The "creative phase" for the gallery occurred during the students' Christmas vacation and was scheduled to avoid interfering with their term-time studies. Some schools accepted "Hype" as part of their curriculum.
- Some of the films submitted were transferred to JVTV, a web-based broadband network of plasma screens in student unions throughout the country.
- The films were also shown in cinemas.

www.hypegallery.com/Phase 2: action and penetration

The start of the second phase saw the opening of the website, on which art from all over the world could be submitted. The first works were printed out and exhibited in Brick Lane. Now the task was to convert the attention generated into additional works, visits, and word-of-mouth recommendations:

- The "HypeGallery" website was opened up to entries from all around the world.
- Participation in the "HypeGallery" was launched in parallel with an online campaign using advertising and banner advertisements on websites popular with the target group.
- A special new contact strategy was implemented for the target group using an outbound e-mail program.
- Publicis showed 60 films in an underground car park in Soho to get young filmmakers interested in short films about "Hype".

www.hypegallery.com/Phase 3: PR and broad effect

In the last phase of the campaign, aimed to exploit multiplier effects in order to generate extra visitors to both the online and offline "HypeGallery", the traditional tools of the PR campaign were also reinforced.

- Visitors to the "HypeGallery" were again targeted with an online campaign via advertising and banners advertisements on websites popular with the target group.
- Printed advertisements again publicized the gallery area in the print media. The works, titles and names of the artists appeared on successive pages together with the internet address hypegallery.com.
- Similar motives were also distributed free of charge as postcards in pubs and bars in and around Brick Lane.

Figure 2-5-4: Cinema short – "When all Hope Plummets"

Figure 2-5-5: Cinema short – "Hairy Pooches"

From a national to an international dimension

Offline communication was only used in the UK, with an emphasis on London. Londoners, of course, also benefited from the gallery's location. However, the website was much more effective in attracting interest. Although the campaign also aimed to encourage work from other parts of the UK, and students even came from as far away as Aberdeen to bring their work in person, the international rollout was actually planned for later. However, once the website received hits from over 140 countries, the campaign soon took on an international dimension of its own.

"Hype" was designed as a toolkit with a view towards the emergence of global spin-offs.

In September 2004, a "HypeGallery" opened in Paris. The intention was to transfer this successful campaign to other markets. One of the aims of the galleries in other countries was to create traffic for the hypegallery.com website and build a unique global depot for new design talents – talents which otherwise would not necessarily receive the appreciation of the public so vital for artists. In Paris, the

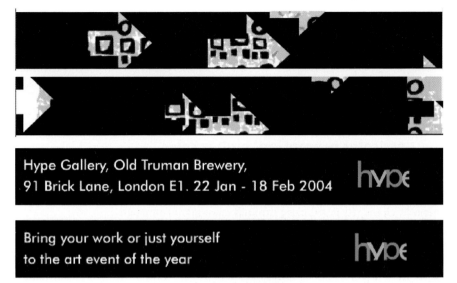

Figure 2-5-6: Advertising banner for Hype on a website

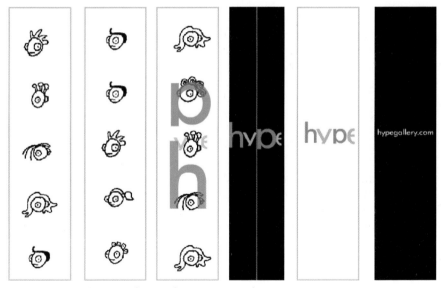

Figure 2-5-7: Advertising banner for Hype on a website

Palais de Tokyo was the gallery location. More than 32,500 excited visitors saw more than 2,300 works. With Moscow the gallery went east in 2005. Demonstrations, flyers and a hype manifest prepared the ground for an "art revolution". The gallery at the ARTPLAY design center attracted 19,000 visitors for 1,700 works of young artists. A month later, "Hype" turned into a truly global phenomenon: In

Singapore, 12,000 visitors went to the Art House for another inspiring 600 works. At the end of 2005, "HypeGallery" returned to Western Europe. Milano became the "Hype Capital". At the beginning of 2006 Amsterdam took over with Berlin following suit in October. Ultimately, www.hypegallery.com became both the center of a worldwide community and a valuable resource for the creative community in its search for new talents – free of charge.

3   Less sales promotion, higher sales

Hewlett-Packard and Publicis have shown how even a brand associated by consumers with less than inspiring , technical products in a saturated market can fundamentally change its positioning through a visionary campaign.

The success of this campaign was based essentially on a radical break from standard radio and TV advertising in favor of consistent direct marketing and the use of innovative means of communication, e.g., hypertags. This prompted an intrinsically inaccessible target group to rediscover and personally experience HP's brand values.

According to research by HP, a total of 135,000 people in the target group came directly into contact with the "Hype" campaign throughout the London campaign alone. They particularly appreciated HP's role as a "facilitator", eschewing a direct sales pitch.

The most important positive result was an intensified affection for HP. The press coverage also reached the target group. In addition, buzz and viral advertising had and will continue to have a significant if unquantifiable effect.

Altogether, in the first year approximately 3,800 works were submitted, leading to the creation of a worldwide address database of 80,000 artists with confirmed registration (double opt-in). The free outbound mailing lists and newsletter went to more than 200,000 people worldwide. The contents, information and links of the "HypeGallery" reached an estimated three million plus viewers worldwide. Approximately 420,000 of these were artists, designers or filmmakers – or people who had a personal and/or professional interest in the arts.

For HP however, the result of a subsequent study was particularly important: the image of HP had changed in the minds of the participants and had now become a synonym for creativity. The long-term strategic goal of the campaign was thus achieved, i.e., the repositioning and positive relaunch of the HP brand in a community that will set the trend for future mass markets. The effective budget for the UK campaign on the basis of various preset criteria was equivalent to £1.6 million.

■ The initial benchmark figure for the cost per visitor to the Brick Lane Gallery was £800. This high number appeared justified to HP because the visitors comprised a highly attractive target group with wide-ranging influence. The unexpectedly high number of visitors ultimately reduced the cost to £400 per visitor.

■ The cost benchmark for each online visitor to the "HypeGallery" was £45. Following 103,000 individual visits, the cost actually fell to £15.50 per visitor. The number of individual visits had quickly risen to 130,245, reducing the cost even further to £12.20. Including the global roll-out this benchmark figure has actually fallen further since 2004.

There were no special benchmarks set for PR reach or buzz. On the basis of studies, however, it has been established that the associated activities reached more than three million people in 142 countries at a cost of £0.53 per person. Viral communication has continued to spread the message even further, although its exact spread cannot be quantified.

The innovative approach, creativity and results of the campaign were publicly recognized with the award of several important prizes by advertising festival juries:

■ Precision Marketing – Grand Prix
■ Precision Marketing – Gold in "Best Interactive Media Initiative"
■ D&AD – Silver in the interactive category
■ Cannes Lions Direct – Gold in the IT Category
■ Cannes Lions Direct – Gold in the "Integrated" category
■ Campaign Direct – Silver in the "Best Use of Interactive" category
■ Campaign Direct – Silver in the "Best IT Product" category

Main results

■ More than 10,000,000 hits on the website from over 150 countries
■ Over 80,000 registered artists in the address database
■ Over 3,800 works of art were submitted
■ Record sales of HP printers and increased sales of other HP products
■ Radical, positive changes in the attitude of the iMac generation to the HP brand

4   Truly amazing resonance

The central task was to implant Hewlett-Packard as a fashionable brand in the minds of the iMac generation, which acts as a pointer to the mass market of the future. These are people with a pronounced mistrust of traditional advertising forms and distinct (non-HP) product preferences in the product ranges concerned. The ignorance of iMac users regarding HP had to be overcome in order for them to experience in person the special advantages of HP printers. This was done through the use of the products in an unorthodox live performance.

The approach had to stand out from traditional forms of advertising, so Publicis communicated with the target group in an innovative fashion, breathing new life into the HP brand.

This was how the idea of the "HypeGallery" developed. It was an art exhibition by the so-called design community in both the virtual and the real worlds. "Hype" was essentially an open gallery area where artists could promote themselves. Publicis exploited this key motivating of the target group in designing the campaign. The target group only noticed the fact that HP was also part of the show when its works of art were printed out in glorious Technicolor on a large-format HP printer.

Figure 2-5-8: Hype postcards as direct mail for acquaintances

The resonance was truly amazing:

▓ The website was accessed more than 10 million times and features a database of over 80,000 registered artists, now well disposed to the HP brand. More than 130,000 individual visitors from 142 countries around the world have visited the website early on. Over 3,800 works of art were uploaded during the UK campaign alone.

▓ Due to its success, the campaign has already been repeated on a global scale. Ultimately, the homepage turned into the center of a worldwide community, and a valuable resource in its search for new talent – all free of charge.

To spread the gallery idea, Publicis used all forms of innovative media and communication channels for direct marketing: clean (legal) graffiti, hypertags (small electronic labels), mail packets, press, radio, cinema, websites, online banner advertisements, viral marketing, fly posting, JVTV (Astra TV), postcards, etc. Both the BBC and Bloomberg TV, among others, reported on the exhibition nationally. There were interviews on local radio and discussions in both weblogs and designer sites around the world.

Alastair Tempest

Robinson lists for efficient direct marketing

6

Overview

- National direct marketing associations in many countries have established what are known as "Robinson" or "preference" services. These services ensure that people who do not wish to be targeted by direct marketing do not receive any such advertising.
- These services are available to all providers of goods and services for the purpose of cleaning up their marketing lists. In some cases, the law in fact requires the use of these services.
- The advertiser can use these services in order to avoid targeting people who would never respond to this kind of advertisement and also to ensure that consumer wishes are respected. Such services are therefore advantageous for both the provider and the consumer.
- Robinson lists help satisfy the statutory requirement to give the consumer the option of blocking the delivery of advertising via what is known as the "opt-out procedure".
- Robinson lists reinforce consumer confidence in direct marketing. Their existence shows consumers that advertisers act responsibly and are sensitive to their wishes in relation to advertising sent to the home.
- Compliance with Robinson lists increases the efficiency of direct marketing activities.

1   Introduction

This chapter discusses the advantages of Robinson lists (also known as preference systems or preference services). The case study concentrates on Robinson lists for direct marketing in Europe, although brief excursions and comparing references are included with respect to North America and the Asia-Pacific region. We begin with a brief overview of the development of direct marketing, outlining the parties concerned and the reasons why it makes sense to use Robinson lists.

As already indicated in other chapters, despite the economic stagnation in Europe over the past ten years, direct marketing continues to grow at a stable and healthy rate. Direct marketing techniques are much better adapted to the overall economic cycle, from boom to recession, than most other forms of marketing, especially with regard to mass media advertising. Even non-commercial users of dialog marketing have boosted their activities. For example, charities and nonprofit organizations, governments and politicians (especially during election campaigns) are now among the heaviest users of direct dialog.

Direct mail, teleservices (inbound and outbound), e-commerce (using the internet for marketing purposes), direct-response TV, and direct response in print and other media are the main direct marketing techniques employed. The adaptability of direct marketing has certainly contributed to the welcome growth in expenditure that has been seen in this field in many countries. However, direct marketing has also benefited enormously from technological advances that have taken place over the past ten years, particularly the evolution of databases and widespread use of the internet. Every economist's dream has become a reality – costs have fallen and productivity has risen!

These new techniques have attracted new users. As always, B2B marketing has led the way. Small and medium-sized companies have found they can compete even without a large advertising budget. A well-structured and maintained database along with a good direct marketing strategy, help them to keep pace with the competition.

Even big brand manufacturers have changed their strategy: they are no longer concentrating on mass media advertising, but are instead turning to integrated marketing strategies – with a focus on customer loyalty. It is expected that big retailers and brand manufacturers will continue to increase their emphasis on direct marketing in the years to come. Direct marketing therefore seems primed for a promising future.

Good results, however, are not possible without hard work. Many postal operators have joined with direct marketing associations in investing in the industry's future. Today, greater value is placed on education and training than ever before. Both are essential in direct marketing, since it is such a complex field. Superior results in direct marketing are found in countries where there is specialized education and training. The advances in technology and subsequent worldwide growth in direct marketing over the past ten years have, however, also led to a few new challenges and unpleasant surprises. With the appropriate level of preparedness, such pitfalls can be avoided.

The rise and temporary fall of the information superhighway (with the internet bubble of the late 1990s) taught some people a valuable lesson about distance selling and the necessity for efficient logistics. Internet marketing (often referred to as e-commerce) had to face the facts. It may have been tedious and laborious, but business had to be built up again from scratch – which says something about the success of this strategy. An unfortunate by-product of the e-communications revolution is email spam - the unsolicited, indiscriminately dispatched emails that tend to clog inboxes.

Spam is the most extreme example of the irresponsible misuse of a direct marketing tool. Direct marketing associations all around the world oppose this damaging form of advertising. One reason for the deluge of spam is the ease with which consumer data can now be collected. This raises the question of privacy protection. Consequently, the challenge for those using direct marketing is to balance effective marketing with respect for the customer. A responsible approach to marketing is required.

Looking at it another way, sending unwanted direct marketing information by any medium, is a waste of advertising money. It can have a negative effect. Some consumers, to use the famous words of Greta Garbo, "just want to be left alone", and reject any advertising contact accordingly.

Sending direct marketing materials to such target groups is a blatant contradiction of the primary goal of direct marketing: identification and specification of target groups in order to achieve the highest possible ROI (return on investment) and long-term customer loyalty.

Regulatory authorities have proposed a radical solution for unwanted direct marketing: make the "opt-in" procedure a general statutory requirement. In Italy, this procedure became law in 1996. It says that direct marketing may only be sent to consumers who, in accordance with the opt-in procedure, have actively chosen to receive such communication. It was passed despite the EU directive of 1995, which explicitly permits (except in cases of sensitive data) use of the "opt-out" procedure for direct marketing. With the opt-out procedure, the consumer has the option to be removed from an advertiser's address lists, but the result of "opt-in" in Italy was a virtual collapse of all direct marketing investment in that country. Lots of large direct marketing companies simply closed up shop and left. Others returned to mass media advertising.

The policy of the regulatory authorities with respect to "invasive" direct marketing media is increasingly focused on asking consumers actively to opt in before they will receive such communication. Some companies have also established internal policies restricting contact to those who register in the company marketing list. This is a business decision that can lead to competitive advantages, although most companies do not have the luxury of being able to target only registered customers. The opt-in/opt-out issue will not be debated here, as it has already been covered in countless publications. Instead, this chapter will concentrate on the opt-out issue and the solutions available in this area.

To identify and remove data on people who do not want to be targeted makes good commercial sense. It is entirely compatible with the basic principles of direct marketing, and is in the interest of both consumers and the providers of goods and services. Maintaining and constantly updating company-owned suppression files is an important element of direct marketing.

2   Suppression files

Suppression files remove data about existing or potential customers from the provider's mailing, telephone, fax and email lists, etc. They are used for both active customers and former or inactive customers who do not want to be targeted. They are also used selectively to reflect the customer's wishes. Perhaps the customer wants a catalog, for example, but opts out of allowing his/her data to be passed on to other companies and/or subsidiaries of the provider. There are several ways for the customer to express his/her wishes, e.g., by checking a box (opt-in or opt-out), or by filling out a questionnaire. With a questionnaire, the advertiser can find out whether the customer is interested in other products. Suppression files can therefore be made as complex and exhaustive as is necessary better to meet customer needs. This benefits both the provider and the customer.

Anyone thinking of using any form of Robinson list/preference system or suppression file has to make sure that they have the ability to suppress a name without deleting it. If a consumer tells a company or operator of a generic Robinson/preference list that s/he no longer wants to be targeted by direct marketing and the data is then completely deleted, it is possible for the following scenario to occur: the next campaign for acquiring new customers is launched and the company rents a list containing the name of that consumer. If this name was suppressed in the company's existing database, it will be recognized and removed. However, if the name has already been deleted, the company will not have this option. For this reason, the EU data protection directive of 1995 clearly refers to the suppression of names. Unfortunately, not all EU member countries have embraced this concept, causing unnecessary consumer irritation. German law, for example, does not require data suppression. This has resulted in a procedure that completely fails to satisfy the objectives of consumer protection.

Suppression files are also essential for registering addresses that are no longer up-to-date ("goneaways"). Over a five-year period, approximately 25-33% of the data stored in consumer databases will change: telephone numbers are switched, people move, marry and adopt new names, are born or die, etc. Email addresses change even more quickly: it is estimated that around 25% of email addresses change every year. Sending further mailings to people, or calling them up when they may have moved or died, is not only a complete waste of money, but can also lead to considerable irritation. We will come back to this issue later on.

In any case, internal suppression files are as relevant for B2B as for B2C marketing. They have the same justification and, if anything, employee turnover is higher than the attrition rate of household addresses. Sending a mailing to Mr. Y as product manager at Company B months after his retirement does not cast the marketer in a positive light. The discussion so far has focused on internal company suppression files. In most countries, data protection legislation requires that these files be updated regularly.

3   Robinson lists/preference services

In the 1970s, leading authorities in the field of direct marketing in the USA recognized that consumers might be interested in the option to blocking delivery of certain types of marketing materials (opt-out system). Marketing lists, in particular those hired or bought from other companies, may contain irrelevant data: hence when marketing gardening equipment, for example, a list of subscribers to a garden magazine would seem to be a valuable source of information. Yet it is quite possible that city-dwellers also purchase garden magazines, even though they live in a tower block. And so the concept of offering customers a selective opt-out facility for direct marketing was born. The files created were called "preference services", and they are by now available for a range of sectors, e.g., DIY, hardware, financial services, etc. Although it was a good idea, the costs for set-up and operation proved to be too high. Every now and then, somebody suggests reintroducing sector-specific preference lists, but their heyday is probably over. List brokers are much more effective at sorting out redundant names and databases.

Nevertheless, the name 'preference service' was retained. In other countries, the same service is known as the Robinson list. This comes from the main character in Daniel Defoe's novel, "Robinson Crusoe". A luckless sailor shipwrecked on a desert island, Robinson wanted no contact with his neighbors (who were cannibals), hence the connection with unwanted advertising contact.

In almost all cases, the consumer can register with the service directly and free of charge, generally in writing. Furthermore, Robinson/preference services increasingly provide for online registration. This is always free for the consumer, as prescribed in most data protection acts. After registration, the consumer is often sent a request for confirmation in order to verify the identity of the registrant. Registration for some preference services/Robinson lists is valid indefinitely, but in others it is only valid for a limited period (usually 2-3 years). After the period ends, the consumer is sent a postcard asking whether s/he would like to reregister. This avoids the problem of changing addresses/telephone numbers, etc. Another issue in compiling Robinson lists is the huge number of variants that a single name can yield, because, in addition to first name and surname, there are also initials, official or unofficial names, and of course typing errors to consider. Consequently, in some Robinson/preference lists, an individual is entered several times so that all possibilities avenues of contact are blocked.

There are preference/Robinson lists for direct mail (mail preference services, MPS), telephone (TPS), fax (FPS), email (eMPS) and SMS, mobile phones. These vary from country to country.

	Mail (MPS)	Telephone (TPS)	Fax (FPS)	E-Mail (eMPS)	SMS/mobile phone (SMSPS/Mobile PS)
Australia*	X	X		X	X
Austria	X			X	
Belgium	X	X		X	X
Canada	X	X	X		
Czech Republic	X	X			
Denmark	X				
Finland	X	X			
France	X	X		X	
Germany	X	X	X	X	X
Greece	X	X	X	X	X
Hungary					
Ireland	X	X	X		X
Italy*	X	X	X	X	X
Netherlands**	X	X		X	X
New Zealand	X	X	X		
Norway	X	X			
Poland	X				
Portugal	X				
Romania					
Russia					
Slovakia	X				
Slovenia	X				
Spain*	X				
Sweden	X	X		X	
Switzerland	X	X			
UK	X	X	X	X	
USA***	X	X		X	

Notes:

*   In these countries, the lists are combined into one service.

**   In the Netherlands, there are also preference services for mobile phones and a market research list.

***   In the USA, there is a mobile preference service (wireless Block), and an overseas preference service is provided in cooperation with various direct marketing associations.

Figure 2-6-1: Preference services (x PS)/Robinson Lists

4   The international arena

The Federation of European Direct and Interactive Marketing (FEDMA) is often asked why there are no international, or at least Europe-wide, Robinson lists. The closest things to international or pan-European files are the rules of the International Federation of Direct Marketing Associations (IFDMA). Within the framework of the IFDMA, there is a general agreement regarding MPS, TPS and eMPS, which has been available for signing since 1996.

IFDMA Agreement (1996)

The following is specified in the IFDMA Agreement:

"[Members undertake] to conduct and manage their business in accordance with the following guidelines:

- Member organizations and the sector in general shall raise the standards and professionalism of direct marketing.
- Represent the positive values of direct marketing to the public and government officials.
- Develop a framework for the implementation of initiatives that will ensure that direct marketing is carried out in a way that creates trust on the part of consumers and corporate clients.
- Formation of an effective lobby to ensure that current and future legislation of national governments meets members' business expectations and represents the balanced interests of all association members.
- Introduction and maintenance of appropriate and effective programs for voluntary self-regulation, such as reasonable codes of practice.
- Introduction and maintenance of consumer preference services (mail and telephone), in order to accommodate the desires and wishes of consumers.
- Improvement of business practice standards through initiatives like the best practice guidelines.
- Introduction, maintenance and improvement of ongoing professional training and education that satisfies the reasonable expectations of employers and enhances the career prospects of direct marketing specialists.
- Creation of a forum for exchanging information and for networking on a national and international level.
- Support for IFDMA members in achieving the above goals, and to reinforce and support unrepresented countries in establishing a representative body for direct marketing."

Every international Robinson list/preference services agreement regulates in detail the sharing of lists for comparing files, and outlines the aspects that need to be taken into account. These rules oblige members of the association to cooperate and exchange data if a provider wishes to advertise in another country by telephone, mail or email.

In all 27 EU countries, in the European Economic Area and also in Switzerland, the law requires that the consumer must always have the right to opt out free of charge. This still applies even if the consumer originally indicated, by opting in, that s/he wanted to receive advertising materials. National data protection authorities generally accept that Robinson/preference lists are essential. This is reflected in the EU directive and the FEDMA date protection code. In some countries, Robinson lists/preference services are obligatory and do not rely on voluntary self-regulation. Other countries have obligatory opt-out lists even though the law prescribes an opt-in approach. This applies to fax marketing, for example, which requires an opt-in approach according to EU provisions[1].

Differences in national legislation are one reason why international or pan-European Robinson lists are practically non-existent. In respect of direct mail, another reason is that there are a variety of different address formats within Europe.

Belgium

Belgium has four separate Robinson/preference lists (see Table 2-6-2): for mail, telephone, email and recently also for SMS (text messages) as well. All lists are maintained by the Belgian Direct Marketing Association.

Denmark

In Denmark, there is only one Robinson list/preference service for direct marketing. This is provided by a government office called the Central Person Register (CPR, Table 2-6-3).

There is no telephone preference service (TPS). According to paragraph 2 of the Danish Consumer Agreements Act (Lov om visse forbrugeraftaler), unsolicited calls to consumers to sell goods or services are generally not permitted. In contrast, unsolicited calls to sell insurance, rescue services, certain foodstuffs, books and newspaper/magazine subscriptions are allowed. Unsolicited calls, mail and faxes to companies are permitted as long as the contact person has not expressly opted out of receiving such communications.

There are also no email, SMS or fax preference services in Denmark. However, since 1 July 2000, the sending of unsolicited advertising via electronic communication media, such as email, SMS, MMS, fax, automatic call systems, etc., has been prohibited. The prohibition applies irrespective of the identity of the recipient.

---

[1] Directires on: Distance Selling (1997); ISDN and Privacy (1997); Distance Marketing of Financial Services (2002), and Privacy and Electronic Communications (2002).

However, since 25 July 2003, it has been permissible to send advertising information by email or SMS/MMS (but not fax) without prior consent, provided the
following conditions are met:

- The recipient purchased goods or services from the company after 25 July 2003.
- The recipient gave, in connection with the purchase, his/her electronic address (telephone number/email address).
- The recipient was informed that the electronic address would be used for
sending advertising information and was advised whether this would be
done by email or SMS/MMS.
- The recipient was, in connection with the purchase, given the opportunity to
refuse receipt of such advertising information.
- The recipient can at a later date, without difficulty or charge, opt out of receiving further advertising information.
- The provider may only advertise goods and services similar to those originally purchased by the recipient.

Complaints regarding unsolicited electronic messages should be addressed to
spam@fs.dk.

France
The Robinson list (La Liste Robinson) is sent out three times a year to companies
who have registered with this service. Registered companies must clean their lists
using the MPS within two months of receiving the latest MPS updates (Table 2-6-4).

Spain
The Spanish Robinson list/preference services include two innovations. First, all
services are combined in one database (similar systems are in place in Italy and
Australia). Second, Spain has both a "positive" and a "negative" list: a conventional
opt-out list, which can be used to opt out of receiving direct marketing, and a positive (or opt-in) list, which consumers use to show that they do wish to receive direct
marketing (Table 2-6-5).

United Kingdom
There are five Robinson lists/preference services, as well as a number of other interesting services. Of the five conventional services, two are prescribed by law, although they are operated under license by the British Direct Marketing Association. Another service deals with fax messages, even though the opt-in system is
legally required for advertising by fax (Table 2-6-6).

British consumers can register with the first-ever global eMPS, established by
the American Direct Marketing Association. Private individuals can register free
of charge by providing their email address, and can opt out of one or more of the
following categories: business to consumers, business to business or all unsolicited
advertising messages by email.

Criterion / List	MPS	TPS	eMPS	SMS
Address	www.robinsonlist.be	www.robinsonlist.be	www.robinsonlist.be	www.robinsonlist.be
Number of people registered	28,012 (December 2005)	14,539 (December 2005)	12,211 (December 2005)	3,466 (December 2005)
Operator	Belgian Direct Marketing Association (BDMA)			
Statutory provision	Not statutory			
National Association Code	Code of Practice of the Belgian Direct Marketing Association (BDMA), requires obligatory application			
Registration	Private individuals only			
Fees	Free			
Consumer contact	www.robinsonlist.be (online registration)			
Corporate contact	www.robinsonlist.be			

Figure 2-6-2: Belgium

Criterion / List	MPS
Address	www.cpr.dk
Number of people registered	+ 700,000 (January 2006)
Operator	Central Person Register (CPR)
Statutory provision	Yes
National Association Code	N/A
Registration	Private individuals only (free)
Fees	Robinson list without search facility: DKK 275 on CD-ROM, subscription (1 year); with search facility: DKK 1,000 on CD-ROM*
Consumer contact	Local town council
Corporate contact	CPR, tel.: 00 45 45 94 03 20, email: kc@cpr.dk

* Prices correct as at January 2006 – including VAT, postage and packing

Figure 2-6-3: Denmark

Criterion / List	La Liste Robinson	e-Robinson
Address	www.fevad.com	www.e-robinson.com
Number of people registered	ca. 170,000 (November 2003)	N/A
Operator	La Fédération des Entreprises de Vente à Distance (FEVAD – Federation of Distance Selling Enterprises) as a member of L'Union Française du Marketing Direct (UFMD – French Direct Marketing Association)	FEVAD
Statutory provision	No	Unknown
National Association Code	Yes	Unknown
Registration	Anyone can register (free)	Anyone can register
Fees	Subscription fee p.a. for companies is either 500 euros (single use) or 747 euros (multiple use).	N/A
Consumer contact	UFMD, Liste Robinson/ Stop Publicité, 60 rue La Boétie, F-75008 Paris, France, Contact person: Véronique Milan, email: vmilan-beslay@fevad.com, tel. +33 1 42 56 54 57.	www.e-robinson.com
Corporate contact	SNA, 103 bis avenue Louis Didier, BP 238, 33506 Libourne Cedex, France, Tel: +33 5 57 55 29 00, Fax: +33 5 57 55 29 29	www.e-robinson.com/form/enterpri.asp

Figure 2-6-4: France

Criterion/List	Opt-out Listas Robinson	MP-List
Address	www.fecemd.org	www.fecemd.org
Number of people registered	37,000 (December 2005)	900 (December 2005)
Operator	Federación de Comercio Electrónico y Márketing Directo (FECEMD)	
Statutory provision	No	
National Association Code	Compulsory for members of the FECEMD	
Registration	Private individuals only (free)	
Fees	For non-member companies who want to buy the list: € 475 plus 16% VAT; free for FECEMD members	
Consumer contact Corporate contact	FECEMD, Avenida Diagonal 437, 5°, 1a, 08036 Barcelona, Spain, tel.: +34 9 3240 4070	

Figure 2-6-5: Spain

The British authorities have recently shown an interest in introducing a mandatory system. As we have seen above, the British telephone preference service (TPS) is mandatory and is operated under license by the British Direct Marketing Association. A new, corporate TPS was introduced this year by the British regulatory body for telecommunications (Ofcom), and is also operated under license by the British Direct Marketing Association. There were lengthy discussions regarding how this service should be set up and the security measures required to prevent misuse. As the British Direct Marketing Association found out when it negotiated the license with Ofcom, there is a need for strict controls and validation on the part of the company. All or some of the company telephone numbers registered in the corporate TPS must be validated in order to prevent a competitor from maliciously registering numbers.

Australia

In Australia, the Data Protection Bill stipulates that companies seeking to acquire new customers must keep lists of consumers who have expressly opted out of receiving offers. Subscription to the service is not a legal requirement, although regular use of the service does help companies to ensure that they are fulfilling their legal obligations. This service does not provide for the removal of consumers from company lists if they are current customers of that company. Nor does it prevent flyers being delivered to households by local retailers (unaddressed mailings), nor telephone calls from market research companies, estate agents and local businesses (Table 2-6-7).

Another issue is the varying price structure for using Robinson lists/preference services. The Australian Robinson lists/preference services, for example, compare favorably in terms of price. This is because in Australia, as in Spain and Italy, there is a central database with a well-structured price list for members and non-members.

Criterion / List	MPS	TPS	Facsimile FPS	eMPS
Addresse	www.mpsonline.org.uk/mpsr	www.tpsonline.org.uk	www.fpsonline.org.uk	www.dmaconsumers.org/emps.html
Number of people registered	2,500,000 entries (January 2006)	11,000,000 entries (January 2006)	1,800,000 entries (January 2006)	Approx. 165,000 addresses registered with eMPS, plus 700 domain names
Operator	(British) DMA	(British) DMA	(British) DMA	DMA USA
Statutory provision	Yes: legislation for advertising, promotions and direct marketing; matching against new customers	The TPS is prescribed by law: matching against new customer lists and regular customer lists	Yes	Required only for campaigns outside of Europe, as by law unsolicited emails within Europe may only be sent to those addressees who agreed to it through double opt-in
National Association Code	Requirement of the DMA's Code of Practice	Requirement of the DMA's Code of Practice	Requirement of the DMA's Code of Practice	Requirement of the DMA's Code of Practice
Registration		Is mainly intended for business customers, but private individuals can also register		any email address may be registered
Fees	MPS subscription can be renewed annually; the current annual fee is £ 595 (January 2006). For a single file, the fee is £150.	a) Annual data delivery (for unlimited access to the complete data via internet download or regular update every 28 days on CD or hard copy): complete file £6,375 (fax: £3,190); partial files £640 (£320) to £5,550 (£390) depending on file size b) Ad-hoc data delivery (for companies that only occasionally require the file): complete file £850 (fax £425; partial files £85 (£45) to £640 (£320) depending on file size c) There is also an online service where companies can compare fax/telephone numbers via a website. The basic fee is £ 50 + VAT per month		Subscription for 12 months: $ 600
Consumer contact	www.mpsonline.org.uk, www.tpsonline.org.uk, tel.: + 44 845 70 34 599, tel.: + 44 845 07 00 707,		www.tpsonline.org.uk/fps/, www.dmaconsumers.org/emps.html tel.: + 44 845 07 00 702	
Corporate contact	www.mpsonline.org.uk, http://corporate.tpsonline.org.uk, corporate.mpsonline.org.uk/fpsC/html/ tel.: + 44 20 72 91 33 27, tel.: + 44 20 72 91 33 26, tel.: + 44 20 72 91 33 26 www.dmaconsumers.org/emps.html			

Figure 2-6-6: United Kingdom

Australia – Do Not Contact Service

A preference system that combines the MPS, TPS, eMPS and mobile phone lists.

- www.adma.com.au
- 113,000 entries (2004)
- Operated by the Australian Direct Marketing Association (ADMA)
- Use is mandated in the code of practice of the ADMA (ADMA members must use the service)
- Only private individuals can register
- Fees (August 2004):

Do not mail/do not call:	$450 (member), $1450 (non-member)
Do not email:	$250 (member), $750 (non-member)
M-marketing opt-out:	$250 (member), $750 (non-member)
Do not email/M-marketing opt-out:	$450 (member), $1450 (non-member)
Full package:	$750 (member), $2500 (non-member)
Note:	All prices are annual fees and exclude goods and services tax.
	Updates are sent out monthly.

- Point of contact for consumers: ADMA – Do Not Contact Service, Kings Cross NSW 1340, Australia; email: info@adma.com.au
- Point of contact for companies: ADMA, PO Box 464, Kings Cross NSW 1340, Australia; email: code@adma.com.au

5   Obligatory lists – the US experience

As mentioned earlier, in some countries there are obligatory systems operated by government offices, or under license by direct marketing associations. In the USA, the statutory provisions introduced in 2003 by the Federal Trade Commission (FTC) and the Federal Communications Commission (FCC) led to the establishment of what are called "Do Not Call" lists. This was the result of continued refusal of a few of the bigger telemarketing companies in the USA to use the telephone preference services (TPS) of the USA Direct Marketing Association (DMA) under a system of voluntary self-regulation. To date, about 100 million telephone numbers have been registered, although some not by the people who actually own them. The call center business in the USA has went into a crisis, and successful initiatives implemented there may well indicate the way forward for regulation in other countries, as well.

Some government agencies in Europe have already indicated that it is probably necessary to follow the USA's lead when it comes to telemarketing – even though the market situation and market size in Europe are totally different. Furthermore, a number of states in the USA have prohibited the sending of unsolicited email messages. They took this step even though the Federal Trade Commission (FTC) had previously indicated that it would not use the authority bestowed upon it by the "Can Spam" Act of 2003 to create an obligatory email preference service across all states. In Europe, the 2002 Directive on Privacy and Electronic Communications already prohibits advertising by unsolicited email. Yet spam remains a serious threat, because it can be sent over the internet from anywhere in the world, evading all regulation. A big problem in connection with the FTC and FCC's Do Not Call lists is the associated cost. Companies that want to perform outbound telemarketing in the USA are now legally obliged to clean up their lists. The fees that the FTC and FCC have established for doing so, however, are very high, and each Do Not Call list purchased can only be used for one marketing campaign. This means that telemarketers cannot simply make a one-off payment and then use the same lists for all their customers. The costs for using a voluntary self-regulation system are much lower, particularly since a call center can reuse the lists numerous times for all its customers.

At this point it may be interesting to note that there is a clear connection between problems in the direct marketing sector and the increase in the number of entries in the Robinson lists. In the UK, for example, improper use of predictive dialers – which organize workflow in call centers by automatically calling the next number in the database after a certain number of rings – has led to a multitude of "dead calls": the called party picks up, but there is nobody on the other end. A press campaign against the use of such dialers soon followed. As a result, the number of TPS entries, i.e., people who did not wish to receive advertising by telephone, increased from under two million to over five million in 2003 alone. In this case, the Robinson list/preference service at least provided the irate citizens with an outlet, avoiding restrictive legislation which could have penalized call center operators for misuse.

6   New Robinson lists: developments

A number of new and innovative Robinson lists/preference services have been around for some time now. In the UK, for example, the British Direct Marketing Association has introduced a "Baby Preference Service".

United Kingdom – Baby Mail Preference Service (Baby MPS)

Parents who do not wish to receive advertising for baby products can register for this service.
- mpsonline.org.uk/bmpsr/
- 2,500 entries (July 2004)
- Operated by the British Direct Marketing Association (DMA)
- Not a legal requirement, but prescribed within the context of the British DMA's Code of Practice (members of the association must compare their lists with these files)
- Fees: unlimited access for one year (£250 +VAT)
- Point of contact for consumers: mpsonline.org.uk/bmpsr/,
  Tel.: + 44 20 72 91 33 10, registration forms are also available from some doctors' surgeries, mother and baby clinics, and gynecological wards.
- Point of contact for companies: www.mpsonline.org.uk/BMPSR/HTML/,
  Tel.: + 44 20 72 91 33 27

Other examples: in the UK, the deceased are also listed in appropriate files. In the past, procedures for identifying the deceased and removing them from direct marketing lists relied on the cooperation of local civil registry offices. But not all authorities were cooperative. Files of the deceased touch on a very sensitive issue and not only because the survivors often protest about receiving mail for a relative who has already passed on (especially if they are being offered life insurance). There are now similar files in a number of other countries, such as Germany, where they are managed by Deutsche Post. Advertisers in the Netherlands have access to similar lists of the deceased.

In the UK, for example, there are two files of the deceased, both operated by commercial organizations.

United Kingdom – the Deceased Register

The "Deceased Register" is a database which lists people who have recently died. The data is collected in collaboration with registrars all over Great Britain. To do this, the registrars in the respective civil registry offices fill in and send postage-paid postcards to the Deceased Register operators. Deaths must ordinarily be registered within five days. The updated data is then made available to companies by the following week.

- www.thedeceasedregister.com
- Operated by Active Media Limited (a member of the Direct Marketing Association, DMA)
- Not required by law
- Point of contact for consumers: Active Media Ltd, Tel.: +44 1332 222700, email: d.reg@activemedia.ltd.uk

Mortascreen™, maintained by Smee and Ford and marketed in cooperation with Millennium ADPM, is another file of the deceased used in Great Britain. It is the biggest file of its type in Europe: every month nearly 40,000 new names are added. Mortascreen™ covers England, Scotland and Wales, whereas the Deceased Register covers the whole of the UK. Further information can be found at www.smeeandford.co.uk/morta.html.

The "Bereavement Register", operated by REaD Group (UK) Ltd, is another file of the deceased from Britain. Further information can be found at www.the-bereavementregister.com/uk.

7   Change of address – moving files

If you have ever moved, you will most likely have worried that mail from your previous address would not be redirected to your new one or that, long after your predecessor moved out, you may still have received that person's mail. The majority of postal companies have their own change of address files. They collect and use this data to help their own delivery systems, but can also use it to advise companies operating door-to-door mailings. In some countries, this system works exceptionally well. In other countries, however, mail redirection and the internal use of change-of-address lists by the postal service is not particularly effective.

With the full support of the whole sector, a new company in the UK, the REaD Group, established a National Suppression File (NSF) in 2002, consisting of confirmed goneaways, returned mail, notifications/deliveries and voter lists.

United Kingdom – National Suppression File (NSF)

The NSF combines various data from the consortium members and can be categorized into four main datasets: confirmed goneaways, returned mail, notifications/ deliveries and voter lists.

- www.readgroup.co.uk
- Introduced by the British Direct Marketing Association, managed by Hays Commercial Services and marketed by the REaD Group
- Not a legal requirement
- Fees: customers can appoint a professional data processor to use the NSF for removing people who have changed address from their mailing files. This involves comparing company files with the NSF, and incurs a fee for each match found. If the customer is a member of the Direct Marketing Association, the fee is £0.17 per match; non-members pay a fee of £0.22 per match. A commission may additionally be payable (around £0.05 per match, at the sole discretion of the data processor).
- Contact: REaD Group, Tel.: +44 1732 460 000, email: sales@readgroup.co.uk

In view of the growing competition, it may be sensible to consider using commercial services such as these. There is also a special Robinson list for "gone aways", the goneaway suppression file (GAS).

United Kingdom – the GAS

The Gone Away Suppression File is the most accurate and comprehensive goneaway file available in Great Britain.

- www.readgroup.co.uk
- Introduced by the British Direct Marketing Association, managed by Hays Commercial Services and marketed by the REaD Group
- 9 million datasets, updated every quarter
- Operated by the REaD Group (UK) Ltd.
- Not a legal requirement
- Fees:
  A. Unspecified and new customer screening: 20p per goneaway identified
  B. Database cleaning: renewable 12-month licenses are available, for apply ing markers to the advertiser's database
- Contact: REaD Group, Tel.: +44 1732 460 000, email: sales@readgroup.co.uk

In Spain, to give another example, goneaway lists are operated by Schober, which offers similar services in several countries. In Germany, Deutsche Post Adress has a very comprehensive change-of-address database.

8   Systems for preventing delivery of unaddressed mailings

An overview of Robinson lists/preference services would not be complete without mentioning unaddressed mailings. In this respect, there are systems available to consumers that enable them to prevent the receipt of unaddressed mail. These are not called Robinson lists, but they have the same effect – they let goods and service providers know who does not want to receive promotional mailings (opt-out system).

In the past ten years, most countries have seen an increase in the volume of unaddressed promotional mailings. This is primarily the result of cheaper printing techniques. Regular mail now has to fight for space in our mailboxes against free newspapers, government brochures and voter information. Inevitably this has led consumers to indicate that they want to be excluded from unaddressed mailings. Several systems, most of them unofficial, were introduced on a national level, but most on a local level. In the USA, all mailboxes belong to the US Postal Service, and placing unaddressed mail into these mailboxes is not permitted. Therefore, the situation in the US has been different from the start. In some European countries, access to private mailboxes is also restricted, for example, in certain apartment blocks.

The issue of unaddressed mailings is particularly sensitive during the holiday season, when mailboxes gradually overflow. Virtually any passer-by can instantly recognize that the owner of the property is away. The Dutch Direct Marketing Association, which operates one of the most developed systems for preventing unaddressed mailings, sees a significant rise in registration requests every year just before vacation. There are two labels available under this system: one is for refusing all unaddressed mailings, including free newspapers, and the other is for refusing unaddressed direct mailings only, but allowing free newspapers. Investigations have revealed that many households only stick these labels on their mailboxes some of the time – usually when they are away on vacation.

9   Implications

There are Robinson lists/preference services in most European Union countries and in the other big markets around the globe (USA, Canada, Australia, Japan, etc.). Poland, too, now also has a working Robinson list/preference service, whereas the system in the Czech Republic is not yet operational. As yet, there are still no Robinson lists/preference systems in Cyprus, Malta, Estonia, Latvia, Lithuania,

Slovenia, Bulgaria, Croatia, Romania or Turkey. This presents a challenge for the European direct marketing sector. Finally, it is worth noting that data protection legislation in most countries actively promotes the use of Robinson lists/preference services by direct marketing companies.

Even in cases where an opt-in approach is required for marketing lists, Robinson lists/preference services have proven useful, e.g., as a service for companies and, in particular, small enterprises such as small private practices (doctors, dentists, lawyers, etc.).

Nevertheless, Robinson lists/preference services do not merely ensure that statutory requirements are met. Operating a Robinson list/preference service offers tangible mutual benefits for both consumers and providers of goods and services. The providers offer the consumers the means, via free registration, to avoid receiving unsolicited direct marketing across a variety of media (mail, telephone, email, fax, SMS and mobile phone). Consumers who sign up for Robinson lists/preference services are not interested in being contacted by the companies. A provider who ignores this information would be wasting the company's resources (print, postage, telephone charges, etc.). The consumer, on the other hand, is grateful to a provider that respects his/her wishes by leaving them alone. The use of Robinson lists/preference services therefore contributes indirectly to brand image.

Efficiency and reliable customer orientation are essential qualities for successful direct marketing, since the possibility always exists that the customer might become annoyed or even alienated in the long run. Indeed, direct customer dialog is typically "pushier" and more personal than the advertisement via the mass media. Consequently the image of direct marketing needs to be characterized by responsible and positive interaction with consumers. Otherwise trust will be lost and the wrath of the legislators incurred. In the USA, for example, the damage caused by the irresponsible use of telephone marketing led to some very restrictive regulations. The European Union reacted in the same way to the problem of email spam. There are many other examples of restrictive provisions that have led to serious practical difficulties – to the detriment of both the consumers and the economy. As long as the sector remains unable to prove unequivocally that it uses personal data in a responsible manner, and consumers remain unconvinced of the advantages of direct marketing, then the healthy growth of the direct marketing sector will remain under threat.

Robinson lists/preference services play a central, crucial role in the preservation, promotion and success of direct marketing, and in doing so benefit all the parties concerned.

10 Summary

Consumers do not always want to receive direct marketing sent by mail, telephone, fax, email, SMS, etc. At the same time, companies must ensure that their direct marketing is effective. It is therefore advantageous to remove the names of any consumers who do not wish to be contacted from marketing lists.

As we have seen, many government bodies have adopted the concept of Robinson lists/preference services to solve certain problems with consumer protection. In the UK, for example, there are two obligatory Robinson lists that telephone marketers are obliged to observe. The consumer TPS list and the corporate TPS list are operated under license by the British Direct Marketing Association, by order of the telecommunications authority (Ofcom). In the USA, the Federal Communications Commission and the Federal Trade Commission (FCC and FTC) instituted Do Not Call lists in 2003, in order to put a stop to the misuse of telemarketing. Some of the telemarketing companies had refused to use the telephone preference service that had already been established by the US Direct Marketing Association. These obligatory Do Not Call lists in the USA have also demonstrated just how expensive regulatory systems can be.

New and innovative Robinson Lists/preference services are now arriving on the market, illustrating that the advertising industry is dealing responsibly with these problems. Over the last four years, a number of commercial organizations in the UK, Germany and Spain, working with the direct marketing sector, have established files containing the names of people who have recently died. Other examples include a baby file and change of address files.

What does the future hold for Robinson lists/preference services? FEDMA believes that national direct marketing associations will continue to be the biggest operators of Robinson lists/preference services. It is unlikely that government agencies or commercial providers will assume these tasks in the long run. However, in view of the challenges faced by the smallest EU countries, for example, it is possible that organizations other than national direct marketing associations will provide significant Robinson lists/preference services.

Today, the most important objective of direct marketing is to ensure that the consumer remains a good and loyal customer. Both parties stand to benefit when advertisers use direct advertising in a responsible manner. Robinson lists/preference services are central to this, and at the same time, they make direct marketing more efficient.

11   References and links

The Direct Marketing Association (DMA)

AUSTRALIA	ADMA	www.adma.com.au
AUSTRIA	DMVÖ	www.dmvoe.at
BELGIUM	BDMA	www.bdma.be
CANADA	CMA	www.the-cma.org
CZECH REP.	ADMAZ	www.admaz.cz
DENMARK	DDMC	www.dmklubben.dk
FINLAND	SSML	www.ssml-fdma.fi
FRANCE	UFMD	www.fevad.com
GERMANY	DDV	www.ddv.de
GREECE	EPAM	(no website)
GREECE	EDEE	www.edee.gr
HUNGARY	DMSZ	www.dmsz.net
IRELAND	IDMA	www.idma.ie
ITALY	AIDIM	www.aidim.it
NETHERLANDS	DDMA	www.ddma.nl
NORWAY	NORDMA	www.nordma.no
POLAND	SMB	www.smb.pl
PORTUGAL	AMD	(no website)
SLOVAKIA	ADIMA	www.klc@hermesplus.sk
SLOVENIA	ZDMS	www.zdms.org
SPAIN	FECEMD	www.fecemd.org
SWEDEN	SWEDMA	www.swedma.se
SWITZERLAND	SDV	www.dmverband.ch
UK	DMA UK	www.dma.org.uk
USA	DMA US	www.the-dma.org
EUROPE	FEDMA	www.fedma.org

12 Examples of Robinson lists

France – Red, Orange and Saffron lists
The Red list is a telephone preference service that enables consumers to opt out of being listed in France Telecom directories. However, because France Telecom does not give out any contact data for people on the Red list, being registered on this list not only blocks unsolicited direct marketing calls, but may also prevent certain telephone calls that would in fact be desirable.

The Orange list is a telephone preference service that enables consumers to opt out of being listed in the direct marketing directories of France Telecom. Unlike the Red list, people entered in the Orange list can still be contacted for purposes other than direct marketing.

The Saffron list, operated by France Telecom, was the French fax preference service. However, it was abandoned, because it has been illegal in France to solicit private individuals with direct marketing via fax without prior consent since 2001. Nevertheless, FEVAD is currently in negotiations with France Telecom regarding a new Saffron list for B2B use.

Points of contact for the Red and Orange lists:

- www.francetelecom.com
- Operated by France Telecom

United Kingdom – Corporate Telephone Preference Service (CTPS)

Since 25 July 2004 companies have been able to register telephone numbers from which they do not wish to receive any unsolicited direct marketing calls.

- www.tpsonline.org.uk/ctps/what/
- Approximately 665,000 entries (January 2006)
- Operated by the Direct Marketing Association (UK)
- Within the scope of the EU directive, the corporate TPS is legally required under the 2004 Privacy and Electronic Communications Act (as amended).
- Registration is open to corporations such as "limited companies" (UK), "limited liability partnerships" (England, Wales and Northern Ireland) or any "partnerships" (Scotland). This also applies to schools, ministries and government agencies, hospitals, public limited companies, and other bodies governed by public law.
- Fees:
  - a) The costs for using the service vary according to the company's require ments. If a company needs a full year's license for the whole of the UK, the price is £3,190 (+ VAT). Partial and ad-hoc files are also available (for a list of costs for the various licenses, visit corporate.mpsonline.org. uk/CTPSC/html/Cost.asp).
  - b) Other options for companies only requiring limited access to the database include an online research service, which costs £50 for each month in which the service is used. This allows for up to 500 numbers to be compared in the corresponding month. (For further details, see corporate.mpsonline.org.uk/CTPSC/html/AdditionalServices.asp)
- Point of contact for companies: tpsonline.org.uk, Tel.: + 44 20 72 91 33 26

Chapter 3:
Marketing facts

Introduction to Chapter 3

Global markets and international competition require worldwide communication strategies. But even though national borders have become ever less important within our multinational economic system, each country nevertheless still has its own requirements and very specific needs with regard to advertising. It is crucial that companies realize this if their customer dialog is to be successful. Mailings are still a very popular form of international advertising. Dialog marketing is currently particularly well received in Eastern and Southern Europe. For example, Poland, with a current growth rate of 5.4%, is one of the strongest national economies among the new member countries of the European Union. This is a good location for international direct marketing to start, since it is already an accepted form of advertising in Poland and has generated good response rates.

The following chapter serves as a tool to support the planning of international direct marketing campaigns and the development of new markets. The data provided below is based on the results of market studies conducted by Deutsche Post AG, in cooperation with TNS Infratest, affording the reader exclusive insider information. This overview from 17 European countries, the United States and six Asian-Pacific countries offers an excellent opportunity to estimate the potential for both, expansion into new markets but also the further development of existing markets. Help is provided in the form of information on purchasing behavior, consumer trends and consumer attitudes towards direct marketing and other media. Altogether, the information provided enables managers to gather a holistic perception of direct marketing opportunities, and presents a framework for one-to-one marketing in individual countries. They also include data concerning the average use of media and advertising expenditure, and should be a useful tool when planning campaigns, since such knowledge is essential if companies are to address a target group successfully.

The first part offers a cross-sectional analysis of the results across individual countries. The major benefit of this article is that it provides a comparison of individual markets across a number of different areas of interest for advertising planners. Examples include how gender or social factors may influence the success of advertising. The following section of the book concentrates on specific details by country, providing a quick overview and a well structured presentation. The accompanying graphics enhance understanding of the information provided when planning successful international advertising campaigns.

Anita Petersen

International dialog marketing: Consumer trends

Operating in globalized markets is no longer the preserve of a few conglomerates. Increasing competitive pressure demands more and more internationally oriented advertising, even from medium-sized companies. Goals are ranging from opening up new markets to ensuring customer loyalty to particular brands and companies, even in remote locations. Internationally, mailings are a favorite advertising medium to pursue these goals. Anyhow, marketers often lack even basic data across countries to optimize their campaigns. Here, a large survey conducted by GfK AG (2004) and TNS Infratest (2005) and the Market Research Service Center (MRSC) on behalf of Deutsche Post AG is a valuable tool. Between April and June 2005, 13,185 consumers in 24 countries were surveyed on their affinity towards mailings, other advertising media and consumer attitudes. The aim of the study was to assess the climate for international dialog marketing in various economic areas. The Asia-Pacific region was added to the scope from the previous year.

This large, computer-aided multi-dimensional survey was carried out (by CATI – i.e., by telephone – or sometimes CAPI, depending on local availability) in the following countries: Australia, Austria, Belgium, Czech Republic, China, Denmark, Finland, France, Germany, Hong Kong, Hungary, Italy, Japan, Netherlands, New Zealand, Norway, Poland, Singapore, Slovakia, Spain, Sweden, Switzerland, UK and the USA. The article makes a comparison of the survey results from 2005 with those of the 2004 survey. It also provides a thorough description of the data that is needed for the results to be implemented when pursuing international direct marketing strategies.

1   The dialog marketing climate: an international comparison

Mailings represent an advertising tool with relatively low "scattering loss" when addressed to specific target groups. However, some of the new EU member states in Eastern Europe still constitute "blind spots" for cross-border media planning. To date, there has been a shortage of available indicators for the success of direct marketing campaigns, as companies tend to keep response rates for individual campaigns a closely-guarded secret. In essence, both the success and efficiency (e.g., in terms of the CPO or CPI) of a particular mailing are determined by design factors and optimal target group selection. Yet it should also be noted that, seen internationally, the popularity of mailings is a universal cultural feature in connection with advertising media. The present study helps to assess the dialog marketing climate on an international level. The details provided by the representative samples surveyed in each country may serve as key indicators of the acceptance of mailings. The respondents' answers were also used to determine "attention rates" and response rates. Here, the attention rate indicates how many recipients actually read advertising mailings regularly and therefore accept this advertising contact. Accordingly, the response rate indicates how many of those who welcome advertising contact also respond to it.

First, it should be noted that across all countries studied, there is a negative correlation between mailing density and the attention rate. This means that the more people receive mailings in a particular country, the lower the rate of those who open the mailings will be. In Eastern Europe, 67% of the population receives mail-

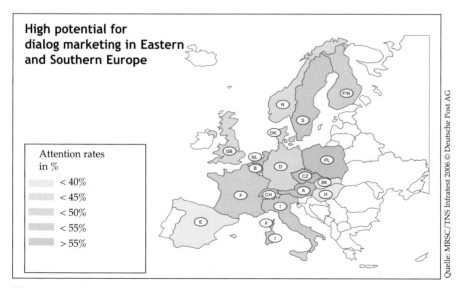

Figure 3-1-1: Attention rates in Europe

ings. In Western Europe, the corresponding figure is a high 87%. Consequently, higher attention rates can be achieved in the Czech Republic, Slovakia, Poland and Hungary, where the markets are less saturated (cf. figure 3-1-1).

The attention rate

Eastern European attention rates, i.e., the willingness to accept advertising contact in the form of mailings, range between 52% in Poland and 68% in Hungary. These are exceptional rates compared with Western Europe, where consumers are considerably more selective and demanding. Here, the attention rates range between 30% in Germany, where consumers are highly skeptical of advertising, and 58% in Spain. Beside the marked East-West divide, there is also a North-South split within Western Europe. In Southern Europe and in Scandinavia, people pay more attention to mailings compared to the Western European average. In Scandinavia, Sweden and Finland stand out with attention rates of over 40%.

In Asia, there is obviously a huge variance in mailing density: whereas 91% of consumers in Japan receive mailings, the population centers in China (the provinces of Beijing, Shanghai and Guangzhou) are much less penetrated by mailings. There only 44% receiving mailings regularly. Singapore and Hong Kong register 71% and 66% respectively. In terms of attention rate, Japan occupies first place in

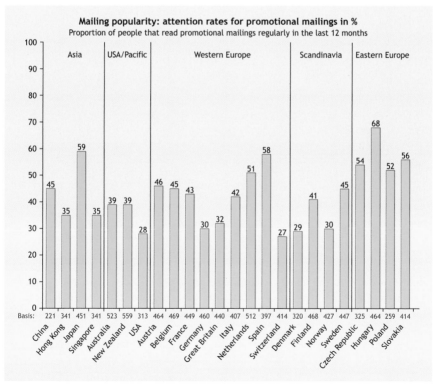

Figure 3-1-2: Attention rates worldwide

Asia with 59% of respondents. In the US/Pacific region, comprised of the US, Australia and New Zealand, a moderate density of mailings produces a very low attention rate of under 40%.

The response rate

The response rate, i.e., the percentage of recipients who have responded to a mailing at least once in 12 months, separates Europe into two camps. High levels of mailing density (cf. figure 3-1-3) are the rule across Europe; With regard to the response rate only Switzerland, Norway, the UK, Germany and Italy fall into the less responsive camp. Having the lowest level of mailing density, the EU member states in Eastern Europe are the most likely to respond to mailings.

Japan is the only non-European country with a high level density and relatively high response rate (29%). This makes this market especially attractive for direct marketing activities. In the US/Pacific region and Asia, on the other hand, response rates around 20% are wide spread.

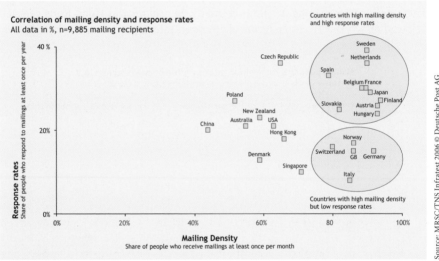

Figure 3-1-3: Relation between mailing density and response rates

There is also an inevitable connection between the response rate to mailings and mail-order popularity in each country – even though not every response is actually an order. Overall however, a small but significant positive correlation can be found between the response rate and the mail-order affinity of respondents across countries.

Japan stands out in this regard, especially in Asia: a high 73% of respondents have ordered by mail in the last 12 months. Large parts of Western Europe, e.g., Germany, France, the UK, Austria and Switzerland, are also especially fond of mail-ordering. The back markers are coming from Southern and Eastern Europe.

The greatest potential for growth seems to be in the Czech Republic, where 51% of the population uses mail-order already.

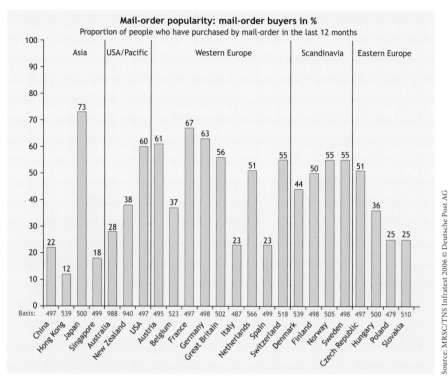

Figure 3-1-4: Mail-order popularity

2   Sociocultural profile of mailing acceptance

For the accurate planning of a campaign, it is of crucial importance not only to know which target groups in the various countries can be addressed through mailings, but which respond favorably. In the following, a person accepting mailings is defined as anyone who regularly accepts advertising contact with promotional mailings (see "attention rate"), i.e., is receptive to this form of advertising message. In all of the countries studied, it seems that a favorable receptiveness of mailings is consistently higher with females. 57.5% of those identified as receptive to mailings are female. At 42.5%, males on the other hand are underrepresented if compared to the overall proportion of males in the sample (48.6%). At the country level, the disproportionate number of females as part of the receptive population is especially noticeable in the US/Pacific region and in Europe. In Asia, on the other hand, mailings are not that much a "women's business": in all four Asian countries studied, men are just as receptive to mailings as are women.

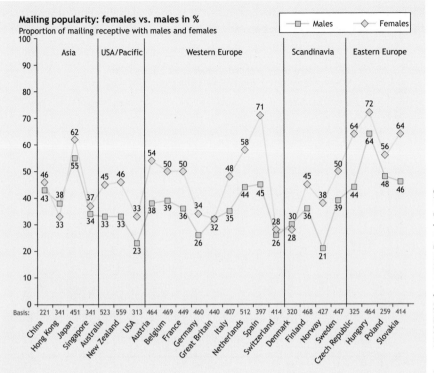

Figure 3-1-5: Mailing popularity by gender

The age distribution (cf. figure 3-1-6) shows that those who are favorable towards mailings are, on average, a few years older than the "neutral" segments. This is generally true in Asia, the US/Pacific region and Eastern Europe. The exceptions to this finding are Sweden, the Netherlands, Belgium, France, Italy and Spain.

The consumer profile of those receptive to mailings is especially interesting. Affinity towards innovation, consumer patriotism, brand loyalty, price orientation and quality awareness all contribute to this profile to differing degrees.

Receptiveness towards promotional mailings goes hand in hand with consumer openness to new products. In practically every case (cf. figure 3-1-7), those who regularly read mailings are also especially keen to try out new products (affinity towards innovation). This visual impression is confirmed by statistical analysis for Germany, Belgium, the Netherlands, Austria, Spain, Poland, the Czech Republic, Hungary, Finland, Sweden, the USA, Australia and Hong Kong. A basic interest in innovative products is thus a constant feature of the consumer profile that is receptive to mailings, making this the ideal target group for direct product communication.

In terms of purchasing decisions, openness to innovation is by no means the only criterion: "price sensitivity" and "brand loyalty" also contribute to the consumer profile. Price sensitivity, a "tendency to choose the cheapest product", definitely

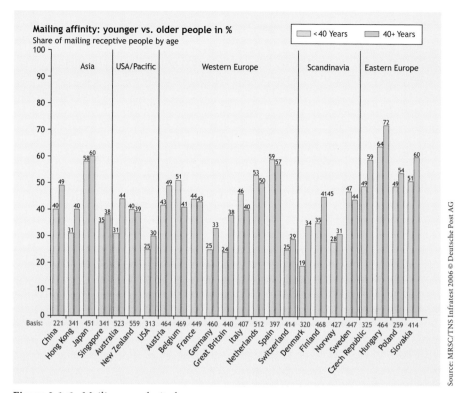

Figure 3-1-6: Mailing popularity by age

does not apply to all countries (cf. figure 3-1-8). Price awareness is especially common in Eastern Europe and Asia, while Western Europe presents a more heterogeneous picture. In general, people receptive to mailings appear to be somewhat more interested in low prices than their neutral/critical compatriots. This is especially true of Europe (exceptions: France, Scandinavia), but the trend can be generally observed in Asia and the Pacific region also (exceptions: the USA and Japan).

Brand loyalty is another prominent feature. In almost all countries, approval ratings are near the top of the scale. It is particularly surprising that, in many regions, target groups receptive to mailings demonstrate greater brand loyalty than less welcoming recipients (cf. figure 3-1-9). In Western Europe as well as in Australia and New Zealand, there are significantly higher values for brand loyalty where there is a pronounced affinity to mailings. This trend is not quite so clear in Eastern Europe and Scandinavia.

In summary, it can be said that those receptive to mailings exhibit a distinctly rational price orientation, as well as greater curiosity about innovative products, and tend to be more loyal to particular brands. The overall picture of consumer attitudes allows only one conclusion: people who are receptive to mailings are more aware as consumers.

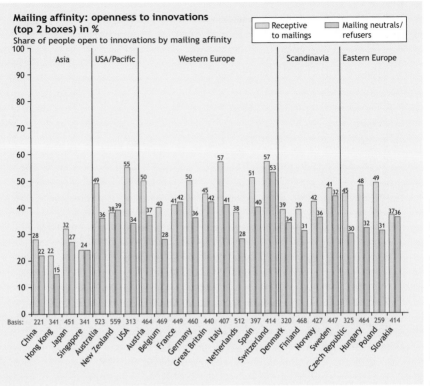

Figure 3-1-7: Mailing affinity and innovation

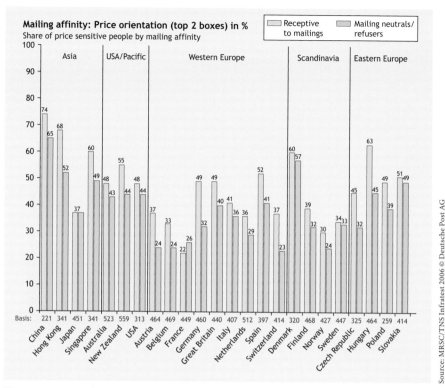

Figure 3-1-8: Mailing affinity and price orientation

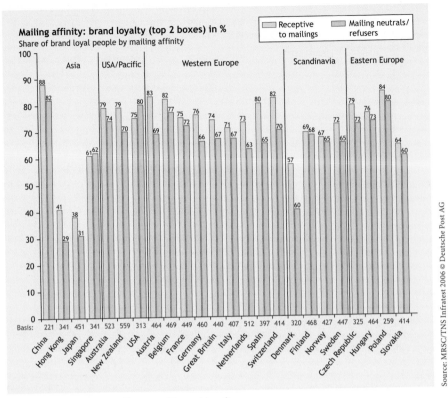

Figure 3-1-9: Mailing affinity and brand loyalty

3   How to gain attention: design features and their impact

Not all design elements make such a powerful impact that the recipient consciously notices and remembers them. Nevertheless, it is important to know what subjective value certain design, address and sender features have for consumer interest in mailings:

- How relevant, for example, is the familiarity of the company sending the mailing, compared to a colorful or witty design?
- What subjective value does the origin of the company have, or is a sophisticated design more important to consumers?
- And of particular relevance: how can the target groups in each country who are less receptive to mailings be addressed?

In general, the profile of the company sending the mailing plays a key role for the target groups in all countries. A good 32% of respondents state that if they are aware of the company, they will be more curious about the mailing. Hence, familiarity is one of the main reasons for opening a promotional mailing (cf. figure 3-1-10). At 30% relevance, product samples enclosed with mailings took second place in the attention ranking. Design features are important to a good quarter of respondents: whether they are witty or colorful, consumers take a careful look before they open a mailing. The origin of the provider, together with personalization, also ranks high among the subjectively important features. A special stamp and the announcement of a lottery were of less subjective relevance.

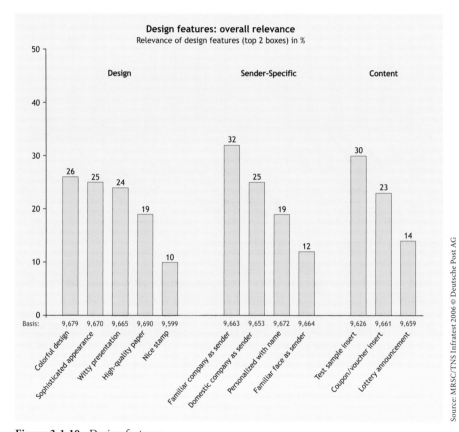

Figure 3-1-10: Design features

Further analysis of the preferences of individual target groups reveals some noticeable differences. It seems that receptive people attribute more relevance to all mailing design features than neutral or unsympathetic target groups. Neutral and unsympathetic recipients are less influenced by the visual aspects, origin or message than those who are receptive to mailings (cf. figure 3-1-11).

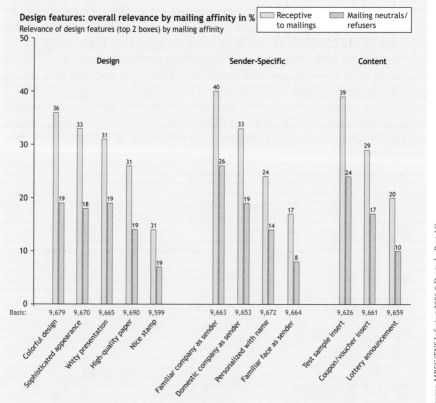

Source: MRSC/TNS Infratest 2006 © Deutsche Post AG

Figure 3-1-11: Design features and mailing affinity

International differences are very noticeable, too. In almost all countries, the company profile proves to be the main attention-grabber (cf. figure 3-1-12), but design features are particularly relevant in the new EU member states in Eastern Europe. With regard to the visual aspects of mailings, for example, people in Eastern and Southern Europe pay particular attention to a "sophisticated appearance". In contrast, Scandinavian, Western European, US-American and Asian consumers are much more restrained in their reaction to the visual impact of mailings (cf. figure 3-1-13). Personalization is also especially important in Eastern Europe (cf. figure 3-1-14). Here again, Scandinavians and Western Europeans seem to feel less personally addressed, while in Asia – apart from Japan – this personalized approach is relatively more important. The tendency of people who are receptive to mailings to respond well to a personalized message can be seen in almost all countries.

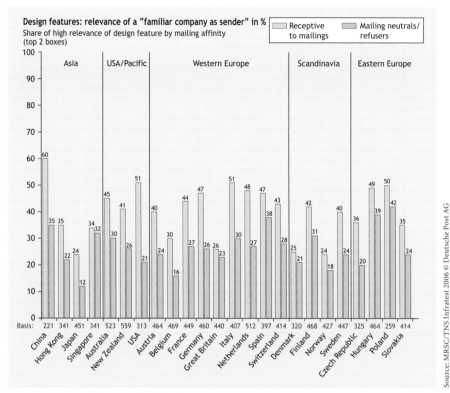

Figure 3-1-12: Relevance of a "familiar company as sender"

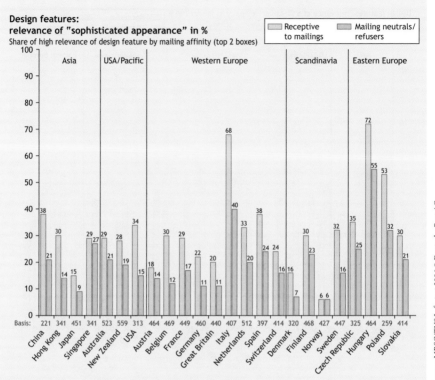

Figure 3-1-13: Relevance of "sophisticated appearance"

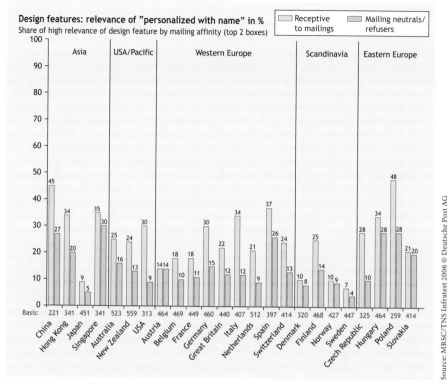

Figure 3-1-14: Relevance of personalization

4   Many ways to get a response: comparison of response channels

What is consumer reaction to promotional mailings?
Which response channels are preferred?

In order to answer these questions, an additional analysis of survey participants has been conducted who had responded to a mailing at least once in the last twelve months (cf. figure 3-1-15). An overview shows that response media are similarly ranked across all countries. Reply cards are at the top of the table in Europe, while electronic and telephone response channels are also very popular in Asia and the US/Pacific region. Email is already in second place among the response media used. An exception to this is Eastern Europe, where people are more likely to pick up the telephone. Fax, on the other hand, is the least favorite response medium in all countries (cf. figure 3-1-15). Given that in some countries the survey sample size is rather small (since only those who responded to a mailing can be included here), country-specific results should only be interpreted as directional information.

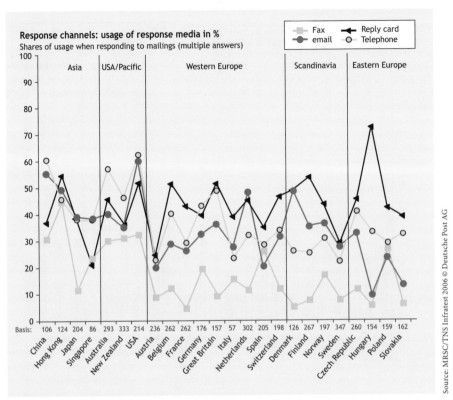

Source: MRSC/TNS Infratest 2006 © Deutsche Post AG

Figure 3-1-15: Comparison of response channels

5   Competition between communication channels: comparison of advertising media

In order to clarify the role of dialog marketing for different advertising media, we need to ascertain the popularity of various advertising media from the customer point of view. An index of acceptance is the percentage of consumers who like rather than merely tolerate advertising in the different media. Similarly, it is necessary to assess the percentage that consistently rejects a certain medium. As Figure 3-1-16 illustrates, press advertising on the whole (for all countries) has the highest acceptance rate (26%). This advertising medium also seems to have little polarization effect: with a solid 37%, it is in the middle of the range in terms of the "tolerance rate" (= neither hard rejection nor expressed preference). As expected, the refusal rate turns out to be relatively low, at 37%. In second place are promotional mailings and TV advertising, with a proportion of refusers of 58% and 59% respectively. A larger proportion are unsympathetic when it comes to radio advertising, with the acceptance rate dropping in comparison with TV advertising and mailings. The

most obvious polarization is found in internet/banner advertising: here the tolerance rate is very low, while the refusal rate climbs to 80%.

If we also look at the information and entertainment aspects, we see a striking
difference between mailings and TV advertising: although both score similarly
overall and in terms of information, TV advertising is perceived as much more
entertaining.

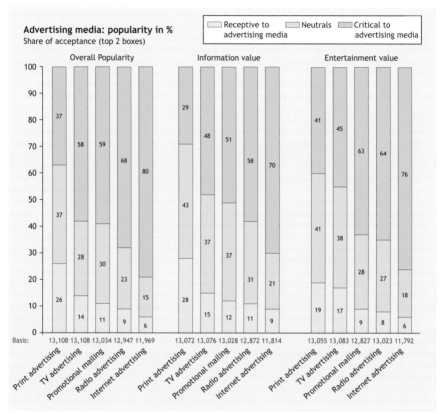

Figure 3-1-16: Comparison of advertising media

There are three possible explanations for the differences in popularity between
advertising media: the first is the invasiveness of an advertising medium, i.e., to
what extent it interferes with the consumption of the media. Press advertising
and mailings score well here, because there is no interruption to media reception,
unlike, for example, commercial breaks on TV and radio or pop-up windows on
the internet. The second aspect is the extent to which advertising contact can be
controlled through one's own behavior. This could be the reason behind the high
refusal rate for internet/banner advertising. Pop-up windows in particular require
active avoidance measures (such as "toggling" or "switching to another window"),

and this, combined with a high level of invasiveness, can provoke resistance A third aspect is the entertainment factor of the advertising media, a feature that may also contribute to the popularity of a medium itself. The findings on the entertainment value of advertising media support this hypothesis. The relatively high acceptance of mailings can be explained mainly by their low invasiveness, together with the high controllability of the advertising contact. An increase in entertainment value can also be expected to result in a much higher level of acceptance of mailings.

Acceptance of mailings also goes hand in hand with general receptiveness to advertising. This becomes obvious when two groups are compared (cf. figures 3-1-17 and 3-1-18): those receptive to mailings are also more receptive to press and TV advertising in general when compared with consumers who are neutral or opposed to advertising by mail. Press advertising is that popular among consumers who are receptive to mailings that it ranks ahead of other media in almost all countries (figure 3-1-17). In Eastern Europe and parts of Central Europe in particular, mailings are clearly preferred over TV advertising, which meets with lower acceptance levels in these regions. Thus, in cross-media campaigns, the best way of reaching target groups who are receptive to mailings is with a combination of press advertising and mailings. In Asia, TV advertising is also highly rated, almost reaching the level of

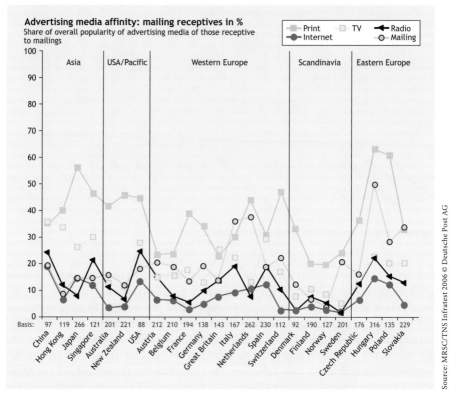

Source: MRSC/TNS Infratest 2006 © Deutsche Post AG

Figure 3-1-17: Acceptance of advertising media amongst those who are receptive to mailings

press advertising. People who are less receptive to advertising by mail are also less receptive to advertising media in general (Figure 3-1-18), although TV and press advertising are the most likely to be accepted by these rather critical consumers. A special case is Japan, where even press advertising must make do with low acceptance rates of well under 30%.

From an international perspective, women show noticeably higher acceptance levels than men for a range of advertising media (cf. figure 3-1-19). Female consumers favor mailings particularly, but also like press advertising. In contrast, males are more receptive – albeit at a low level – to internet/banner advertising than females. However, overall the relative media popularity scale is similar for both groups: press advertising enjoys the highest level of acceptance, followed by TV advertising and promotional mailings. Radio and banner advertising fall well behind the other media.

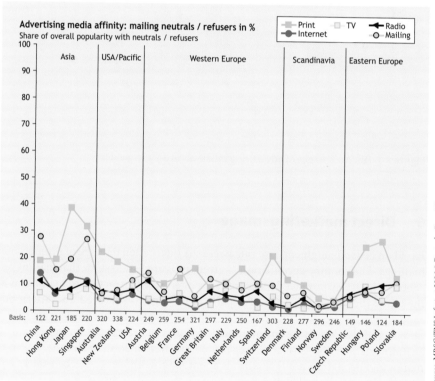

Figure 3-1-18: Acceptance of advertising media and mailing affinity

Source: MRSC/TNS Infratest 2006 © Deutsche Post AG

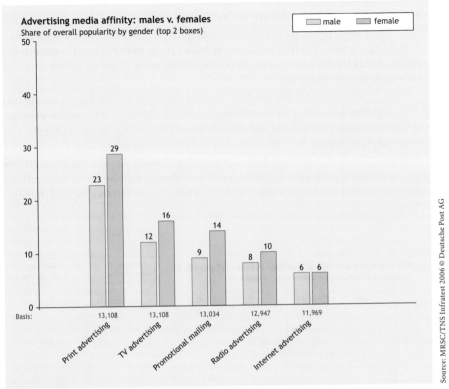

Figure 3-1-19: Acceptance of advertising media according to gender

6   Direct marketing image

Based on general judgments, we can assess the international image of promotional mailings. The country-specific results given in figure 3-1-20 show that mailing acceptance is largely product dependent. This interest-led attraction to mailings is at the top of the image profile in large parts of the regions surveyed. In Eastern Europe especially, people are also enthusiastic about mailings that have an appealing design, and they are more curious about mailings in general. In Western Europe, Scandinavia and the US/Pacific region, people have a similar attitude to direct marketing: people are not that curious about mailings in general. Their interest is very much only aroused by the product.

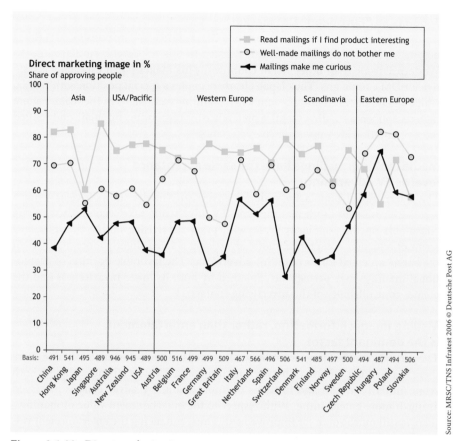

Figure 3-1-20: Direct marketing image

7 Summary

A number of trends in internationally oriented dialog marketing can be deduced from these findings. These can serve as a valuable basis for successful cross-border direct marketing strategies.

Dialog marketing climate: strong potential
for dialog marketing in Eastern and Southern Europe and Asia

The attention paid by consumers to dialog marketing is very satisfactory in large parts of Europe. Up to 68% of mailing recipients within a country consciously make advertising contact with mailings, and regularly read promotional mailings with interest. There is a large potential in Eastern (Hungary, the Czech Republic, Slovakia and Poland) and Southern Europe (Spain and Italy). This is also valid for Asia and Japan in particular, where there is a high level of acceptance of mailings.

Japan is an "European" DM market

Japan is the only non-European country with receptive and responsive consumers despite having a high level of mailing density. In this respect it is similar rather to Western Europe than other Asian countries. This makes Japan especially attractive for DM campaigns. Thus Japan clearly occupies a special position within Asia, which should be taken into account when planning campaigns in the Asian region: high receptiveness to direct mail, a preference for responding by email, and limited price orientation are important characteristics.

Media ranking: mailings have the same acceptance level as TV advertising

The international popularity scale for advertising media shows a clear pattern across all countries. Both mailings and TV advertising take second place among consumers on the popularity scale, with press advertising taking first place. In terms of reluctant acceptance, radio advertising is rated slightly more highly than the barely accepted forms of online advertising. The favorable position of promotional mailings may perhaps be explained by both its lower invasiveness and the greater controllability of the advertising contact.

Mailing image: information, rather than entertainment, is the dominant factor

The perception of mailings is strongly influenced by their informational value. Here there is a striking difference between mailings and TV advertising: although both score similarly overall and in terms of information, TV advertising is perceived as much more entertaining. With respect to the entertainment value of mailings, there is still much room for improvement. Thus, enhancing the entertainment value of promotional mailings can be seen as the main challenge, and would involve increasing the emotional rather than the rational side of their image.

Cross-media campaigns: those who are receptive to mailings are more receptive to advertising media in general

With respect to cross-media campaigns, it is especially relevant that those receptive to mailings do not respond selectively to certain media, but are generally receptive to advertising. However, a combination of mailing and press advertising is slightly more effective in reaching target groups who, based on their subjective acceptance of advertising contact, are receptive to mailings.

Consumers who are receptive to mailings are more aware as consumers

In each country, consumer attitudes within target groups most receptive to mailings are more clearly profiled than those of the remaining respondents. Whichever way you look at it, people who are receptive to mailings are also more receptive to innovation and to new products. They are also intensely loyal to the brands they value and at the same time price sensitive consumers. The upshot is that they are aware and receptive consumers with a distinct profile.

Women are more receptive to advertising than men

It is easier to reach women with mailings than men – women generally pay more attention to them. In all countries surveyed, women are disproportionately represented among consumers most receptive to mailings. The reluctance of men is, however, also applicable to other advertising media: women also tend to have a more positive attitude towards press, TV and radio advertising.

Design features:
sender familiarity is more important than appearance,
samples and coupons gain the interest of consumers

In terms of consumer interest, the outward appearance of mailings has only secondary importance to the subjective relevance of the features of advertising letters. Colorful, witty and entertaining designs take second place in the majority of countries. Consumers consider it much more relevant that they can recognize the sender as a trusted, familiar provider. Hence, familiarity plays the most important role for consumers. Consumers in all countries are also especially keen on sampling: enclosed samples and coupons arouse increased interest everywhere. Additionally, some consumers value a personalized message. This attitude is most pronounced in Eastern and Southern Europe, where a higher value is also placed on design features. Contrary to other regions, in some Eastern European countries a "sophisticated design" is the most important attribute. These aspects should be given particular consideration when considering the obvious potential for mailing campaigns in Eastern Europe.

Anyone seeking to open up new markets or expand into existing markets may use the facts and findings of this study as a basis for their plans. The greater our knowledge about overseas markets, the easier it is to reach the right consumers with the right advertising message, and the greater the chances are of building up successful cross-border business.

Direct marketing data and facts from 24 countries

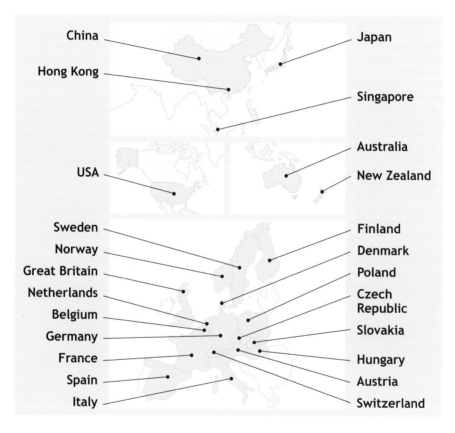

Conquering new markets requires advertising. This chapter provides crucial information: data, facts and trends from 17 European countries, 6 from Asia-Pacific and the USA. It contains selected economic and sociodemographic information, as well as information on direct marketing affinities, use of advertising media and important consumer attitudes.

China

Zhongguo, the "Central Country" (or mainland China as it is called in English), has made an impressive transition from an agricultural economy to a booming industrialized nation. GDP in 2005 is nearly 9.5% above the figure for the previous year. The record-setting pace of economic development has a positive effect on the purchasing power of the Chinese consumer which makes this a very attractive market indeed. However, success will come only to those companies that make careful preparations to operate in this multi-ethnic country where the business environment is dominated by personal relationships. Direct marketing with colorful, personalized mailings which inspire trust and confidence is one way to achieve access to this consumer market.

Demographic data

Area	9,572,419 square kilometers
Population	1,300 million
Number of households	351.2 million
Average household size	3.4 persons
Number of internet users	94.0 million
Major cities/metropolitan areas (residents)	Shanghai (12,887,000), Beijing (10,839,000), Tientsin (9,156,000), Wuhan (5,169,000), Chongqing (4,900,000), Shenyang (4,828,000)
Population age 0-14	279.0 million
Population age 15-64	922.0 million
Population age 65 and up	99.0 million

(Source: Fischer Weltalmanach 2005, Bundesagentur für Außenwirtschaft 2005)

Direct marketing trends

The mailing density in China is well below the average for Asia: 15% receive mailings frequently (Asia: 35%), 29% rarely (Asia: 33%) and 56% almost never (Asia: 32%).

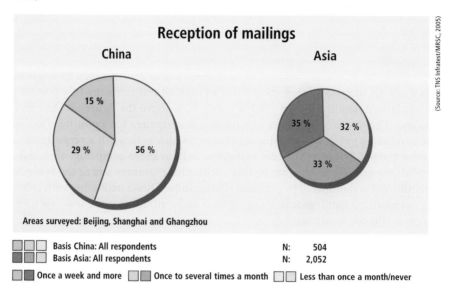

Chinese consumers respond slightly above the average for Asia: 45% read their mailings regularly (Asia: 44%), 20% respond at least once a year (Asia: 19%) and 7% even more frequently (Asia: 6%). Trust plays a large role in China: 46% value a well-

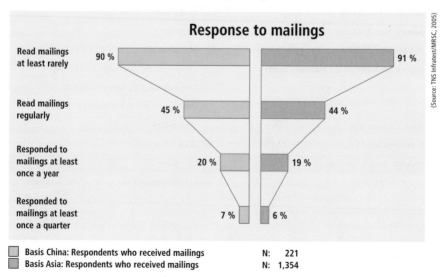

known sender and 35% would like to be addressed personally. However, less known companies can persuade consumers with a good design – in particular, colorful

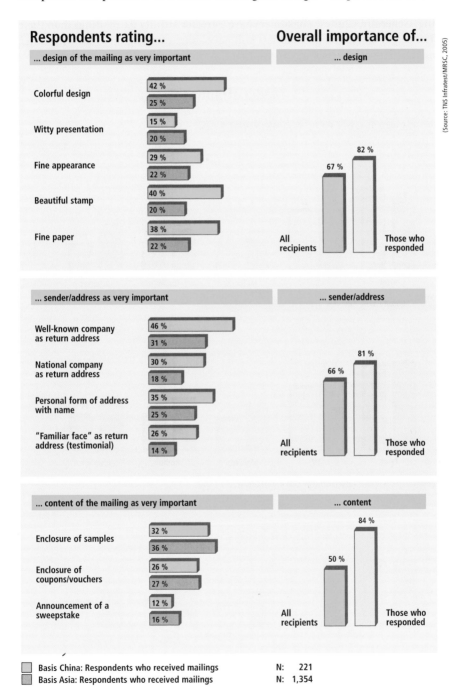

(Source: TNS Infratest/MRSC, 2005)

Respondents rating...

... design of the mailing as very important

Colorful design — 42 % / 25 %

Witty presentation — 15 % / 20 %

Fine appearance — 29 % / 22 %

Beautiful stamp — 40 % / 20 %

Fine paper — 38 % / 22 %

Overall importance of...

... design

All recipients 67 % — Those who responded 82 %

... sender/address as very important

Well-known company as return address — 46 % / 31 %

National company as return address — 30 % / 18 %

Personal form of address with name — 35 % / 25 %

"Familiar face" as return address (testimonial) — 26 % / 14 %

... sender/address

All recipients 66 % — Those who responded 81 %

... content of the mailing as very important

Enclosure of samples — 32 % / 36 %

Enclosure of coupons/vouchers — 26 % / 27 %

Announcement of a sweepstake — 12 % / 16 %

... content

All recipients 50 % — Those who responded 84 %

Basis China: Respondents who received mailings   N: 221
Basis Asia: Respondents who received mailings   N: 1,354

design (42%), the stamp's appearance (40%) and the quality of the paper (38%) meet with a great response. Print media captures first place in terms of popularity (29%), informational content (38%) and entertainment value (29%), followed by TV advertising. Generally, Chinese consumers have a greater affinity for mailings than their Asian neighbors, although mailings still have some catching up to do with other forms of advertising when it comes to entertainment value.

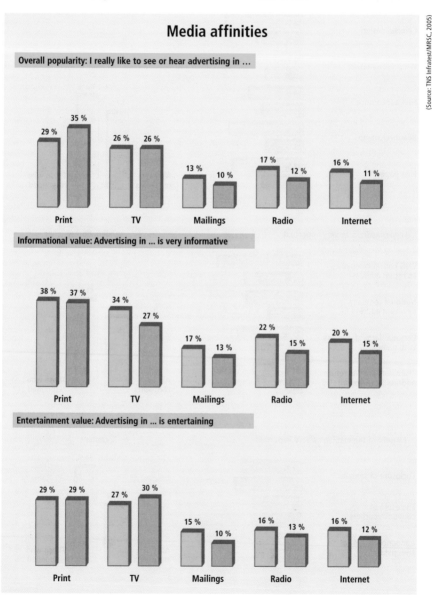

(Source: TNS Infratest/MRSC, 2005)

Consumer trends

Established brands enjoy almost unreserved loyalty among 83% of the Chinese surveyed. In addition, price (69%) determines whether they buy a product, although 54% of consumers are also willing to pay extra for quality. A striking 29% prefer products from their own country.

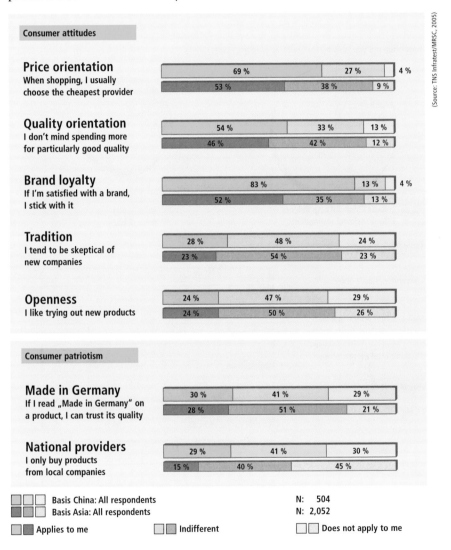

Consumer attitudes

Price orientation
When shopping, I usually choose the cheapest provider
69 % | 27 % | 4 %
53 % | 38 % | 9 %

Quality orientation
I don't mind spending more for particularly good quality
54 % | 33 % | 13 %
46 % | 42 % | 12 %

Brand loyalty
If I'm satisfied with a brand, I stick with it
83 % | 13 % | 4 %
52 % | 35 % | 13 %

Tradition
I tend to be skeptical of new companies
28 % | 48 % | 24 %
23 % | 54 % | 23 %

Openness
I like trying out new products
24 % | 47 % | 29 %
24 % | 50 % | 26 %

Consumer patriotism

Made in Germany
If I read „Made in Germany" on a product, I can trust its quality
30 % | 41 % | 29 %
28 % | 51 % | 21 %

National providers
I only buy products from local companies
29 % | 41 % | 30 %
15 % | 40 % | 45 %

Basis China: All respondents   N: 504
Basis Asia: All respondents   N: 2,052

■ Applies to me   □ Indifferent   □ Does not apply to me

(Source: TNS Infratest/MRSC, 2005)

Mail-order affinity

The Chinese market is far from being saturated with regard to mail-ordering: Only 6% shop frequently this way, 16% rarely and 78% never. Conventional mail-ordering (62%) is just ahead of the internet (60%) as a channel. However, the most popular way of placing orders is through the internet, albeit with a below-average rating of 51%.

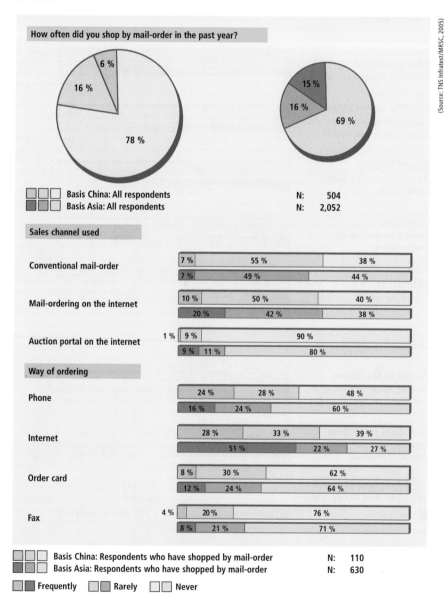

(Source: TNS Infratest/MRSC, 2005)

Hong Kong

Hong Kong has one of the world's best infrastructures of information technology. This indicates a market that despite being a part of greater China deserves special attention. This international financial capital is considered to be extremely secure. It can claim a GDP for 2005 that has grown more than 7% from the previous year and consumer spending here, badly shaken during the Asian market crisis, has been on the rise since 2004. Effective direct marketing requires a targeted offer that acknowledges the following: selecting the target group with interest in the product is success factor number one, sampling of products achieves additional consideration.

Demographic data

Area	1,095 square kilometers
Population	6.9 million
Number of households	2.2 million
Average household size	3.1 persons
Number of households with internet connection	1.1 million
Major cities/metropolitan areas (residents)	Kowloon (2,021,669), Victoria-City (1,063,646), Tuen Mun (522,370), Sha Tin (475,177), Tai Po (350,448), Tseung Kwan O (342,913)
Population age 0-14	1.0 million
Population age 15-64	5.1 million
Population age 65 and up	0.8 million

(Source: Fischer Weltalmanach 2005, Bundesagentur für Außenwirtschaft 2005, ITU 2006)

Direct marketing trends

Hong Kong appears split three ways with regard to mailing density: 31% receive mailings at least once a week, 35% at least once a month and 34% as good as never.

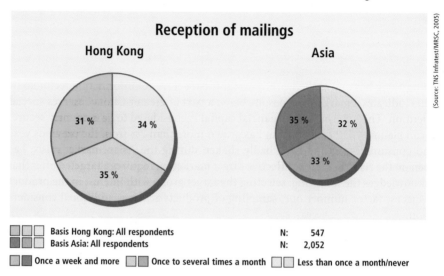

(Source: TNS Infratest/MRSC, 2005)

Just about all those surveyed in Hong Kong read their mailings at least rarely and 35% who receive them even do so regularly. Their response is around the average for Asia: 18% respond at least once a year (Asia: 19%) and 5% even more frequently (Asia: 6%). Hong Kong's consumers (67% of respondents) like their mailings to

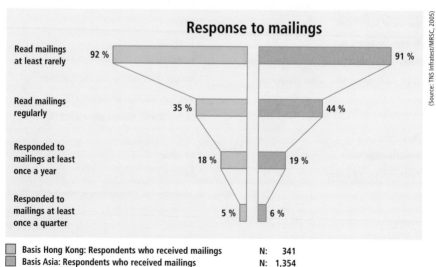

(Source: TNS Infratest/MRSC, 2005)

contain more: They especially like receiving samples (32%) and redeeming coupons (26%). A quarter tends to give personalized mailings more of a chance. This

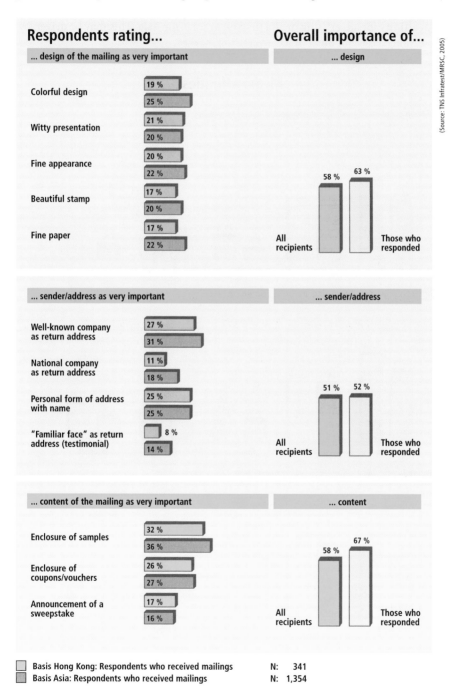

Respondents rating...

... design of the mailing as very important

- Colorful design: 19 %, 25 %
- Witty presentation: 21 %, 20 %
- Fine appearance: 20 %, 22 %
- Beautiful stamp: 17 %, 20 %
- Fine paper: 17 %, 22 %

... sender/address as very important

- Well-known company as return address: 27 %, 31 %
- National company as return address: 11 %, 18 %
- Personal form of address with name: 25 %, 25 %
- "Familiar face" as return address (testimonial): 8 %, 14 %

... content of the mailing as very important

- Enclosure of samples: 32 %, 36 %
- Enclosure of coupons/vouchers: 26 %, 27 %
- Announcement of a sweepstake: 17 %, 16 %

Overall importance of...

... design

- All recipients: 58 %
- Those who responded: 63 %

... sender/address

- All recipients: 51 %
- Those who responded: 52 %

... content

- All recipients: 58 %
- Those who responded: 67 %

Basis Hong Kong: Respondents who received mailings   N: 341
Basis Asia: Respondents who received mailings   N: 1,354

(Source: TNS Infratest/MRSC, 2005)

is also true for well-known companies (27%). Print is popular – at least among a quarter of those surveyed. TV advertising ranks second (23%) and fares around the same for informational content (24%). Generally, Hong Kong's consumers have less of an affinity for advertising media than on average for Asia. This may be driven by the advanced development of its advertising market.

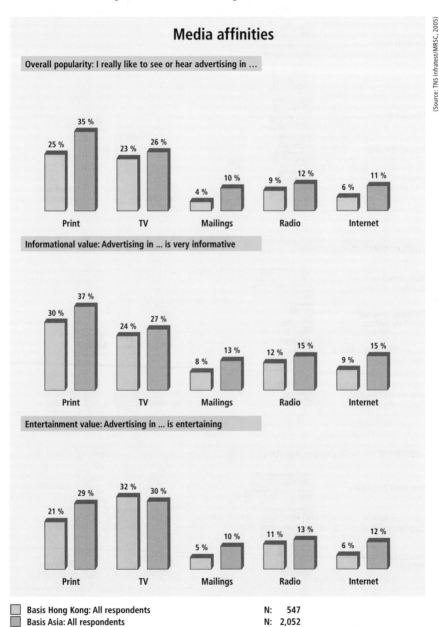

(Source: TNS Infratest/MRSC, 2005)

Media affinities

Overall popularity: I really like to see or hear advertising in …

	Print	TV	Mailings	Radio	Internet
Hong Kong	25 %	23 %	4 %	9 %	6 %
Asia	35 %	26 %	10 %	12 %	11 %

Informational value: Advertising in … is very informative

	Print	TV	Mailings	Radio	Internet
Hong Kong	30 %	24 %	8 %	12 %	9 %
Asia	37 %	27 %	13 %	15 %	15 %

Entertainment value: Advertising in … is entertaining

	Print	TV	Mailings	Radio	Internet
Hong Kong	21 %	32 %	5 %	11 %	6 %
Asia	29 %	30 %	10 %	13 %	12 %

☐ Basis Hong Kong: All respondents   N: 547
■ Basis Asia: All respondents   N: 2,052

Consumer trends

Price determines purchasing behavior: 54% of consumers state that they usually choose the cheapest provider. Nevertheless, quality also counts (42%). And that is a feature seen as being offered by foreign companies, too. Only 10% prefer products from national providers.

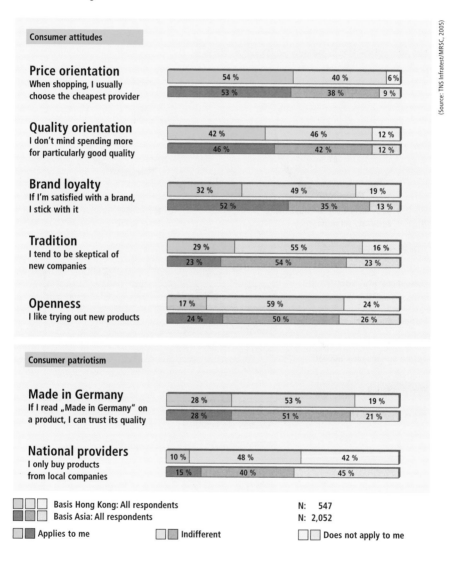

(Source: TNS Infratest/MRSC, 2005)

Consumer attitudes

Price orientation
When shopping, I usually
choose the cheapest provider

54 % | 40 % | 6 %
53 % | 38 % | 9 %

Quality orientation
I don't mind spending more
for particularly good quality

42 % | 46 % | 12 %
46 % | 42 % | 12 %

Brand loyalty
If I'm satisfied with a brand,
I stick with it

32 % | 49 % | 19 %
52 % | 35 % | 13 %

Tradition
I tend to be skeptical of
new companies

29 % | 55 % | 16 %
23 % | 54 % | 23 %

Openness
I like trying out new products

17 % | 59 % | 24 %
24 % | 50 % | 26 %

Consumer patriotism

Made in Germany
If I read „Made in Germany" on
a product, I can trust its quality

28 % | 53 % | 19 %
28 % | 51 % | 21 %

National providers
I only buy products
from local companies

10 % | 48 % | 42 %
15 % | 40 % | 45 %

Basis Hong Kong: All respondents   N: 547
Basis Asia: All respondents   N: 2,052

Applies to me   Indifferent   Does not apply to me

Mail-order affinity

There are still prospects for mail-order in Hong Kong, as only a few consumers currently use it: only 3% order frequently, 10% rarely and a full 87% have never used this channel. Mail-ordering by internet (57%) is ahead of conventional mail-ordering (51%). There are similar preferences with regard to the way consumers place orders – 76% do so online.

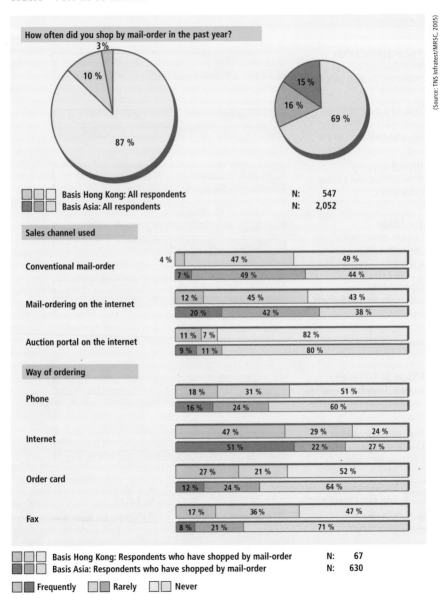

(Source: TNS Infratest/MRSC, 2005)

Japan

Japan's economy is on the rebound: in 2005, the Japanese economy grew by nearly 3% over the previous year and is expected to grow by another 2.4% in the year 2006. The consumer confidence index once again reflects a positive trend and spending in this sector over the next few years is expected to increase by 1.5% annually. Patience – coupled with respect – is rewarded in Japan and this is true for business as well. The Japanese are receptive to direct marketing and like mailings, especially those that include a product sample.

Demographic data

Area	377,837 square kilometers
Population	127.7 million
Number of households	46.8 million
Average household size	2.7 persons
Number of households with internet connection	41.2 million
Major cities/metropolitan areas (residents)	Tokyo (8,025,538), Yokohama (3,433,612), Osaka (2,484,326), Nagoya (2,109,681), Sapporo (1,822,992), Kobe (1,478,390)
Population age 0-14	17.7 million
Population age 15-64	85.0 million
Population age 65 and up	25.0 million

(Source: Fischer Weltalmanach 2005, Bundesagentur für Außenwirtschaft 2005)

Direct marketing trends

Japan's mailing density is clearly above the average for Asia: More than half of those surveyed say they receive mailings at least once a week (Asia: 35%), 39% at least once a month (Asia: 33%) and only 9% almost never (Asia: 32%).

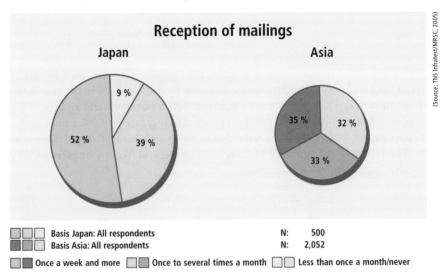

Mailings in Japan reach the majority of consumers: 95% read them occasionally and more than half regularly. Response is also well above the reference value for Asia: 29% respond at least once a year (Asia: 19%) and 9% even more frequently (Asia: 6%). It is better if the mailing contains something: 64% of respondents are then positive about receiving one. Both samples (42%) and coupons (31%) are par-

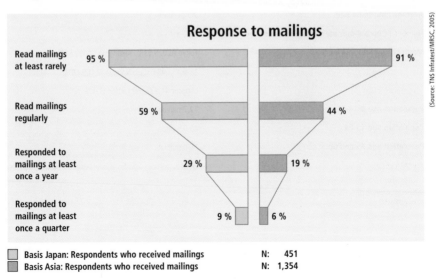

ticularly popular. Almost all the other features of direct mail are of lesser relevance to Japanese consumers than to their Asian neighbors. However, a witty presentation (22%) can bring them out of their shell.

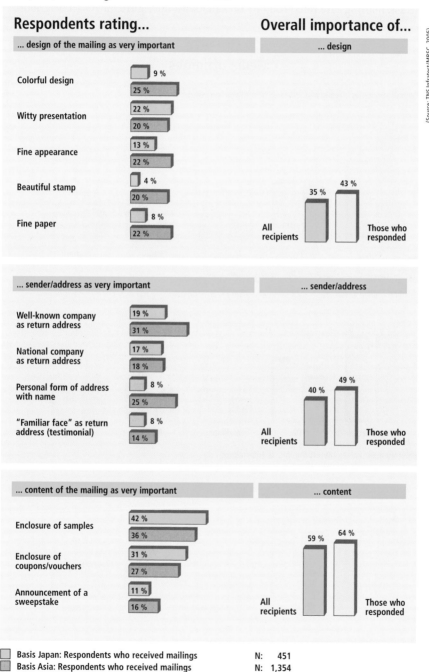

Respondents rating...

... design of the mailing as very important

	Japan	Asia
Colorful design	9 %	25 %
Witty presentation	22 %	20 %
Fine appearance	13 %	22 %
Beautiful stamp	4 %	20 %
Fine paper	8 %	22 %

... sender/address as very important

	Japan	Asia
Well-known company as return address	19 %	31 %
National company as return address	17 %	18 %
Personal form of address with name	8 %	25 %
"Familiar face" as return address (testimonial)	8 %	14 %

... content of the mailing as very important

	Japan	Asia
Enclosure of samples	42 %	36 %
Enclosure of coupons/vouchers	31 %	27 %
Announcement of a sweepstake	11 %	16 %

Overall importance of...

... design

All recipients 35 %
Those who responded 43 %

... sender/address

All recipients 40 %
Those who responded 49 %

... content

All recipients 59 %
Those who responded 64 %

(Source: TNS Infratest/MRSC, 2005)

Basis Japan: Respondents who received mailings — N: 451
Basis Asia: Respondents who received mailings — N: 1,354

Print wins – print media (49%) are well ahead, at least in terms of overall popularity. When it comes to entertainment value (36%), they also have a large lead over TV advertising (29%), which generally fares more poorly than the Asian mean. In contrast, mailings are rated roughly on a par with the figure for Asian neighbors.

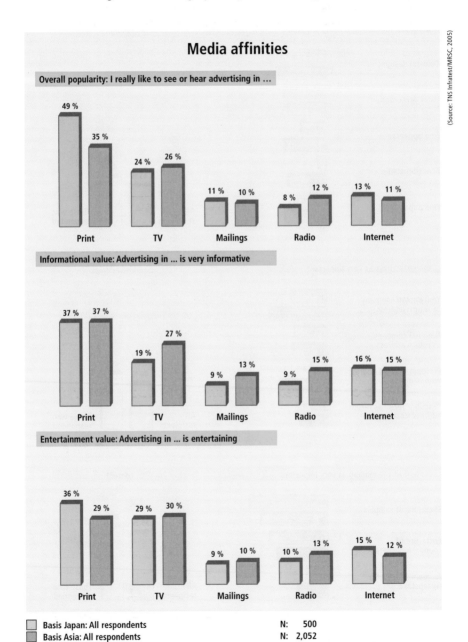

(Source: TNS Infratest/MRSC, 2005)

Consumer trends

Good news for entrepreneurs: Living in an importing nation, Japanese consumers are open to something new – only 16% tend to be skeptical about new providers. And neither do companies from other countries need to be afraid of consumer patriotism: Only 9% have a preference for national providers. Basically, price (37%), quality (36%) and the brand (35%) have a relatively equivalent influence on purchasing decisions.

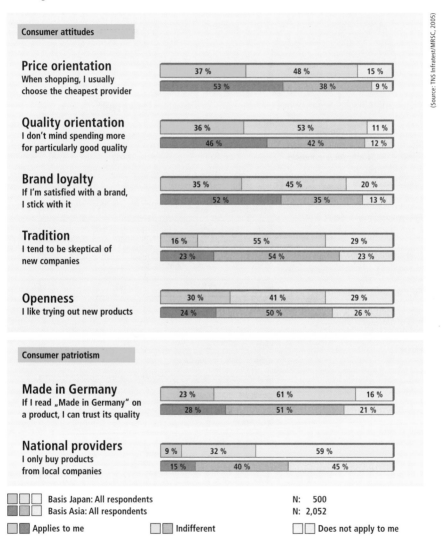

Consumer attitudes			

Price orientation
When shopping, I usually choose the cheapest provider
| 37 % | 48 % | 15 % |
| 53 % | 38 % | 9 % |

Quality orientation
I don't mind spending more for particularly good quality
| 36 % | 53 % | 11 % |
| 46 % | 42 % | 12 % |

Brand loyalty
If I'm satisfied with a brand, I stick with it
| 35 % | 45 % | 20 % |
| 52 % | 35 % | 13 % |

Tradition
I tend to be skeptical of new companies
| 16 % | 55 % | 29 % |
| 23 % | 54 % | 23 % |

Openness
I like trying out new products
| 30 % | 41 % | 29 % |
| 24 % | 50 % | 26 % |

Consumer patriotism			

Made in Germany
If I read „Made in Germany" on a product, I can trust its quality
| 23 % | 61 % | 16 % |
| 28 % | 51 % | 21 % |

National providers
I only buy products from local companies
| 9 % | 32 % | 59 % |
| 15 % | 40 % | 45 % |

☐☐☐ Basis Japan: All respondents   N: 500
■☐☐ Basis Asia: All respondents   N: 2,052

☐■ Applies to me   ☐☐ Indifferent   ☐☐ Does not apply to me

(Source: TNS Infratest/MRSC, 2005)

Mail-order affinity

Almost half of Japanese respondents use mail-order frequently, 26% rarely and 27% never. Most prefer the internet as both a sales channel (77%) and a method of ordering (84%).

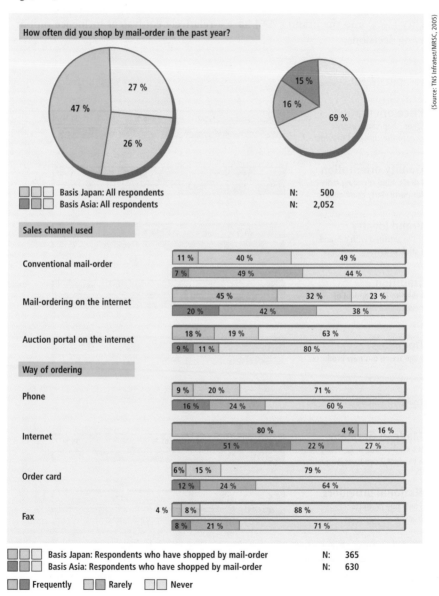

(Source: TNS Infratest/MRSC, 2005)

How often did you shop by mail-order in the past year?

27 %
47 %
26 %

15 %
16 %
69 %

☐☐☐ Basis Japan: All respondents   N: 500
■■☐ Basis Asia: All respondents   N: 2,052

Sales channel used

Conventional mail-order
| 11 % | 40 % | 49 % |
| 7 % | 49 % | 44 % |

Mail-ordering on the internet
| 45 % | 32 % | 23 % |
| 20 % | 42 % | 38 % |

Auction portal on the internet
| 18 % | 19 % | 63 % |
| 9 % | 11 % | 80 % |

Way of ordering

Phone
| 9 % | 20 % | 71 % |
| 16 % | 24 % | 60 % |

Internet
| 80 % | 4 % | 16 % |
| 51 % | 22 % | 27 % |

Order card
| 6 % | 15 % | 79 % |
| 12 % | 24 % | 64 % |

Fax
| 4 % | 8 % | 88 % |
| 8 % | 21 % | 71 % |

☐☐☐ Basis Japan: Respondents who have shopped by mail-order   N: 365
■■☐ Basis Asia: Respondents who have shopped by mail-order   N: 630

■■ Frequently   ☐☐ Rarely   ☐☐ Never

Singapore

Possessing very few natural resources, this city state has managed to achieve an economic prosperity based on know-how that is without equal. In 2005, the GDP grew by 6.4% over the previous year. Private-sector spending increased nearly 9% in 2005 which is mainly attributed to the improved situation in the job market and multiplied further still by higher base wage rates. Communications here should consider the cultural diversity which Singapore represents. These various segmentation opportunities are very promising for successful direct marketing: A very good response can be expected, for example, from mailings that include product samples.

Demographic data

Area	682.7 square kilometers
Population	3.4 million
Number of households	0.9 million
Average household size	3.7 persons
Number of internet users	2.1 million
Major cities/metropolitan areas (residents)	Singapore is a city-state
Population age 0-14	0.7 million
Population age 15-64	2.4 million
Population age 65 and up	0.3 million

(Source: Fischer Weltalmanach 2005, Bundesagentur für Außenwirtschaft 2005)

Direct marketing trends

The mailing density in Singapore is slightly above the average for Asia: 41% receive mailings at least once a week (Asia: 35%), 30% at least once a month (Asia: 33%) and only 29% as good as never (Asia: 32%).

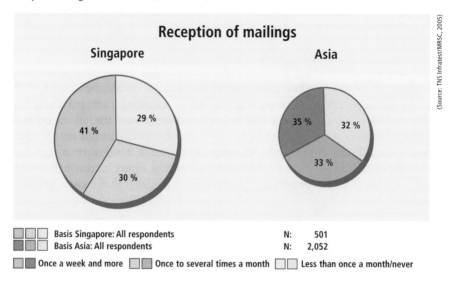

Singaporean consumers respond to mailings with somewhat more restraint than their Asian neighbors: Fewer consumers read them – 85% of recipients read them occasionally and 35% regularly. 10% respond to their mailings at least once a year (Asia: 19%) and 4% even more frequently (Asia: 6%). Mailings in Singapore can persuade mainly by their content, an important factor for 85% of those who respond.

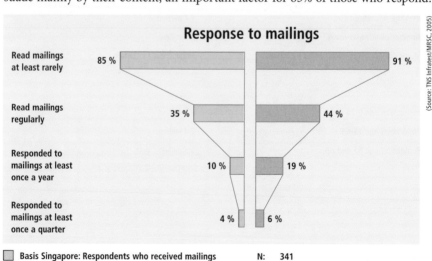

37% of those surveyed like samples to be enclosed. One-third of consumers tend to trust well-known senders or a personal form of address (31%). Less well-known

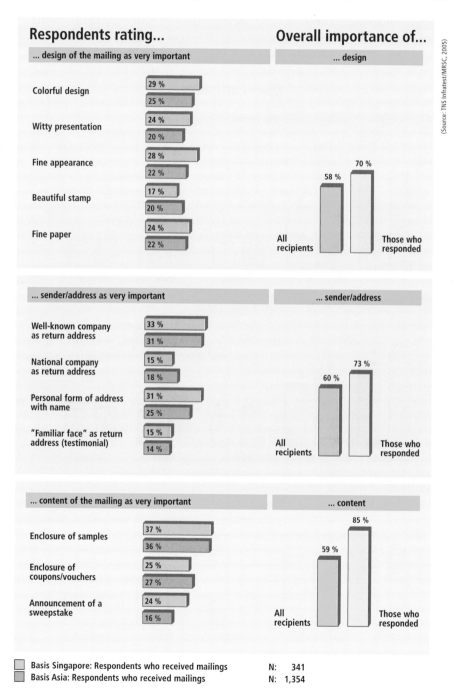

(Source: TNS Infratest/MRSC, 2005)

Respondents rating...

... design of the mailing as very important

Colorful design — 29 % / 25 %

Witty presentation — 24 % / 20 %

Fine appearance — 28 % / 22 %

Beautiful stamp — 17 % / 20 %

Fine paper — 24 % / 22 %

... sender/address as very important

Well-known company as return address — 33 % / 31 %

National company as return address — 15 % / 18 %

Personal form of address with name — 31 % / 25 %

"Familiar face" as return address (testimonial) — 15 % / 14 %

... content of the mailing as very important

Enclosure of samples — 37 % / 36 %

Enclosure of coupons/vouchers — 25 % / 27 %

Announcement of a sweepstake — 24 % / 16 %

Overall importance of...

... design

All recipients 58 % — Those who responded 70 %

... sender/address

All recipients 60 % — Those who responded 73 %

... content

All recipients 59 % — Those who responded 85 %

Basis Singapore: Respondents who received mailings   N: 341
Basis Asia: Respondents who received mailings   N: 1,354

companies should make an effort to design lavish mailings in order to make a positive impression.

Print media are not only popular in Singapore (37%), but are also highly rated for their informational content (41%). Moreover, those surveyed regard print media as being just as entertaining as TV advertising (31% in each case). Mailings rank third in terms of informational value, just ahead of radio and the internet.

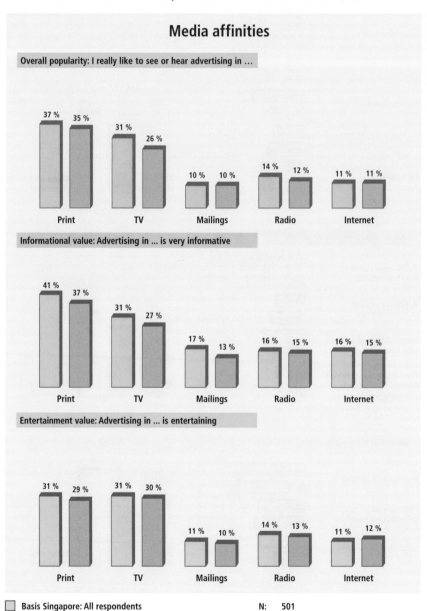

Media affinities

Overall popularity: I really like to see or hear advertising in ...

Print 37 % / 35 %
TV 31 % / 26 %
Mailings 10 % / 10 %
Radio 14 % / 12 %
Internet 11 % / 11 %

Informational value: Advertising in ... is very informative

Print 41 % / 37 %
TV 31 % / 27 %
Mailings 17 % / 13 %
Radio 16 % / 15 %
Internet 16 % / 15 %

Entertainment value: Advertising in ... is entertaining

Print 31 % / 29 %
TV 31 % / 30 %
Mailings 11 % / 10 %
Radio 14 % / 13 %
Internet 11 % / 12 %

Basis Singapore: All respondents   N: 501
Basis Asia: All respondents   N: 2,052

(Source: TNS Infratest/MRSC, 2005)

Consumer trends

Brand awareness (59%) is more pronounced in Singapore than in the Asian reference countries (52%) – as is the willingness to pay extra for quality products (51% compared with 46% for Asia). Only 10% display consumer patriotism and the vast majority welcomes new providers with open arms.

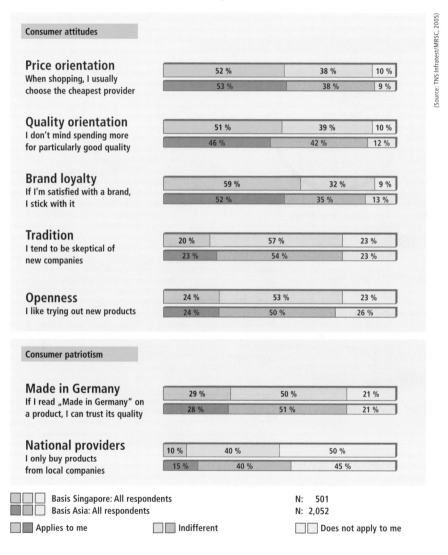

(Source: TNS Infratest/MRSC, 2005)

Consumer attitudes

Price orientation
When shopping, I usually choose the cheapest provider
- 52 % | 38 % | 10 %
- 53 % | 38 % | 9 %

Quality orientation
I don't mind spending more for particularly good quality
- 51 % | 39 % | 10 %
- 46 % | 42 % | 12 %

Brand loyalty
If I'm satisfied with a brand, I stick with it
- 59 % | 32 % | 9 %
- 52 % | 35 % | 13 %

Tradition
I tend to be skeptical of new companies
- 20 % | 57 % | 23 %
- 23 % | 54 % | 23 %

Openness
I like trying out new products
- 24 % | 53 % | 23 %
- 24 % | 50 % | 26 %

Consumer patriotism

Made in Germany
If I read „Made in Germany" on a product, I can trust its quality
- 29 % | 50 % | 21 %
- 28 % | 51 % | 21 %

National providers
I only buy products from local companies
- 10 % | 40 % | 50 %
- 15 % | 40 % | 45 %

☐☐☐ Basis Singapore: All respondents   N: 501
■■☐ Basis Asia: All respondents   N: 2,052

☐■ Applies to me   ☐■ Indifferent   ☐☐ Does not apply to me

Mail-order affinity

Mail-ordering in the city-state reaches only a small portion of the population by Asian standards: Just 4% order frequently this way, 14% rarely and 82% never. Conventional mail-ordering (59%) and mail-ordering over the internet (57%) are roughly neck and neck. The most popular way of ordering is via the internet: 46% say they order online frequently.

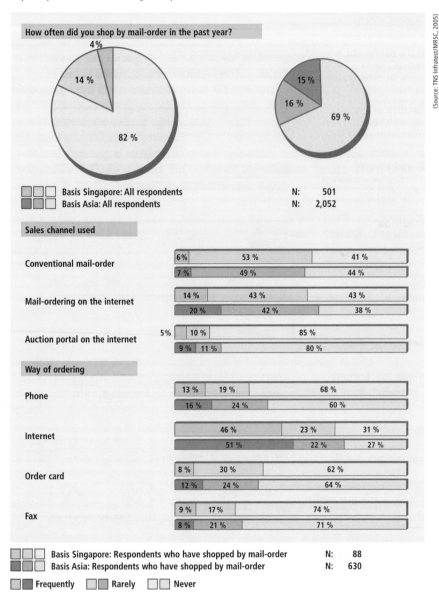

(Source: TNS Infratest/MRSC, 2005)

Australia

5

Australia is enjoying a period of solid economic growth accompanied by a very positive job market. In 2005, the GDP increased by 2.5% from the previous year. A country of many nationalities, Australia absorbs numerous immigrants each year which demands selective target-group marketing. Here, direct marketing has a good chance for success: one of every two people responding to surveys – males and females of all ages alike – reports his/her curiosity is generally increased by mailings. This is even more effective when well prepared mailings present a special offer targeted at the specific product interests of the recipient.

Demographic data

Area	7,692,030 million square kilometers
Population	19.2 million
Number of households	7.5 million
Average household size	2.6 persons
Number of households with internet connection	3.5 million
Major cities/metropolitan areas (residents)	Sydney (4,154,700), Melbourne (3,488,800), Brisbane (1,653,400), Perth (1,397,000), Adelaide (1,110,500), Newcastle (494,400)
Population age 0-14	4.0 million
Population age 15-64	12.8 million
Population age 65 and up	2.4 million

(Source: Fischer Weltalmanach 2005, Bundesagentur für Außenwirtschaft 2005)

Direct marketing trends

Australian respondents receive mailings more rarely than the average for USA/Pacific: 32% frequently (USA/Pacific: 35%), 23% rarely (USA/Pacific: 24%) and 45% as good as never (USA/Pacific: 41%).

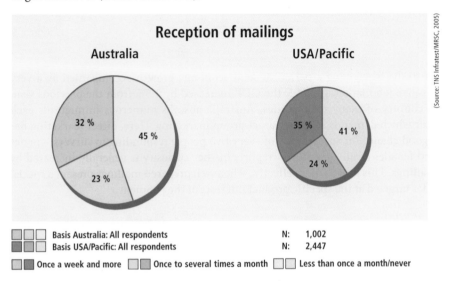

The response of Australians is roughly the same as that for USA/Pacific: Only regular readers (39%) have a higher percentage (USA/Pacific: 35%), whereas the figure for those who respond with a lower frequency (21%) is slightly below the average for the region (22%). 10% respond to mailings several times a year.

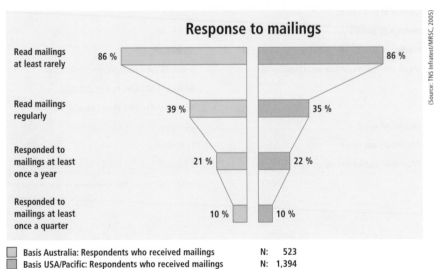

It is somewhat easier for well-known companies to garner the attention of Australians surveyed (36%). A total of 70% of respondents say that the sender and form of address have a very high priority. However, less well-known senders can also appeal to Australians through use of creativity and wit (32%).

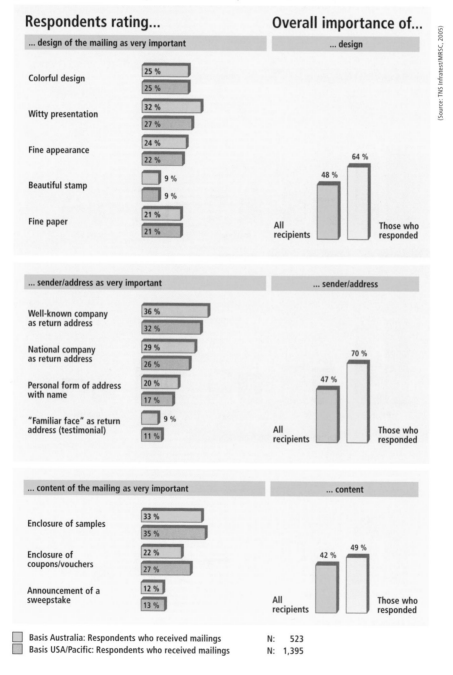

(Source: TNS Infratest/MRSC, 2005)

Respondents rating...

... design of the mailing as very important

Colorful design	25 % / 25 %
Witty presentation	32 % / 27 %
Fine appearance	24 % / 22 %
Beautiful stamp	9 % / 9 %
Fine paper	21 % / 21 %

... sender/address as very important

Well-known company as return address	36 % / 32 %
National company as return address	29 % / 26 %
Personal form of address with name	20 % / 17 %
"Familiar face" as return address (testimonial)	9 % / 11 %

... content of the mailing as very important

Enclosure of samples	33 % / 35 %
Enclosure of coupons/vouchers	22 % / 27 %
Announcement of a sweepstake	12 % / 13 %

Overall importance of...

... design
- All recipients 48 %
- Those who responded 64 %

... sender/address
- All recipients 47 %
- Those who responded 70 %

... content
- All recipients 42 %
- Those who responded 49 %

Basis Australia: Respondents who received mailings   N: 523
Basis USA/Pacific: Respondents who received mailings   N: 1,395

Advertising in newspapers is more popular than all other media among Australia's consumers with regard to informational content (36%), popularity (33%) and entertainment value (22%). Second place in the popularity ratings is shared by mailings (10%) and TV spots (10%). Advertising over the internet is below the average for USA/Pacific in all areas.

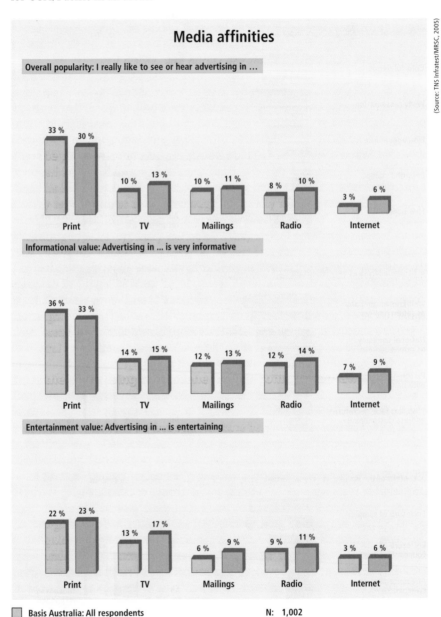

(Source: TNS Infratest/MRSC, 2005)

Consumer trends

Australian consumers are just as brand-conscious (75%) as those surveyed from the reference countries. 60% are swayed by quality when they shop, and 45% by price. Good news for marketers: 40% of respondents regard themselves as open to new products.

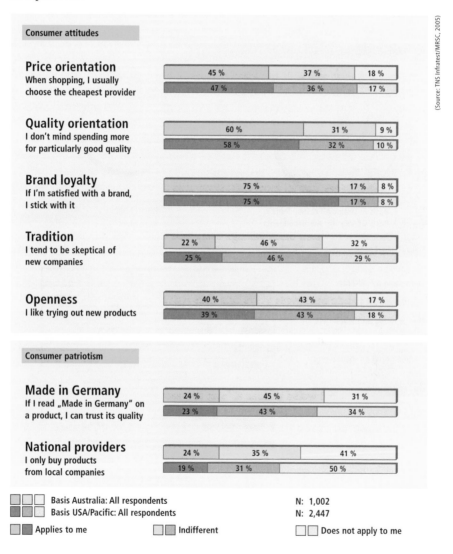

(Source: TNS Infratest/MRSC, 2005)

Consumer attitudes

Price orientation
When shopping, I usually choose the cheapest provider
45 % | 37 % | 18 %
47 % | 36 % | 17 %

Quality orientation
I don't mind spending more for particularly good quality
60 % | 31 % | 9 %
58 % | 32 % | 10 %

Brand loyalty
If I'm satisfied with a brand, I stick with it
75 % | 17 % | 8 %
75 % | 17 % | 8 %

Tradition
I tend to be skeptical of new companies
22 % | 46 % | 32 %
25 % | 46 % | 29 %

Openness
I like trying out new products
40 % | 43 % | 17 %
39 % | 43 % | 18 %

Consumer patriotism

Made in Germany
If I read „Made in Germany" on a product, I can trust its quality
24 % | 45 % | 31 %
23 % | 43 % | 34 %

National providers
I only buy products from local companies
24 % | 35 % | 41 %
19 % | 31 % | 50 %

Basis Australia: All respondents   N: 1,002
Basis USA/Pacific: All respondents   N: 2,447

Applies to me   Indifferent   Does not apply to me

Mail-order affinity

Mail-order seems to have a rather small following in Australia: Only 10% ordered goods frequently by this channel, 19% rarely and 71% never. Mail-ordering over the internet (13%) is just ahead of conventional mail-ordering (12%) and internet auction portals (11%). Most of those surveyed (45%) also used the internet frequently as a mean of ordering.

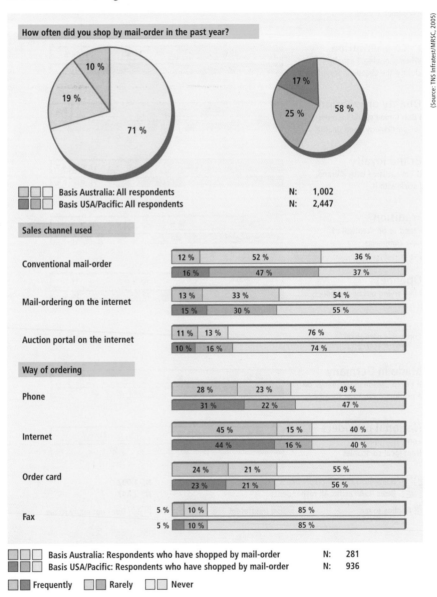

(Source: TNS Infratest/MRSC, 2005)

New Zealand

6

Again in 2005, the New Zealand economy was one that can be diagnosed as being very healthy. Thanks to solid corporate profits and a positive wage situation for employees, the willingness to invest remains high. The increase from last year in the value of the GDP was 3.6%. International comparisons show consumers in New Zealand respond positively to mailings: one out of ten recipients reacts to a mailing at least once per quarter – most often when the letter is direct, informative and designed with a personal touch.

Demographic data

Area	270,534 million square kilometers
Population	4.0 million
Number of households	1.5 million
Average household size	2.7 persons
Number of households with internet connection	0.6 million
Major cities/metropolitan areas (residents)	Auckland (337,382), Christchurch (322,188), Manukau (281,607), North Shore (184,287), Waitakere (167,172), Wellington (165,945)
Population age 0-14	0.8 million
Population age 15-64	2.7 million
Population age 65 and up	0.5 million

(Source: Fischer Weltalmanach 2005, Bundesagentur für Außenwirtschaft 2005, OECD 2005)

Direct marketing trends

The mailing density in New Zealand is right around the reference value: 38% receive mailings at least once a week (USA/Pacific: 35%), 21% at least once a month (USA/Pacific: 24%) and 41% as good as never (identical to USA/Pacific).

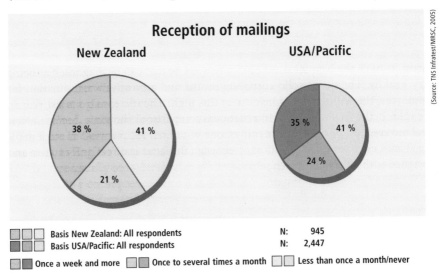

(Source: TNS Infratest/MRSC, 2005)

New Zealand consumers have a little higher affinity towards mailings than the average for the USA/Pacific: 90% read mailings now and again (USA/Pacific: 86%) and 39% regularly (USA/Pacific: 35%). 23% respond at least once a year (USA/Pacific: 22%) and 11% even more frequently (USA/Pacific: 10%). 65% of those who

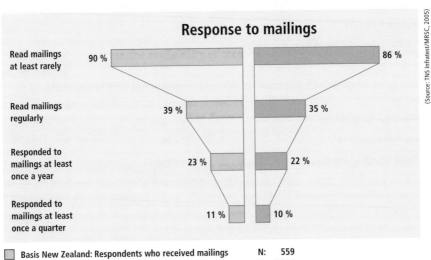

(Source: TNS Infratest/MRSC, 2005)

respond feel the content of a mailing to be extremely important: For example, one-third of New Zealanders likes enclosed samples. 32% tend to trust direct mail from

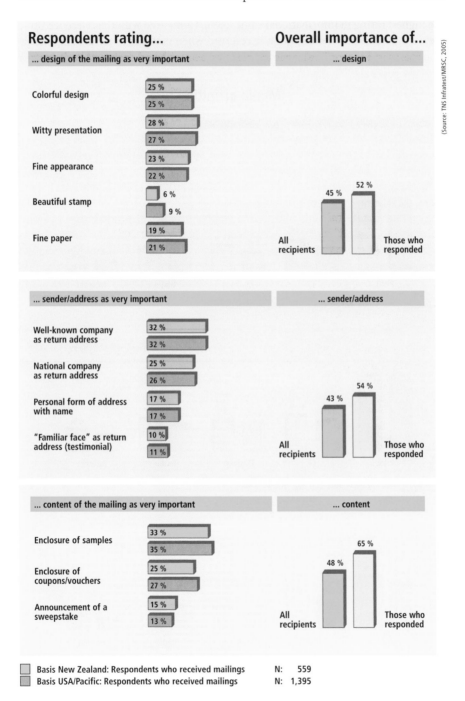

(Source: TNS Infratest/MRSC, 2005)

a well-known company – national providers (25%) also have good chances. 28% attach importance to a witty presentation.

Print advertising wins in all areas among New Zealand consumers – achieving the highest rating in informational value (33%). Compared with the reference value, New Zealanders are seemingly more reserved when it comes to advertising media. In particular, TV spots and advertising over the internet are less popular here.

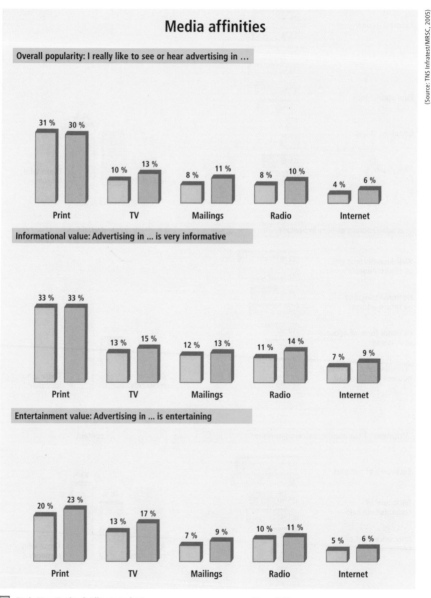

(Source: TNS Infratest/MRSC, 2005)

Consumer trends

New Zealanders have a pronounced brand awareness (73%), however, quality (59%) and price (49%) shape their consumption habits. A gratifying 39% like trying out new products. A pleasing point for international providers: Only 14% of those surveyed have a preference for New Zealand companies.

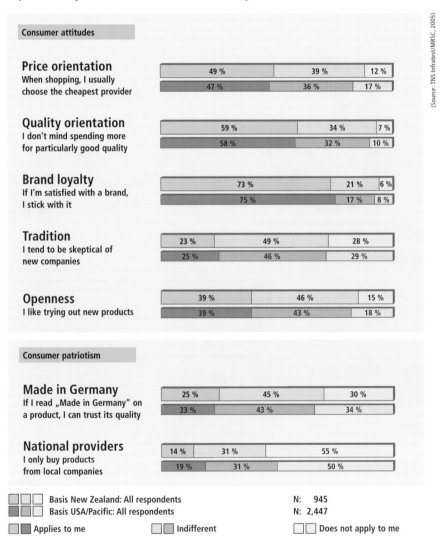

(Source: TNS Infratest/MRSC, 2005)

Mail-order affinity

Affinity for mail-order is somewhat below the average for the USA/Pacific: 11% order frequently by this channel (USA/Pacific: 17%), 27% rarely (USA/Pacific: 25%) and 62% never (USA/Pacific: 58%). Conventional mail-order (68%) is well ahead of the internet (38%). Most of those surveyed (52%) like ordering online, although the internet platform and e-auctions are not as established as in the rest of the USA/Pacific region.

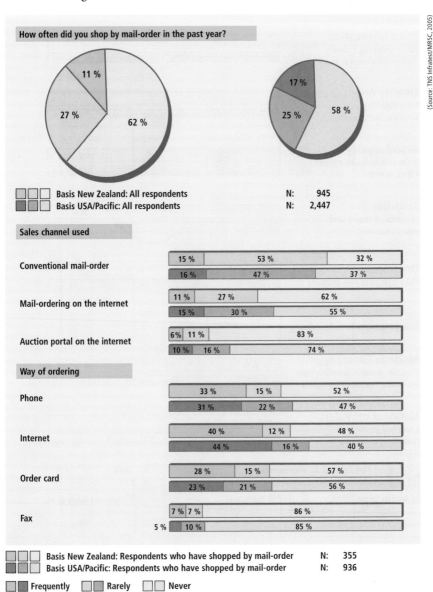

(Source: TNS Infratest/MRSC, 2005)

How often did you shop by mail-order in the past year?

11 %
27 %
62 %

17 %
25 %
58 %

☐☐☐ Basis New Zealand: All respondents   N: 945
■■☐ Basis USA/Pacific: All respondents   N: 2,447

Sales channel used

Conventional mail-order
15 %   53 %   32 %
16 %   47 %   37 %

Mail-ordering on the internet
11 %   27 %   62 %
15 %   30 %   55 %

Auction portal on the internet
6% 11 %   83 %
10 % 16 %   74 %

Way of ordering

Phone
33 %   15 %   52 %
31 %   22 %   47 %

Internet
40 %   12 %   48 %
44 %   16 %   40 %

Order card
28 %   15 %   57 %
23 %   21 %   56 %

Fax
7 % 7 %   86 %
5 %   10 %   85 %

☐☐☐ Basis New Zealand: Respondents who have shopped by mail-order   N: 355
■■☐ Basis USA/Pacific: Respondents who have shopped by mail-order   N: 936

■■ Frequently   ☐☐ Rarely   ☐☐ Never

USA

Some experts expect the economy to lose some of the dynamics of its upswing, even though the projected increase in GDP was 3.5% for 2005 in comparison to the previous year. Consumer spending still consistently breaks the 3% barrier and is projected to increase even further in 2006. The average American consumer is confronted each day with more than 100 TV commercials. For this reason, direct marketing, with its unlimited opportunities to deliver personalized messages, is especially effective at gaining their attention. The recipients of sales letters put great stock in the content of the mailings: product samples and coupons are equally well received and, especially by the female audience, are rewarded with high response rates.

Demographic data

Area	9.8 million square kilometers
Population	291.1 million
Number of households	108.4 million
Average household size	2.7 persons
Number of households with internet connection	55.0 million
Major cities/metropolitan areas (residents)	New York (8,084,316), Los Angeles (3,798,981), Chicago (2,886,251), Houston (2,009,834), Philadelphia (1,492,231), Phoenix (1,371,960)
Population age 0-14	61.0 million
Population age 15-64	193.0 million
Population age 65 and up	36.0 million

(Source: Fischer Weltalmanach 2005, Bundesagentur für Außenwirtschaft 2005)

Direct marketing trends

American consumers receive direct mail a little more frequently on average: 36% at least once a week (USA/Pacific: 35%) and 27% at least once a month (USA/Pacific: 24%). 37% state that they almost never receive any mailings (USA/Pacific: 41%).

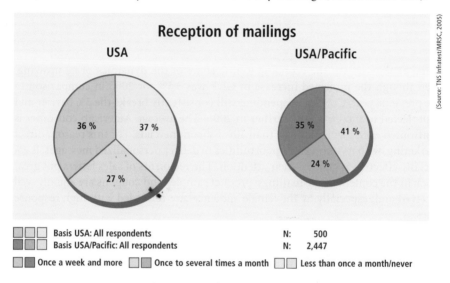

82% of those surveyed read their mailings at least rarely and 28% do so regularly. Their response is just under the USA/Pacific average. 21% respond at least once a year (USA/Pacific: 22%) and 9% more frequently (USA/Pacific: 10%). The mailing's

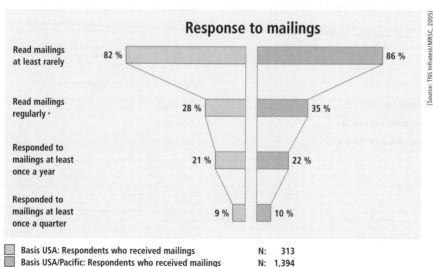

content has the most relevance for 75% of respondents: In particular, samples (37%) and coupons (36%) enjoy great popularity. A well-known company can score points

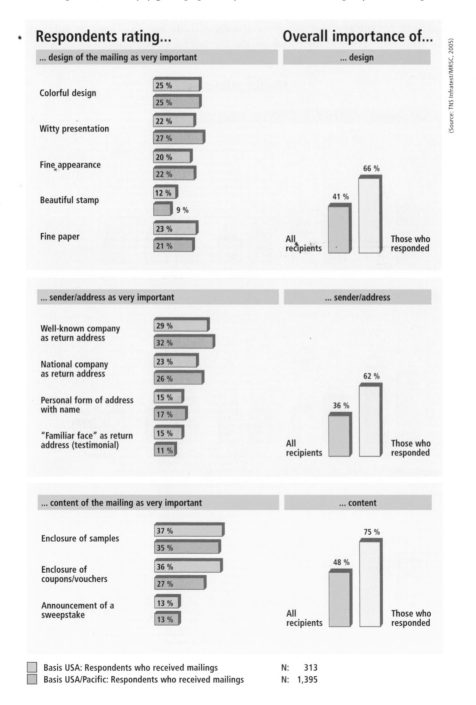

- **Respondents rating...**

... design of the mailing as very important

Colorful design: 25 % / 25 %

Witty presentation: 22 % / 27 %

Fine appearance: 20 % / 22 %

Beautiful stamp: 12 % / 9 %

Fine paper: 23 % / 21 %

... sender/address as very important

Well-known company as return address: 29 % / 32 %

National company as return address: 23 % / 26 %

Personal form of address with name: 15 % / 17 %

"Familiar face" as return address (testimonial): 15 % / 11 %

... content of the mailing as very important

Enclosure of samples: 37 % / 35 %

Enclosure of coupons/vouchers: 36 % / 27 %

Announcement of a sweepstake: 13 % / 13 %

Overall importance of...

... design

All recipients: 41 %
Those who responded: 66 %

... sender/address

All recipients: 36 %
Those who responded: 62 %

... content

All recipients: 48 %
Those who responded: 75 %

(Source: TNS Infratest/MRSC, 2005)

Basis USA: Respondents who received mailings — N: 313
Basis USA/Pacific: Respondents who received mailings — N: 1,395

with 29% of American consumers, while a quarter of those surveyed prefer a colorful design.

Print media come first in all three areas. In comparison with the reference value, American consumers have an above-average affinity for TV. However, mailings also meet with approval slightly above the average for USA/Pacific.

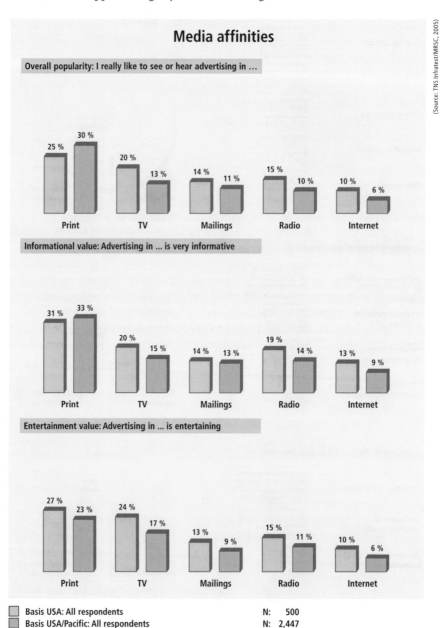

(Source: TNS Infratest/MRSC, 2005)

Media affinities

Overall popularity: I really like to see or hear advertising in …

25 % 30 % Print
20 % 13 % TV
14 % 11 % Mailings
15 % 10 % Radio
10 % 6 % Internet

Informational value: Advertising in … is very informative

31 % 33 % Print
20 % 15 % TV
14 % 13 % Mailings
19 % 14 % Radio
13 % 9 % Internet

Entertainment value: Advertising in … is entertaining

27 % 23 % Print
24 % 17 % TV
13 % 9 % Mailings
15 % 11 % Radio
10 % 6 % Internet

Basis USA: All respondents   N: 500
Basis USA/Pacific: All respondents   N: 2,447

Consumer trends

American consumers show an above-average loyalty to brands: 77% stick with a brand if they are satisfied with it (USA/Pacific: 75%). However, quality (54%) and price (47%) play a decisive role in consumer behavior. New products go over well among 39% of Americans. More than half (54%) say that they do not have any preference for products from America.

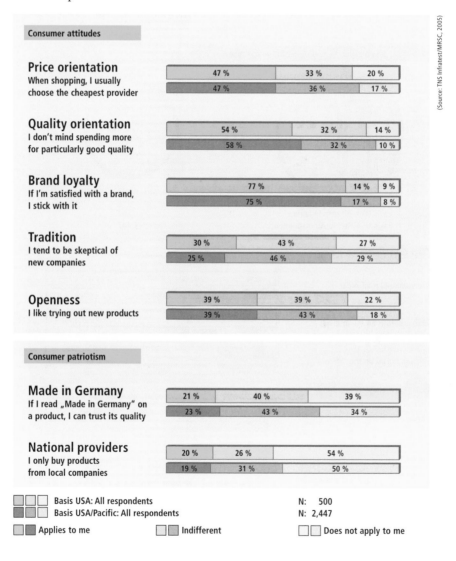

(Source: TNS Infratest/MRSC, 2005)

Consumer attitudes

Price orientation
When shopping, I usually choose the cheapest provider

| 47 % | 33 % | 20 % |
| 47 % | 36 % | 17 % |

Quality orientation
I don't mind spending more for particularly good quality

| 54 % | 32 % | 14 % |
| 58 % | 32 % | 10 % |

Brand loyalty
If I'm satisfied with a brand, I stick with it

| 77 % | 14 % | 9 % |
| 75 % | 17 % | 8 % |

Tradition
I tend to be skeptical of new companies

| 30 % | 43 % | 27 % |
| 25 % | 46 % | 29 % |

Openness
I like trying out new products

| 39 % | 39 % | 22 % |
| 39 % | 43 % | 18 % |

Consumer patriotism

Made in Germany
If I read „Made in Germany" on a product, I can trust its quality

| 21 % | 40 % | 39 % |
| 23 % | 43 % | 34 % |

National providers
I only buy products from local companies

| 20 % | 26 % | 54 % |
| 19 % | 31 % | 50 % |

Basis USA: All respondents   N: 500
Basis USA/Pacific: All respondents   N: 2,447

Applies to me   Indifferent   Does not apply to me

Mail-order affinity

Mail-order enjoys above-average popularity among American consumers: 31% use this channel frequently (USA/Pacific: 17%), 29% now and again (USA/Pacific: 25%) and only 40% never (USA/Pacific: 58%). Conventional mail-ordering and shopping via the internet are neck and neck in the popularity ratings (20% each). As could be expected, the country where eBay was invented makes great use of online auction houses. The internet is the most frequently used method of ordering (49%).

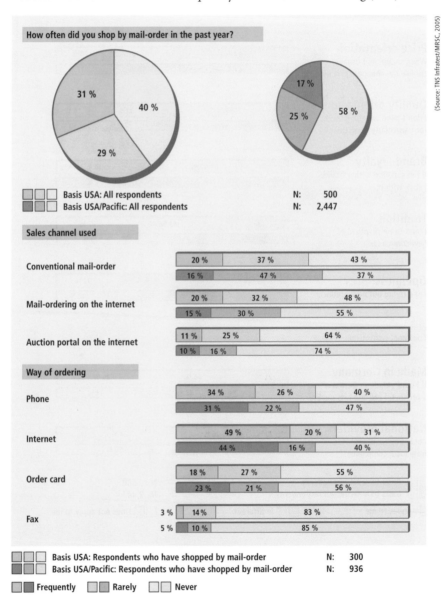

(Source: TNS Infratest/MRSC, 2005)

Austria

8

The forecasts of economic growth in Austria for 2006 remain at approximately 2.4%. The government here is placing hope on a tax reform package that is designed to deliver equal support to both the employer and the employee. Higher wages and salaries of up to 2.5% are expected to have a positive effect on private investment, so that the increase in consumption is projected to be approximately 2.3% in 2006 over one year earlier. The country is also gaining importance as an economic center due to its central European location. The Austrians are positively inclined to direct marketing and 17% of the mailing recipients respond several times per quarter to commercial mailings.

Demographic data

Area	83,871 square kilometers
Population	8.1 million
Number of households	3.3 million
Average household size	2.4 persons
Number of households with internet connection	1.4 million
Major cities/metropolitan areas (residents)	Vienna (1,550,123), Graz (226,244), Linz (183,504), Salzburg (142,662), Innsbruck (113,392), Klagenfurt (90,141)
Population age 0-14	1.3 million
Population age 15-64	5.5 million
Population age 65 and up	1.3 million

(Source: Fischer Weltalmanach 2005, Bundesagentur für Außenwirtschaft 2005)

Direct marketing trends

Austrians receive direct mail more frequently than most other Western Europeans: 84% even receive mailings several times a week.

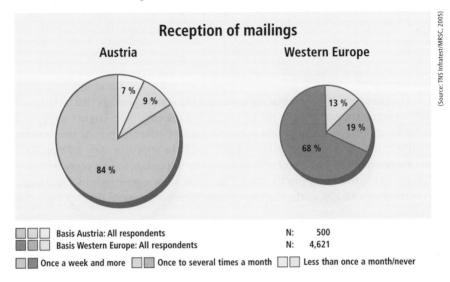

Despite the volume of mailings, 93% of Austrian recipients read them, and almost half do so regularly. Of those who receive them and read them regularly, an astounding 17% respond several times a year. This intensity far exceeds the average

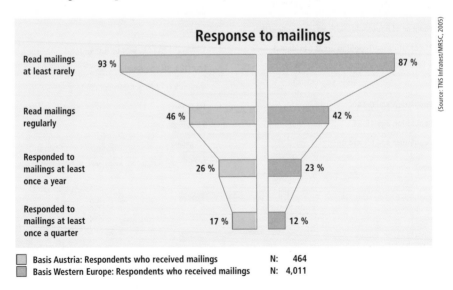

for Western Europe. The sender is crucial: A well-known sender (31%) and the nationality (25%) play an important role for many mailing recipients, especially those

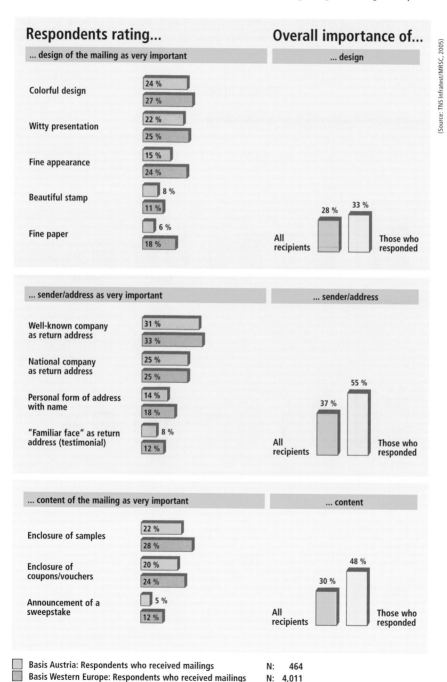

(Source: TNS Infratest/MRSC, 2005)

who respond. Austrians value a distinguished design and fine paper less than the average for Western Europe.

16% of Austrian respondents rate the informational value of mailings. 18% find TV advertising entertaining and print advertising wins the popularity stakes among 17% of those surveyed. A striking point in comparison with Western Europe is the above-average positive assessment of radio advertising in Austria.

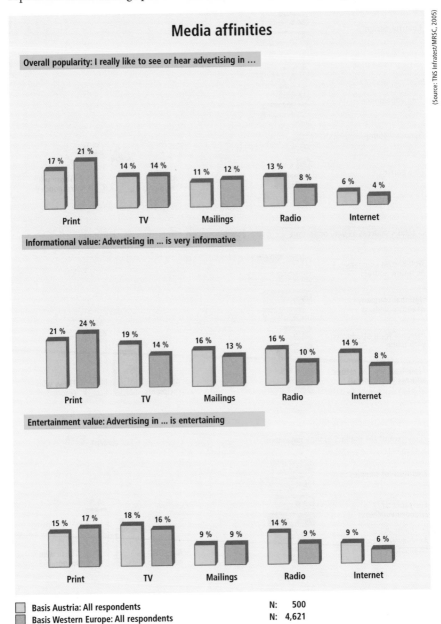

Media affinities

Overall popularity: I really like to see or hear advertising in ...

Print: 17 %, 21 %
TV: 14 %, 14 %
Mailings: 11 %, 12 %
Radio: 13 %, 8 %
Internet: 6 %, 4 %

Informational value: Advertising in ... is very informative

Print: 21 %, 24 %
TV: 19 %, 14 %
Mailings: 16 %, 13 %
Radio: 16 %, 10 %
Internet: 14 %, 8 %

Entertainment value: Advertising in ... is entertaining

Print: 15 %, 17 %
TV: 18 %, 16 %
Mailings: 9 %, 9 %
Radio: 14 %, 9 %
Internet: 9 %, 6 %

Basis Austria: All respondents   N: 500
Basis Western Europe: All respondents   N: 4,621

(Source: TNS Infratest/MRSC, 2005)

Consumer trends

The brand (75%) and quality (69%) are the decisive factors that sway shoppers. Like their Swiss neighbors, few Austrians (30%) pay attention to very low prices. Products "Made in Germany" can score more points on average than in Western Europe.

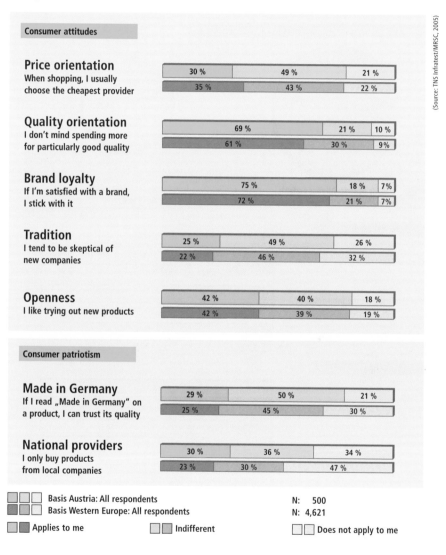

Consumer attitudes

Price orientation
When shopping, I usually choose the cheapest provider
30 % | 49 % | 21 %
35 % | 43 % | 22 %

Quality orientation
I don't mind spending more for particularly good quality
69 % | 21 % | 10 %
61 % | 30 % | 9 %

Brand loyalty
If I'm satisfied with a brand, I stick with it
75 % | 18 % | 7 %
72 % | 21 % | 7 %

Tradition
I tend to be skeptical of new companies
25 % | 49 % | 26 %
22 % | 46 % | 32 %

Openness
I like trying out new products
42 % | 40 % | 18 %
42 % | 39 % | 19 %

Consumer patriotism

Made in Germany
If I read „Made in Germany" on a product, I can trust its quality
29 % | 50 % | 21 %
25 % | 45 % | 30 %

National providers
I only buy products from local companies
30 % | 36 % | 34 %
23 % | 30 % | 47 %

(Source: TNS Infratest/MRSC, 2005)

Basis Austria: All respondents   N: 500
Basis Western Europe: All respondents   N: 4,621

Applies to me   Indifferent   Does not apply to me

Mail-order affinity

The share of mail-order shoppers in Austria (61%) is above the average for Western Europe. 27% use this channel frequently. Austrians prefer conventional mail-order (28%). The phone (45%) heads the list of most popular ordering channels, followed by the internet (30%) and the order card (23%).

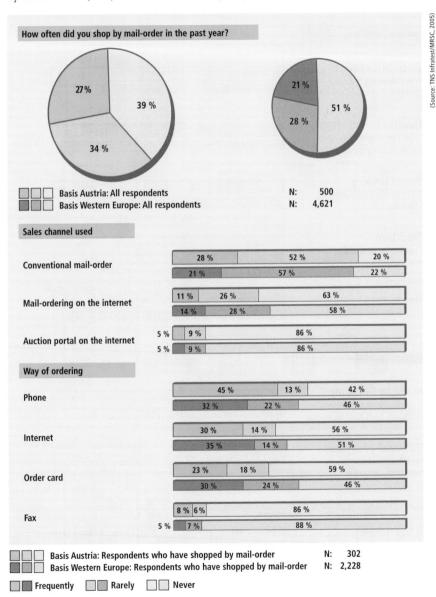

(Source: TNS Infratest/MRSC, 2005)

Belgium

9

Solid growth is projected for the Belgian economy over the coming years. The GDP is projected to increase each year from 2005 to 2010 by approximately 2.2%. The positive economic outlook is strengthening consumer confidence and is reflected in the forecasts of 2.3% growth in private consumption in 2006 over the previous year. Here, direct marketing has overtaken TV-ads in the rankings: In the category of overall acceptance, amusement and information value, mailings are now preferred over TV-commercials.

Demographic data

Area	32,545 square kilometers
Population	10.4 million
Number of households	3.9 million
Average household size	2.7 persons
Number of households with internet connection	1.5 million
Major cities/metropolitan areas (residents)	Brussels (978,384), Antwerp (448,709), Ghent (226,220), Charleroi (200,578), Liège (185,131), Bruges (116,836)
Population age 0-14	1.8 million
Population age 15-64	6.8 million
Population age 65 and up	1.8 million

(Source: Fischer Weltalmanach 2005, Bundesagentur für Außenwirtschaft 2005)

Direct marketing trends

Two-thirds of all Belgian respondents receive direct mail more than once a week, slightly below the average for Western Europe (68%). However, the density of mailings in Belgium is generally higher than in Western Europe: Only 11% of Belgian consumers receive direct mail rarely or never (13% in Western Europe).

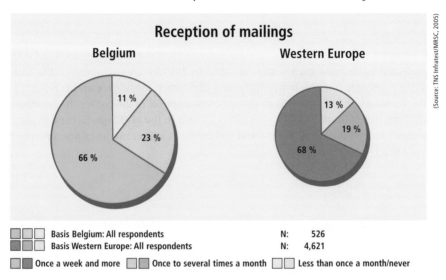

Mailings are certainly paid a great deal of attention in Belgium: A hefty 91% of recipients read them at least now and again. The response to mailings is also higher in Belgium than in neighboring Western European countries: 30% respond to them at least once a year and a full 16% do so several times a quarter. Esthetics

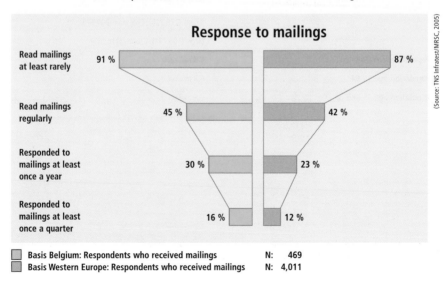

play a major role in Belgium. And as long as the content is right, international senders can also capture the attention of Belgians – especially if recipients are able

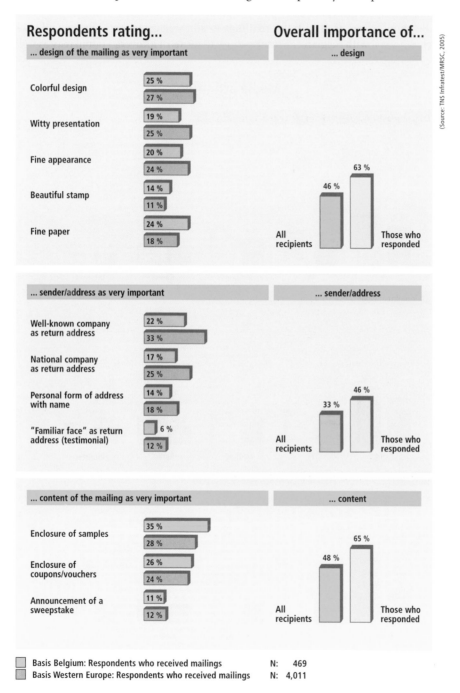

Respondents rating...

... design of the mailing as very important

Colorful design — 25 % / 27 %
Witty presentation — 19 % / 25 %
Fine appearance — 20 % / 24 %
Beautiful stamp — 14 % / 11 %
Fine paper — 24 % / 18 %

... sender/address as very important

Well-known company as return address — 22 % / 33 %
National company as return address — 17 % / 25 %
Personal form of address with name — 14 % / 18 %
"Familiar face" as return address (testimonial) — 6 % / 12 %

... content of the mailing as very important

Enclosure of samples — 35 % / 28 %
Enclosure of coupons/vouchers — 26 % / 24 %
Announcement of a sweepstake — 11 % / 12 %

Overall importance of...

... design

All recipients 46 % — Those who responded 63 %

... sender/address

All recipients 33 % — Those who responded 46 %

... content

All recipients 48 % — Those who responded 65 %

(Source: TNS Infratest/MRSC, 2005)

Basis Belgium: Respondents who received mailings — N: 469
Basis Western Europe: Respondents who received mailings — N: 4,011

to test the product by means of an enclosed sample (35%). One thing is clear from the analysis of Belgians who respond: The form of address and sender (46%) are nowhere near as relevant as design (63%) and content (65%).

Belgium proves its affinity for mailings in all three categories: Direct mail goes over quite well with Belgian consumers, both in terms of its overall popularity as well

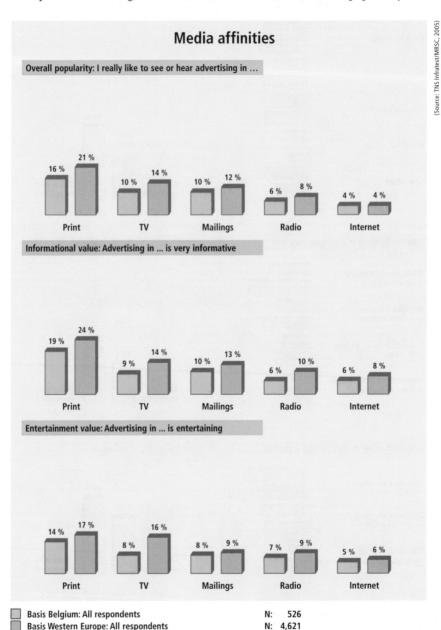

(Source: TNS Infratest/MRSC, 2005)

as its informational and entertainment value. A striking feature is that TV advertising is ousted from 2nd place by mailings when it comes to informational value.

Consumer trends

If you want to have success in Belgium, you should build on brand values. Hardly any other Western European country is so loyal to brands (79%) and so little price-oriented (28%) as Belgium. When it comes to the importance of quality, Belgians (62%) concur with their neighbors in Western Europe (61%). National providers are not preferred: Over half of consumers do not attach importance to the products they buy being of Belgian origin.

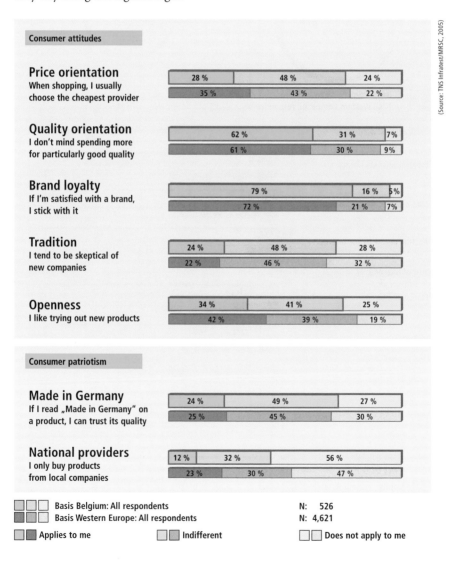

(Source: TNS Infratest/MRSC, 2005)

Consumer attitudes

Price orientation
When shopping, I usually choose the cheapest provider
28 % | 48 % | 24 %
35 % | 43 % | 22 %

Quality orientation
I don't mind spending more for particularly good quality
62 % | 31 % | 7%
61 % | 30 % | 9%

Brand loyalty
If I'm satisfied with a brand, I stick with it
79 % | 16 % | 5%
72 % | 21 % | 7%

Tradition
I tend to be skeptical of new companies
24 % | 48 % | 28 %
22 % | 46 % | 32 %

Openness
I like trying out new products
34 % | 41 % | 25 %
42 % | 39 % | 19 %

Consumer patriotism

Made in Germany
If I read „Made in Germany" on a product, I can trust its quality
24 % | 49 % | 27 %
25 % | 45 % | 30 %

National providers
I only buy products from local companies
12 % | 32 % | 56 %
23 % | 30 % | 47 %

Basis Belgium: All respondents — N: 526
Basis Western Europe: All respondents — N: 4,621

Applies to me   Indifferent   Does not apply to me

Mail-order affinity

Only 11% of Belgian consumers shop by mail-order and a huge 63% have never used this channel, both of which are below the average for Western Europe. The few who do order by catalog prefer the order card (46%) as the mean of responding.

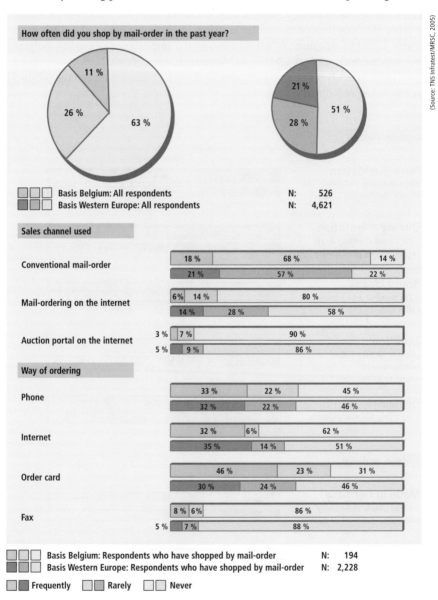

(Source: TNS Infratest/MRSC, 2005)

Despite the small, mid-year slump in the French economy in 2005, a positive investment impulse was observed from the private household and business segments. Not least on account of the increase in basic wages, the growth in private consumption for 2006 – as already seen in 2005 – is expected to be approximately 2% over the previous year. In France, direct marketing has established itself as being both long term and successful: Provided an interest in the product exists, mailings - especially those with coupons included - can be expected to have a large resonance.

Demographic data

Area	543,965 square kilometers
Population	62.4 million
Number of households	25.5 million
Average household size	2.4 persons
Number of households with internet connection	7.7 million
Major cities/metropolitan areas (residents)	Paris (2,115,757), Marseille (797,700), Lyon (416,263), Toulouse (390,712), Nice (341,016), Strasbourg (268,683)
Population age 0-14	15.7 million
Population age 15-64	36.6 million
Population age 65 and up	10.1 million

(Source: Fischer Weltalmanach 2005, Bundesagentur für Außenwirtschaft 2005)

Direct marketing trends

90% of those surveyed receive direct mail. In France, its distribution therefore slightly above the average for Western Europe (87%). However, French consumers (62%) do not receive mailings as frequently as their Western European neighbors (68%).

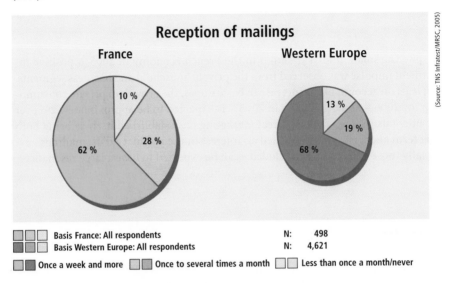

89% of French mailing recipients read them, 43% even regularly. 30% of those surveyed who receive mailings and read them regularly respond at least once a year – a figure well above the mean for Western Europe (23%). A large number (13%) respond several times a quarter. Whereas the French attach equal value to design

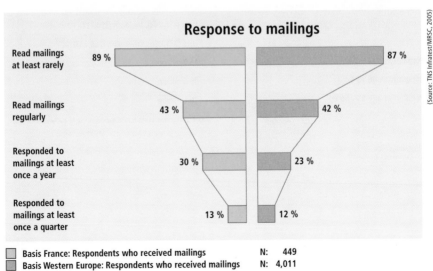

and personal form of address of a mailing as their neighbors in Western Europe on average, they stand out with their preference for couponing (40% compared with

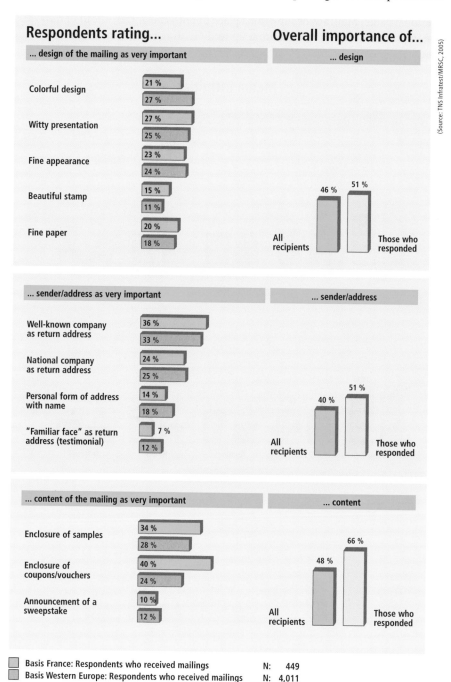

(Source: TNS Infratest/MRSC, 2005)

Respondents rating...

... design of the mailing as very important

Colorful design	21 %
	27 %
Witty presentation	27 %
	25 %
Fine appearance	23 %
	24 %
Beautiful stamp	15 %
	11 %
Fine paper	20 %
	18 %

... sender/address as very important

Well-known company as return address	36 %
	33 %
National company as return address	24 %
	25 %
Personal form of address with name	14 %
	18 %
"Familiar face" as return address (testimonial)	7 %
	12 %

... content of the mailing as very important

Enclosure of samples	34 %
	28 %
Enclosure of coupons/vouchers	40 %
	24 %
Announcement of a sweepstake	10 %
	12 %

Overall importance of...

... design

All recipients	Those who responded
46 %	51 %

... sender/address

All recipients	Those who responded
40 %	51 %

... content

All recipients	Those who responded
48 %	66 %

Basis France: Respondents who received mailings   N: 449
Basis Western Europe: Respondents who received mailings   N: 4,011

24%). Above all, the content of the mailing is crucial in capturing the attention of 66% of those who respond to mailings.

Print is the number 1 in France when it comes to overall popularity and informational value. Mailings occupy third place in both categories, ahead of radio and the internet, but have some catching up to do with regard to entertainment value compared with print and TV.

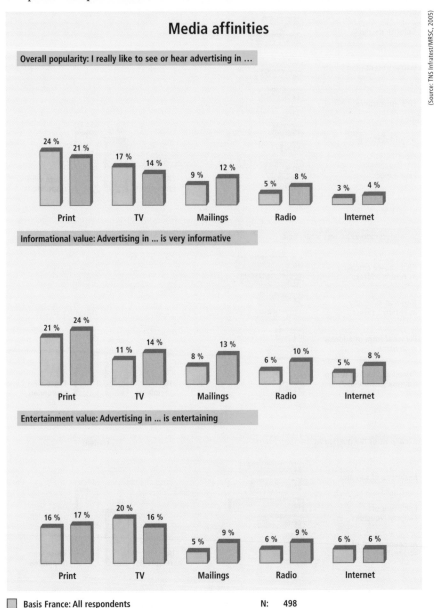

Media affinities

Overall popularity: I really like to see or hear advertising in ...

| Print | TV | Mailings | Radio | Internet |
| 24 % 21 % | 17 % 14 % | 9 % 12 % | 5 % 8 % | 3 % 4 % |

Informational value: Advertising in ... is very informative

| Print | TV | Mailings | Radio | Internet |
| 21 % 24 % | 11 % 14 % | 8 % 13 % | 6 % 10 % | 5 % 8 % |

Entertainment value: Advertising in ... is entertaining

| Print | TV | Mailings | Radio | Internet |
| 16 % 17 % | 20 % 16 % | 5 % 9 % | 6 % 9 % | 6 % 6 % |

☐ Basis France: All respondents   N: 498
☐ Basis Western Europe: All respondents   N: 4,621

(Source: TNS Infratest/MRSC, 2005)

Consumer trends

Brand loyalty is quite large in France: 75% of respondents remain loyal to a brand if they are satisfied with it. In contrast, only a quarter make a decision to purchase on the basis of a low price. Quality is far more important to the French (54%). Consumer patriotism is more pronounced among the French than their Western European neighbors: A quarter prefer national providers.

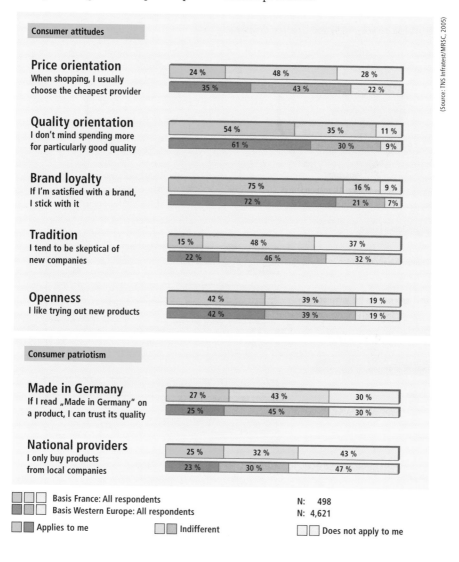

(Source: TNS Infratest/MRSC, 2005)

Consumer attitudes

Price orientation
When shopping, I usually
choose the cheapest provider
- 24 % | 48 % | 28 %
- 35 % | 43 % | 22 %

Quality orientation
I don't mind spending more
for particularly good quality
- 54 % | 35 % | 11 %
- 61 % | 30 % | 9 %

Brand loyalty
If I'm satisfied with a brand,
I stick with it
- 75 % | 16 % | 9 %
- 72 % | 21 % | 7%

Tradition
I tend to be skeptical of
new companies
- 15 % | 48 % | 37 %
- 22 % | 46 % | 32 %

Openness
I like trying out new products
- 42 % | 39 % | 19 %
- 42 % | 39 % | 19 %

Consumer patriotism

Made in Germany
If I read „Made in Germany" on
a product, I can trust its quality
- 27 % | 43 % | 30 %
- 25 % | 45 % | 30 %

National providers
I only buy products
from local companies
- 25 % | 32 % | 43 %
- 23 % | 30 % | 47 %

☐☐☐ Basis France: All respondents   N: 498
■☐☐ Basis Western Europe: All respondents   N: 4,621

☐■ Applies to me   ☐☐ Indifferent   ☐☐ Does not apply to me

Mail-order affinity

The majority of French shop by mail-order at least occasionally. However, the internet has not achieved such a breakthrough as a sales channel to date; respondents prefer the conventional catalog. A third of all those who shop by mail-order frequently switch to the internet, although 45% of French prefer ordering using the order card – far higher than the average for Western Europeans.

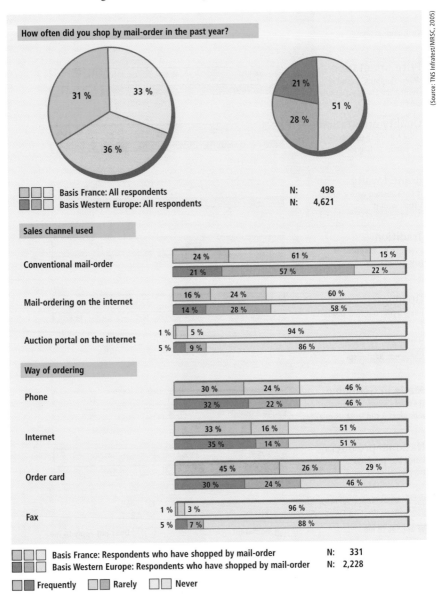

(Source: TNS Infratest/MRSC, 2005)

Germany

11

Germany is hoping for world class consumer spending in 2006, encouraged by the World Soccer Championships as a strong motor for consumption. By the same time, the new coalition government gives hope for a sustainable improvement in the economic situation. Direct marketing continues to gain in significance. Targeted mailings that hit the product interests of the recipients and reflect a high degree of personalization can still achieve a respectable success even in this country where mailing density is quite high.

Demographic data

Area	357,027 square kilometers
Population	82.5 million
Number of households	38.9 million
Average household size	2.1 persons
Number of households with internet connection	18.2 million
Major cities/metropolitan areas (residents)	Berlin (3,392,425), Hamburg (1,728,806), Munich (1,234,692), Cologne (968,639), Frankfurt am Main (643,726), Dortmund (590,831)
Population age 0-14	12.1 million
Population age 15-64	55.5 million
Population age 65 and up	14.9 million

(Source: Fischer Weltalmanach 2005, Bundesagentur für Außenwirtschaft 2005)

Direct marketing trends

Just about every German knows what mailings are – a full 73% receive them at least once a week, above the average for Western Europe (68%). Only 8% of Germans surveyed state that they have almost never received direct mail.

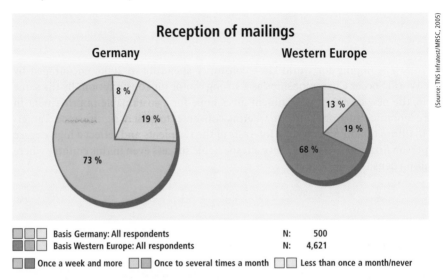

A full 87% of German recipients of mailings can be reached through this mean and 30% have taken to reading them frequently. Compared with Western Europe (42%) however, there is a larger portion of Germans that read direct mail rarely. Their response is also slightly below the Western European mean: 7% of those surveyed who receive mailings and read them regularly responded frequently to them last year.

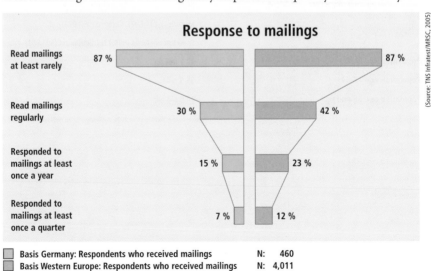

Recipients of mailings in Germany feel it is particularly important for the sender to be well-known and the mail to contain a personal form of address. Less importance

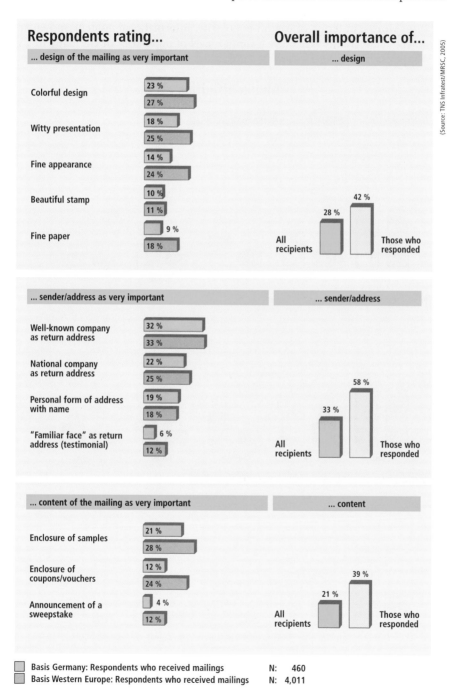

Respondents rating...

... design of the mailing as very important

Colorful design	23 %
	27 %
Witty presentation	18 %
	25 %
Fine appearance	14 %
	24 %
Beautiful stamp	10 %
	11 %
Fine paper	9 %
	18 %

... sender/address as very important

Well-known company as return address	32 %
	33 %
National company as return address	22 %
	25 %
Personal form of address with name	19 %
	18 %
"Familiar face" as return address (testimonial)	6 %
	12 %

... content of the mailing as very important

Enclosure of samples	21 %
	28 %
Enclosure of coupons/vouchers	12 %
	24 %
Announcement of a sweepstake	4 %
	12 %

Overall importance of...

... design

All recipients	Those who responded
28 %	42 %

... sender/address

All recipients	Those who responded
33 %	58 %

... content

All recipients	Those who responded
21 %	39 %

(Source: TNS Infratest/MRSC, 2005)

Basis Germany: Respondents who received mailings   N: 460
Basis Western Europe: Respondents who received mailings   N: 4,011

is attached to design features than on average in Western Europe. However, 21% of respondents rate samples as very important. The sender, form of address and content of the mailing have a much greater importance for those who respond.

Print wins – in terms of overall popularity, informational content and entertainment value. Mailings achieve a similar level of popularity in Germany to TV

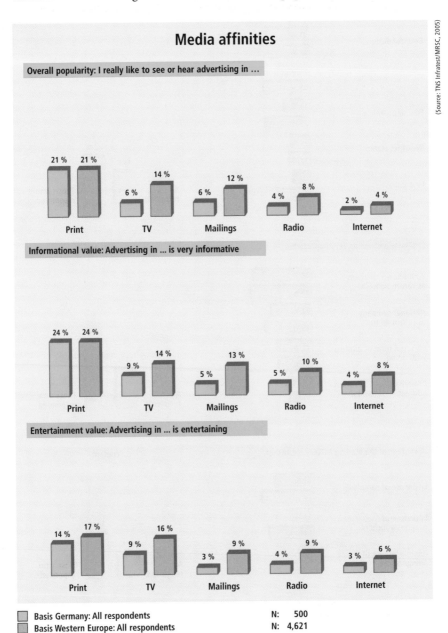

Media affinities

Overall popularity: I really like to see or hear advertising in ...

Print: 21 %, 21 %
TV: 6 %, 14 %
Mailings: 6 %, 12 %
Radio: 4 %, 8 %
Internet: 2 %, 4 %

Informational value: Advertising in ... is very informative

Print: 24 %, 24 %
TV: 9 %, 14 %
Mailings: 5 %, 13 %
Radio: 5 %, 10 %
Internet: 4 %, 8 %

Entertainment value: Advertising in ... is entertaining

Print: 14 %, 17 %
TV: 9 %, 16 %
Mailings: 3 %, 9 %
Radio: 4 %, 9 %
Internet: 3 %, 6 %

Basis Germany: All respondents   N: 500
Basis Western Europe: All respondents   N: 4,621

(Source: TNS Infratest/MRSC, 2005)

advertising and are regarded as being just as informative. Apart from print, Germans rate all media far more critically than the average for Western Europe.

Consumer trends

If the brand delivers what it promises, it can enjoy everlasting loyalty among 69% of German consumers. The main factor here is special quality, for which 61% are also willing to pay extra. In this regard, Germans concur with their Western European neighbors. The number of those who rely solely on "Made in Germany" as a sign of quality has fallen compared with the previous year (from 32% to 23%). This and the openness towards international products among 42% of German consumers should entice foreign providers into the German market.

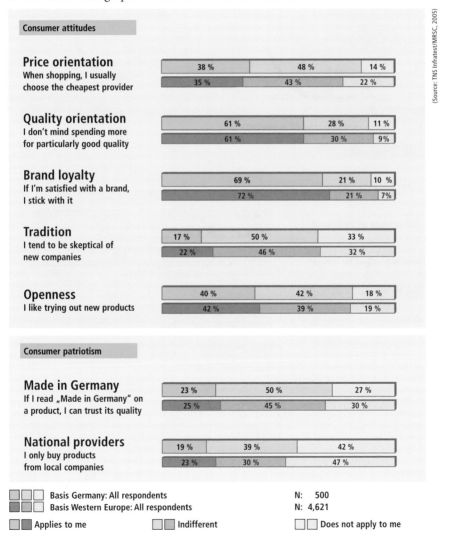

(Source: TNS Infratest/MRSC, 2005)

Consumer attitudes

Price orientation
When shopping, I usually choose the cheapest provider
- 38 % | 48 % | 14 %
- 35 % | 43 % | 22 %

Quality orientation
I don't mind spending more for particularly good quality
- 61 % | 28 % | 11 %
- 61 % | 30 % | 9 %

Brand loyalty
If I'm satisfied with a brand, I stick with it
- 69 % | 21 % | 10 %
- 72 % | 21 % | 7%

Tradition
I tend to be skeptical of new companies
- 17 % | 50 % | 33 %
- 22 % | 46 % | 32 %

Openness
I like trying out new products
- 40 % | 42 % | 18 %
- 42 % | 39 % | 19 %

Consumer patriotism

Made in Germany
If I read „Made in Germany" on a product, I can trust its quality
- 23 % | 50 % | 27 %
- 25 % | 45 % | 30 %

National providers
I only buy products from local companies
- 19 % | 39 % | 42 %
- 23 % | 30 % | 47 %

Basis Germany: All respondents   N: 500
Basis Western Europe: All respondents   N: 4,621

Applies to me   Indifferent   Does not apply to me

Mail-order affinity

Compared with Western Europe, mail-ordering in Germany is extremely popular: 34% of Germans use this channel frequently to order goods. The conventional catalog is still clearly preferred for ordering (29%), and not the internet (15%). Orders are placed most frequently by phone (49%), with the internet coming second. The order card is used more rarely (21%) compared with the rest of Western Europe.

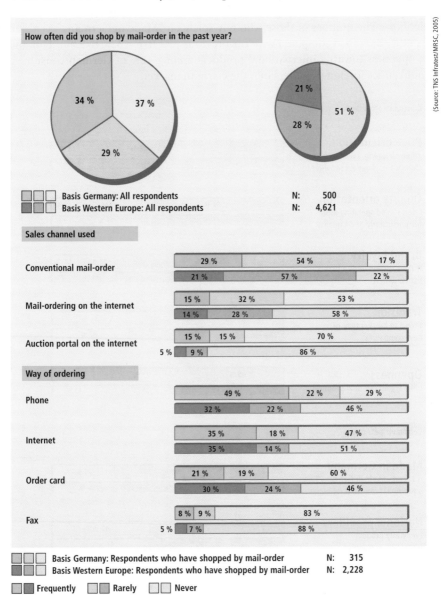

(Source: TNS Infratest/MRSC, 2005)

Great Britain

12

The pleasant, positive trend visible in the economy now for over ten years continued in 2005. Both the consumer goods sector as well as the entire health industry registered big gains. Confidence is also observed above all in the communications and IT industries. The rising trend is continuing: private consumption in 2006 should hit 2.4% compared to the previous year. This growth is slightly better than that achieved in 2005 (2.2%). This country is known for its peculiar brand of humor. A similar subtle, disarming approach in direct marketing will also have a positive effect on the response rates.

Demographic data

Area	242,910 square kilometers
Population	58.8 million
Number of households	25.2 million
Average household size	2.3 persons
Number of households with internet connection	12.6 million
Major cities/metropolitan areas (residents)	London (7,357,100), Birmingham (1,010,400), Leeds (726,100), Glasgow (609,400), Sheffield (530,100), Bradford (486,100)
Population age 0-14	11.9 million
Population age 15-64	36.1 million
Population age 65 and up	10.8 million

(Source: Fischer Weltalmanach 2005, Bundesagentur für Außenwirtschaft 2005)

Direct marketing trends

65% of the British surveyed receive direct mail more than once a week, roughly on a par with the Western European mean. The number of British who receive mailings never or rarely (13%) matches the average for Western Europe exactly.

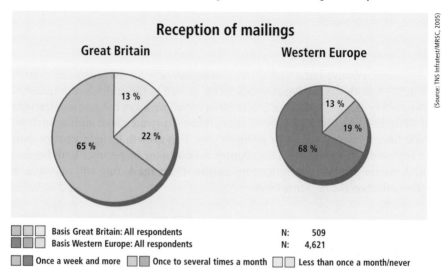

British recipients of direct mail are somewhat restrained in their response: 15% of those surveyed who receive mailings and read them regularly respond at least once a year. Compared with Western Europe, the British read their mailings less often (74% versus 87%) and do not respond as frequently (7% to 12%). British recipients

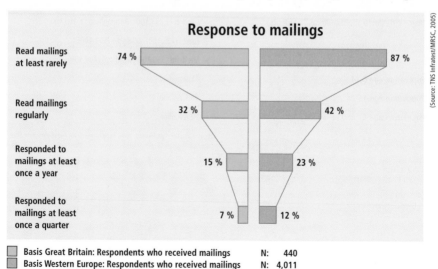

of direct mail concur with their Western European neighbors with regard to the relevance of samples (27%) and coupons (22%). In particular, those who respond

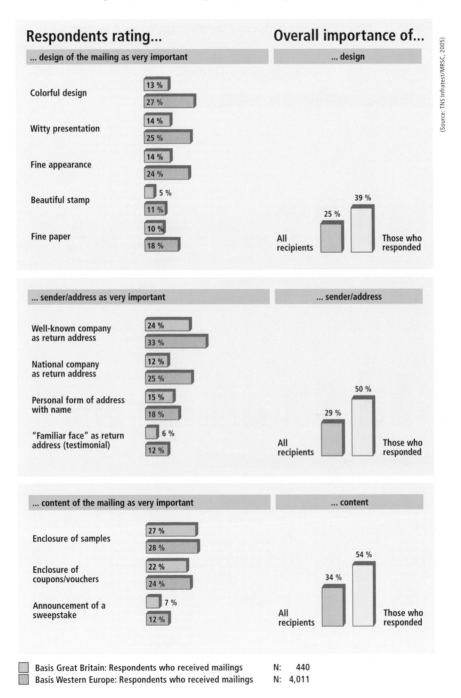

(Source: TNS Infratest/MRSC, 2005)

Respondents rating...

... design of the mailing as very important

Colorful design — 13 % / 27 %

Witty presentation — 14 % / 25 %

Fine appearance — 14 % / 24 %

Beautiful stamp — 5 % / 11 %

Fine paper — 10 % / 18 %

... sender/address as very important

Well-known company as return address — 24 % / 33 %

National company as return address — 12 % / 25 %

Personal form of address with name — 15 % / 18 %

"Familiar face" as return address (testimonial) — 6 % / 12 %

... content of the mailing as very important

Enclosure of samples — 27 % / 28 %

Enclosure of coupons/vouchers — 22 % / 24 %

Announcement of a sweepstake — 7 % / 12 %

Overall importance of...

... design

All recipients 25 % — Those who responded 39 %

... sender/address

All recipients 29 % — Those who responded 50 %

... content

All recipients 34 % — Those who responded 54 %

Basis Great Britain: Respondents who received mailings   N: 440
Basis Western Europe: Respondents who received mailings   N: 4,011

to mailings (54%) rate their content as especially important. The British consider design features to be of lesser importance than do other Western Europeans.

TV advertising is top in terms of overall popularity (17%) and entertainment value (22%). These figures are both above the mean for Western Europe.

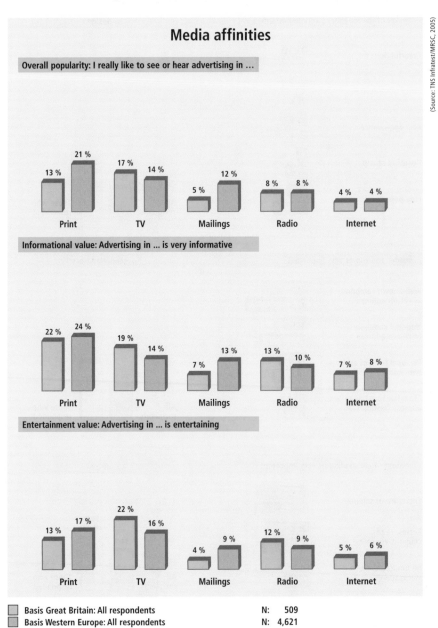

Media affinities

Overall popularity: I really like to see or hear advertising in …

| Print | TV | Mailings | Radio | Internet |

Informational value: Advertising in … is very informative

Entertainment value: Advertising in … is entertaining

☐ Basis Great Britain: All respondents   N: 509
☐ Basis Western Europe: All respondents   N: 4,621

(Source: TNS Infratest/MRSC, 2005)

Consumer trends

Price orientation (43%) occupies third place when it comes to choice of provider, after brand loyalty (71%) and quality orientation (62%). This means that the British attach far greater importance to a good buy than do Western Europeans on average (35%). However, they are more tolerant with regard to nationality – 62% of consumers do not make their choice based on whether a product is British.

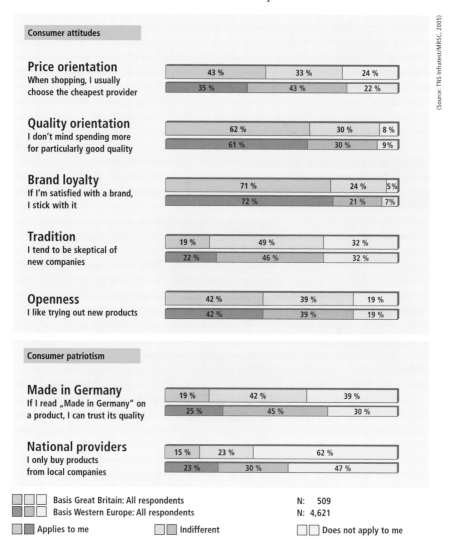

Consumer attitudes

Price orientation
When shopping, I usually
choose the cheapest provider

43 %   33 %   24 %
35 %   43 %   22 %

Quality orientation
I don't mind spending more
for particularly good quality

62 %   30 %   8 %
61 %   30 %   9%

Brand loyalty
If I'm satisfied with a brand,
I stick with it

71 %   24 %   5%
72 %   21 %   7%

Tradition
I tend to be skeptical of
new companies

19 %   49 %   32 %
22 %   46 %   32 %

Openness
I like trying out new products

42 %   39 %   19 %
42 %   39 %   19 %

Consumer patriotism

Made in Germany
If I read „Made in Germany" on
a product, I can trust its quality

19 %   42 %   39 %
25 %   45 %   30 %

National providers
I only buy products
from local companies

15 %   23 %   62 %
23 %   30 %   47 %

☐☐☐ Basis Great Britain: All respondents   N: 509
■■☐ Basis Western Europe: All respondents   N: 4,621

☐■ Applies to me   ☐■ Indifferent   ☐☐ Does not apply to me

(Source: TNS Infratest/MRSC, 2005)

Mail-order affinity

The British like using mail-order for occasional purchases: Only 43% have never used this channel – far less than the average for Western Europe (51%). They also like to use the internet (48%) or the phone (44%) for placing orders.

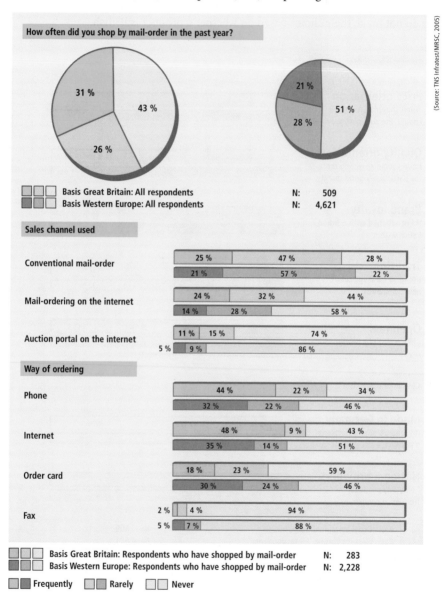

(Source: TNS Infratest/MRSC, 2005)

13

Italy

The Italian economy was still struggling to pick up the pace in 2005 because of increasing competitive pressures stemming from lower prices in Asia. Now however, several large-scale projects such as the "Citta della Moda" in Milan are expected to propel economic growth forward. Private consumption is projected to increase by almost 1% in 2006 over the previous year. Direct marketing, with its potential for personalized messages, not only addresses the regional differences of the Italian people, but is also well received among the consumers there. For example, with respect to the scale of popularity, direct mailings rank higher than both TV and print media advertising.

Demographic data

Area	301,336 square kilometers
Population	58.1 million
Number of households	23.5 million
Average household size	2.6 persons
Number of households with internet connection	9.0 million
Major cities/metropolitan areas (residents)	Rome (2,540,829), Milan (1,247,052), Naples (1,008,419), Turin (861,644), Palermo (682,901), Genoa (604,732)
Population age 0-14	8.7 million
Population age 15-64	35.7 million
Population age 65 and up	13.7 million

(Source: Fischer Weltalmanach 2005, Bundesagentur für Außenwirtschaft 2005, OECD 2005)

Direct marketing trends

The figures for Italian consumers are roughly on a par with the Western European average: 65% of those surveyed receive mailings at least once a week (Western Europe: 68%) and 15% as good as never (Western Europe: 13%).

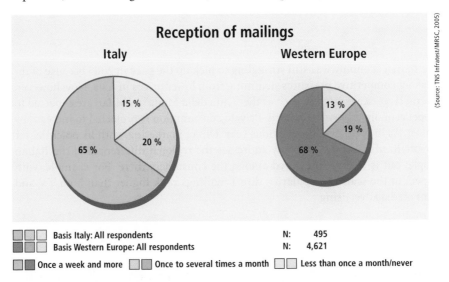

The strikingly low willingness to respond in Italy (despite a fundamental openness for mailings) was reviewed in a validation study. It appears that elections in Italy significantly influenced the first figure due to an increase in election advertising (time of the survey: April 2005). The validation survey (July 2005) shows a far higher willingness to respond among the population. To boost the response by

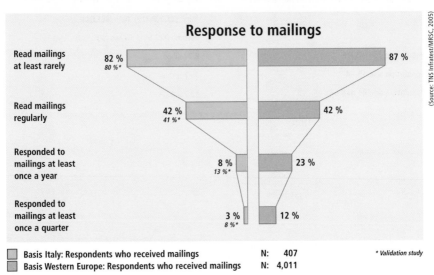

Italians, one should clearly pay attention to design and content, two factors that have top priority for 80% of respondents. 45% of those surveyed like prize drawings, 42%

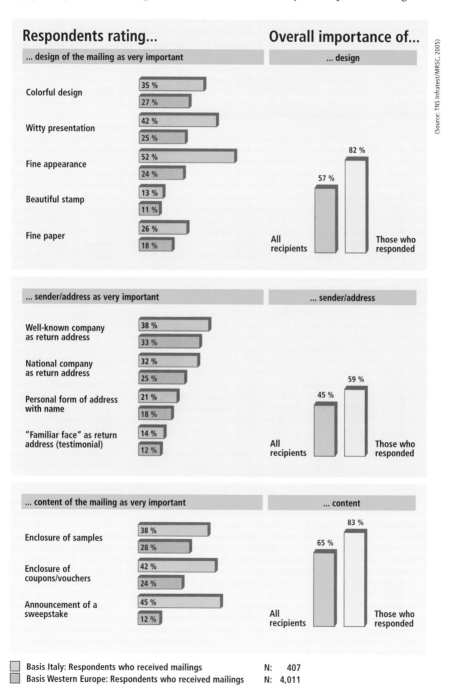

(Source: TNS Infratest/MRSC, 2005)

Respondents rating...

... design of the mailing as very important

Colorful design — 35 % / 27 %

Witty presentation — 42 % / 25 %

Fine appearance — 52 % / 24 %

Beautiful stamp — 13 % / 11 %

Fine paper — 26 % / 18 %

Overall importance of...

... design

57 % All recipients

82 % Those who responded

... sender/address as very important

Well-known company as return address — 38 % / 33 %

National company as return address — 32 % / 25 %

Personal form of address with name — 21 % / 18 %

"Familiar face" as return address (testimonial) — 14 % / 12 %

... sender/address

45 % All recipients

59 % Those who responded

... content of the mailing as very important

Enclosure of samples — 38 % / 28 %

Enclosure of coupons/vouchers — 42 % / 24 %

Announcement of a sweepstake — 45 % / 12 %

... content

65 % All recipients

83 % Those who responded

Basis Italy: Respondents who received mailings   N: 407
Basis Western Europe: Respondents who received mailings   N: 4,011

enclosed coupons and 38% samples. A fine presentation also goes over well with 52% of Italian consumers.

Despite their currently restrained willingness to respond to offerings, Italian consumers certainly do have an affinity for mailings: They are more popular (20%) than all other media and come second in terms of informational value (23%), ahead of TV

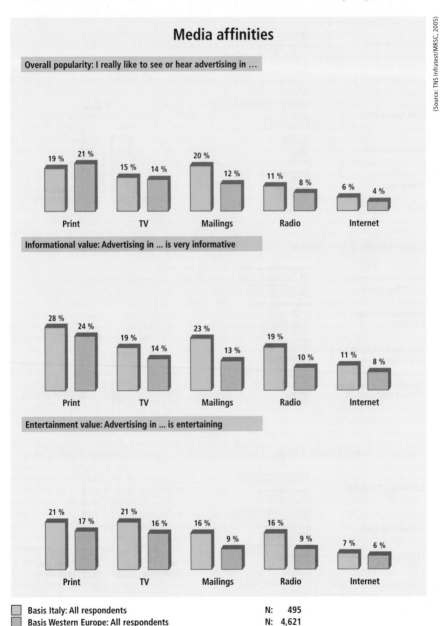

Media affinities

Overall popularity: I really like to see or hear advertising in ...

Informational value: Advertising in ... is very informative

Entertainment value: Advertising in ... is entertaining

Basis Italy: All respondents   N: 495
Basis Western Europe: All respondents   N: 4,621

(Source: TNS Infratest/MRSC, 2005)

spots (19%). In contrast, those surveyed feel that print and TV advertising are the most entertaining (21% each).

Consumer trends

Good news for companies: Almost half of all Italians surveyed (48%) like trying out new products, although national products have things a little easier. 42% prefer Italian providers – a level of customer patriotism far above the Western European average (23%). However, it is mainly the brand (69%) and quality (54%) that sway purchasing decisions.

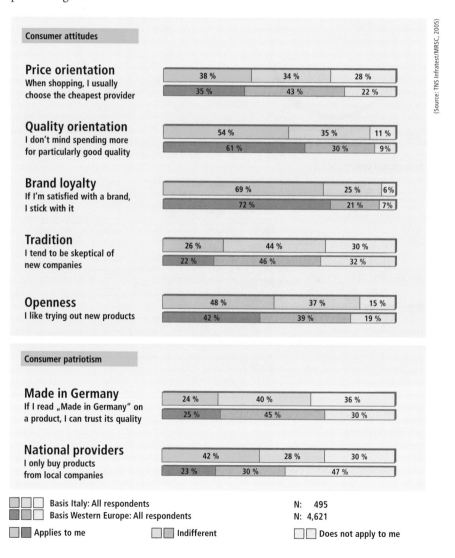

(Source: TNS Infratest/MRSC, 2005)

Mail-order affinity

Very few Italian consumers use mail-order: 77% never order by this channel and only 5% shop frequently this way – well below the average for Western Europe. Conventional mail-order (11%) is just ahead of internet sales (10%). The order card (22%), internet (22%) and phone (21%) are equally popular ways of ordering.

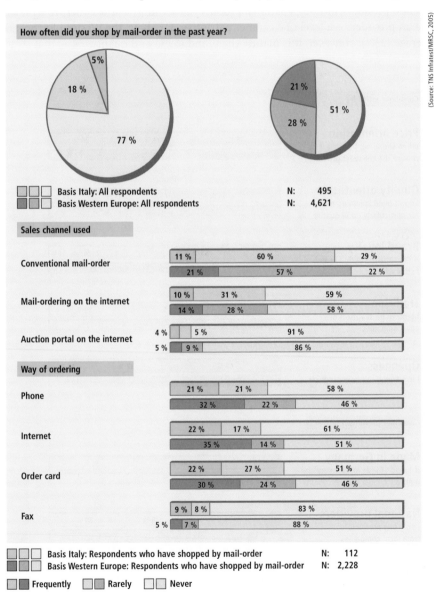

(Source: TNS Infratest/MRSC, 2005)

The Netherlands

14

The upturn forecasted for 2005 did not materialize, but by the end of the year and into the year 2006, the economy of The Netherlands should begin to advance. The upswing will be driven especially by a rising demand for investment goods. Direct marketing reflects a positive message: of the 77% of the Dutch population that receive direct mailings, 21% say they respond favorably several times per quarter – a percentage far above the average in western Europe and good enough for 2nd place among all the countries served by this publication. Straightforwardness is just as important here for direct marketing as it is for routine business transactions.

Demographic data

Area	41,526 square kilometers
Population	16.3 million
Number of households	7.0 million
Average household size	2.3 persons
Number of households with internet connection	2.3 million
Major cities/metropolitan areas (residents)	Amsterdam (736,562), Rotterdam (559,651), The Hague (457,726), Utrecht (265,151), Eindhoven (206,118), Tilburg (197,917)
Population age 0-14	3.0 million
Population age 15-64	11.0 million
Population age 65 and up	2.3 million

(Source: Fischer Weltalmanach 2005, Bundesagentur für Außenwirtschaft 2005)

Direct marketing trends

Direct mail is widespread in the Netherlands: 77% of the Dutch respondents state that they receive mailings several times a week; only one-tenth hardly ever receive any advertising by mail. This means that the mailing density is well above the average for Western Europe.

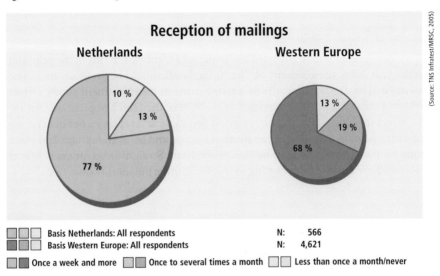

The vast majority of Dutch recipients of direct mail reads it, while more than half (51%) regularly scrutinize mailings. A gratifying 21% of those who receive mailings and read them regularly respond several times a year. This intensity far exceeds the European average (by almost 100%). Design counts! The Dutch are attracted if

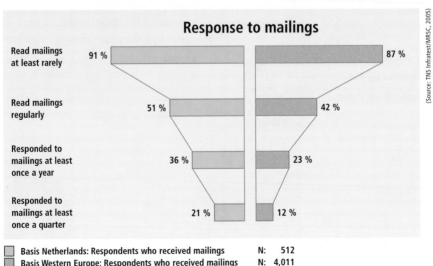

mailings are colorful (29%) and they like them to have a fine presentation (26%). A well-known sender plays a major role for 38% of those surveyed. In contrast with

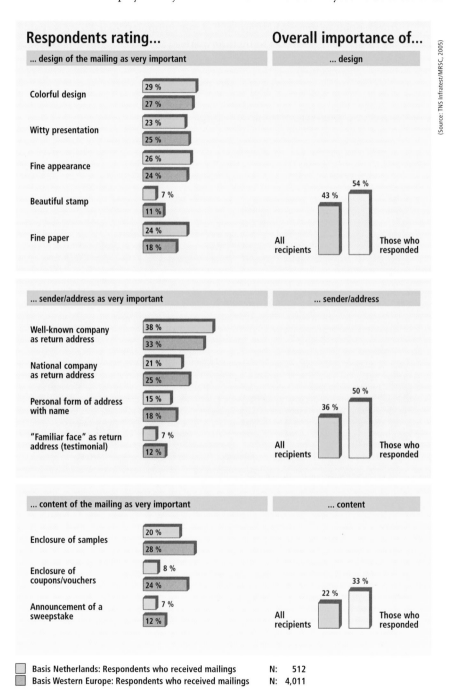

Respondents rating...

... design of the mailing as very important

Colorful design — 29 % / 27 %

Witty presentation — 23 % / 25 %

Fine appearance — 26 % / 24 %

Beautiful stamp — 7 % / 11 %

Fine paper — 24 % / 18 %

... sender/address as very important

Well-known company as return address — 38 % / 33 %

National company as return address — 21 % / 25 %

Personal form of address with name — 15 % / 18 %

"Familiar face" as return address (testimonial) — 7 % / 12 %

... content of the mailing as very important

Enclosure of samples — 20 % / 28 %

Enclosure of coupons/vouchers — 8 % / 24 %

Announcement of a sweepstake — 7 % / 12 %

Overall importance of...

... design

All recipients: 43 %
Those who responded: 54 %

... sender/address

All recipients: 36 %
Those who responded: 50 %

... content

All recipients: 22 %
Those who responded: 33 %

Basis Netherlands: Respondents who received mailings   N: 512
Basis Western Europe: Respondents who received mailings   N: 4,011

(Source: TNS Infratest/MRSC, 2005)

the trend for Western Europe, however, the Dutch are hard to inspire with coupons (8%) or prize drawings (7%).

Direct mailings have overtaken TV advertising in the Netherlands, at least from the consumer's point of view: Mailings are far more popular than TV advertising (24% versus 10%), are regarded as more informative (20% to 8%) and even surpass

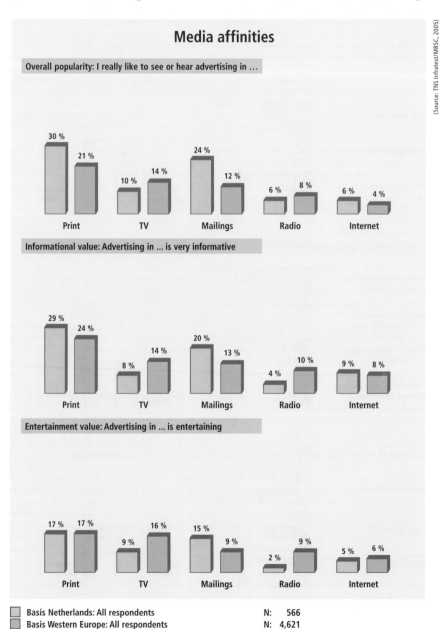

(Source: TNS Infratest/MRSC, 2005)

Media affinities

Overall popularity: I really like to see or hear advertising in ...

| Print | TV | Mailings | Radio | Internet |

Informational value: Advertising in ... is very informative

Entertainment value: Advertising in ... is entertaining

Basis Netherlands: All respondents   N: 566
Basis Western Europe: All respondents   N: 4,621

TV in terms of entertainment value (15% to 9%). These figures are well above the mean for Western Europe.

Consumer trends

The majority of Dutch (67%) remain loyal to their brand if they are satisfied with it. Above all, they attach a great deal of importance to quality (57%). This attitude is roughly in line with the average for Western Europe. Yet Dutch consumers do not share their neighbors' view regarding one point: Buying a product just because the provider is local is something only 9% would do (Western Europe: 23%).

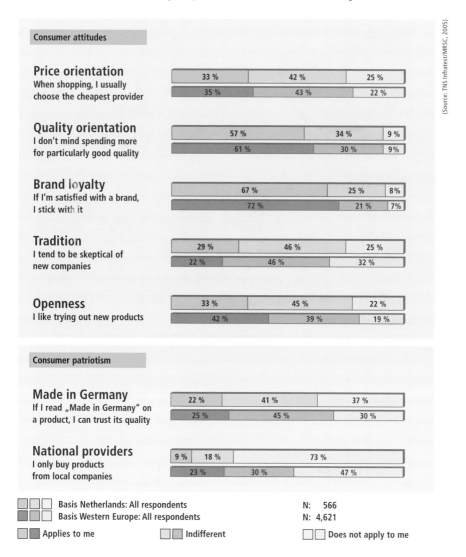

(Source: TNS Infratest/MRSC, 2005)

Mail-order affinity

Around half of the respondents shop by mail-order, albeit not regularly. Internet portals are more popular compared with the rest of Western Europe (51% to 42%), whereas conventional catalogs are used slightly less than the average (72% to 78%). For ordering too, the Dutch tend to choose the internet ahead of the order card or hotline.

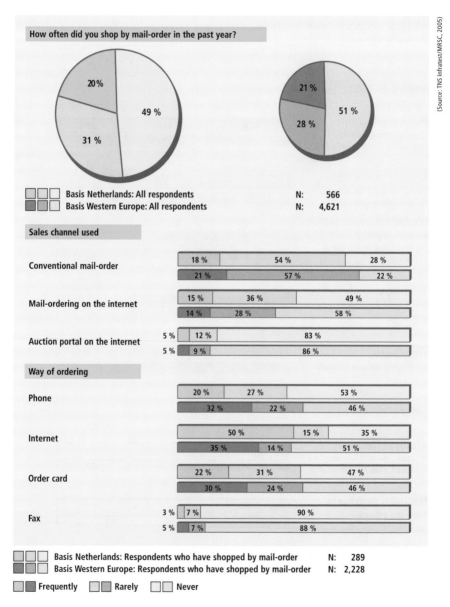

(Source: TNS Infratest/MRSC, 2005)

How often did you shop by mail-order in the past year?

20 %
49 %
31 %

21 %
51 %
28 %

☐☐☐ Basis Netherlands: All respondents   N: 566
■■☐ Basis Western Europe: All respondents   N: 4,621

Sales channel used

Conventional mail-order
18 %   54 %   28 %
21 %   57 %   22 %

Mail-ordering on the internet
15 %   36 %   49 %
14 %   28 %   58 %

Auction portal on the internet
5 %   12 %   83 %
5 %   9 %   86 %

Way of ordering

Phone
20 %   27 %   53 %
32 %   22 %   46 %

Internet
50 %   15 %   35 %
35 %   14 %   51 %

Order card
22 %   31 %   47 %
30 %   24 %   46 %

Fax
3 %   7 %   90 %
5 %   7 %   88 %

☐☐☐ Basis Netherlands: Respondents who have shopped by mail-order   N: 289
■■☐ Basis Western Europe: Respondents who have shopped by mail-order   N: 2,228

■■ Frequently   ☐☐ Rarely   ☐☐ Never

15

Spain

The Spanish economy appears to be in an updraft. The GDP has been increasing at a rate of 3.3% in 2005 and is expected to grow by the same rate in 2006. An important lynchpin and the largest source of income for the Spanish economy remains, as in the past, tourism. Private consumption also showed satisfactory development and in 2006 – as was the case in 2005 – it is expected to grow more than 3% over the previous year. The Spanish consumer can be reached by direct marketing – especially colorful mailings are met here with curiosity and wide acceptance. Nearly 60% of the Spanish recipients take the time to read the direct mailing.

Demographic data

Area	504,782 square kilometers
Population	42.9 million
Number of households	14.2 million
Average household size	2.9 persons
Number of households with internet connection	3.5 million
Major cities/metropolitan areas (residents)	Madrid (3,016,788), Barcelona (1,527,190), Valencia (791,871), Seville (704,114), Saragossa (620,419), Malaga (535,686)
Population age 0-14	6.2 million
Population age 15-64	29.7 million
Population age 65 and up	7.2 million

(Source: Fischer Weltalmanach 2005, Bundesagentur für Außenwirtschaft 2005)

Direct marketing trends

More than half of all Spanish surveyed (55%) receive direct mail at least once a week, above the average for Western Europe. Only 21% state they almost never receive mailings.

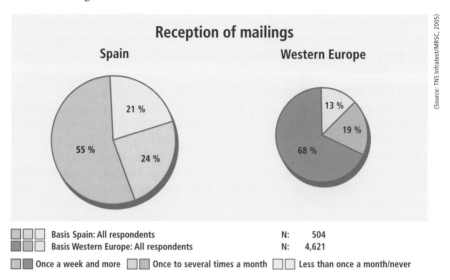

(Source: TNS Infratest/MRSC, 2005)

The Spanish surveyed who read mailings – a pleasing 58% do so regularly – respond to them more often than their neighbors in Western Europe: 33% at least once a year (Western Europe: 23%) and 14% more frequently (Western Europe: 12%). You can score points with Spanish consumers by means of the right sender

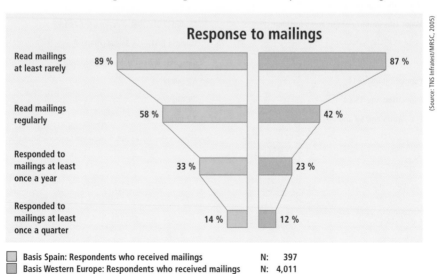

(Source: TNS Infratest/MRSC, 2005)

and a suitable form of address – top priorities for 78% of respondents. A well-known testimonial persuades 49%, compared with an average of 12% in Western Europe.

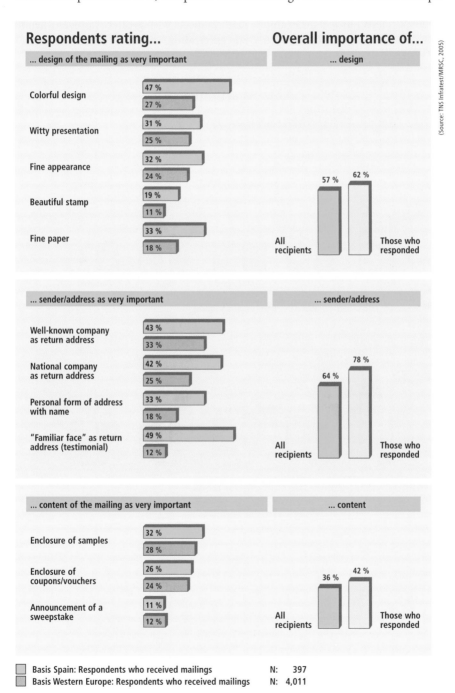

Respondents rating...

... design of the mailing as very important

Colorful design	47 % / 27 %
Witty presentation	31 % / 25 %
Fine appearance	32 % / 24 %
Beautiful stamp	19 % / 11 %
Fine paper	33 % / 18 %

Overall importance of...

... design

All recipients 57 % — Those who responded 62 %

... sender/address as very important

Well-known company as return address	43 % / 33 %
National company as return address	42 % / 25 %
Personal form of address with name	33 % / 18 %
"Familiar face" as return address (testimonial)	49 % / 12 %

... sender/address

All recipients 64 % — Those who responded 78 %

... content of the mailing as very important

Enclosure of samples	32 % / 28 %
Enclosure of coupons/vouchers	26 % / 24 %
Announcement of a sweepstake	11 % / 12 %

... content

All recipients 36 % — Those who responded 42 %

(Source: TNS Infratest/MRSC, 2005)

Basis Spain: Respondents who received mailings   N: 397
Basis Western Europe: Respondents who received mailings   N: 4,011

Design is also important to most Spanish (62% of respondents): A colorful mailing (47%) goes over far better with them compared with their neighbors (27%).

Overall, the Spanish have a greater affinity for advertising media than the average for Western Europe: for example, mailing meets with greater approval when it comes to informational content (16%) and entertainment value (16%). TV advertising also has an above-average following in Spain.

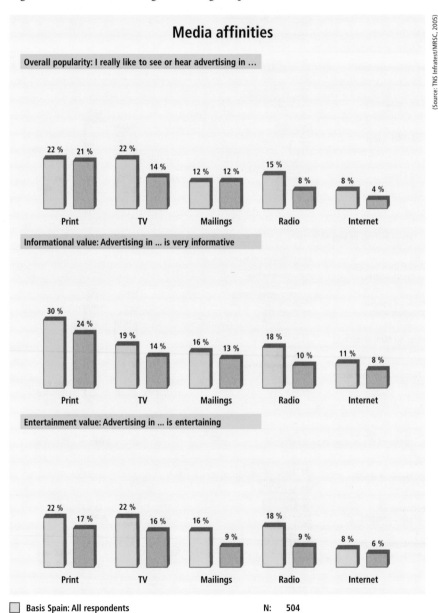

(Source: TNS Infratest/MRSC, 2005)

Media affinities

Overall popularity: I really like to see or hear advertising in …

	Print	TV	Mailings	Radio	Internet
Spain	22 %	22 %	12 %	15 %	8 %
Western Europe	21 %	14 %	12 %	8 %	4 %

Informational value: Advertising in … is very informative

	Print	TV	Mailings	Radio	Internet
Spain	30 %	19 %	16 %	18 %	11 %
Western Europe	24 %	14 %	13 %	10 %	8 %

Entertainment value: Advertising in … is entertaining

	Print	TV	Mailings	Radio	Internet
Spain	22 %	22 %	16 %	18 %	8 %
Western Europe	17 %	16 %	9 %	9 %	6 %

Basis Spain: All respondents   N: 504
Basis Western Europe: All respondents N: 4,621

Consumer trends

The brand (74%) and quality (66%) decisively shape the behavior of Spanish consumers. Price (51%) plays a greater role than among their Western European neighbors (35%). However, new providers also have good opportunities: Almost half of those surveyed (47%) like trying out new products, despite the fact that consumer patriotism (36%) is more prevalent than in the rest of Western Europe (23%).

(Source: TNS Infratest/MRSC, 2005)

Mail-order affinity

Compared with Western Europe, far fewer Spanish shop by mail-order: Only 6% frequently (Western Europe: 21%) and 76% never (Western Europe: 51%). 77% of users prefer conventional mail-order. The most popular way of ordering is the order card (63%).

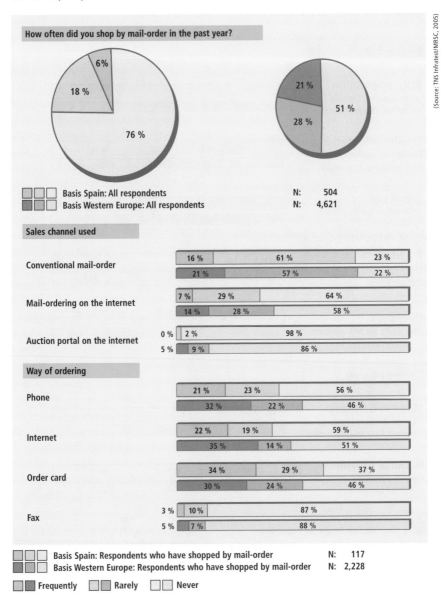

(Source: TNS Infratest/MRSC, 2005)

Switzerland

16

Exports and private consumption are expected to continue to fuel the economic growth in Switzerland – even when this proceeds at a moderate pace. The Swiss are hoping for an upturn in consumer sentiment thanks to the slight drop in the numbers of unemployed and higher real wages. Accordingly, growth for 2006 is forecasted at 2% higher than the previous year. The generally positive attitude of the quality minded Swiss consumer is reflected by their assessment of their living conditions: on a scale of 1 to 10, this is rated on average at 8.4. A colorful and witty approach to direct marketing finds success and success factor number one is choosing the right words for the target group.

Demographic data

Area	41,285 square kilometers
Population	7.4 million
Number of households	3.1 million
Average household size	2.4 persons
Number of households with internet connection	2.7 million
Major cities/metropolitan areas (residents)	Zurich (342,518), Geneva (177,535), Basel (165,051), Bern (122,707), Lausanne (116,232), Winterthur (90,152)
Population age 0-14	1.2 million
Population age 15-64	5.0 million
Population age 65 and up	1.2 million

(Source: Fischer Weltalmanach 2005, Bundesagentur für Außenwirtschaft 2005)

Direct marketing trends

Two-thirds (67%) of all Swiss surveyed state that they receive direct mail at least once a week, just slightly below the average for Western Europe (68%). However, an above-average number of Swiss (20%) almost never receive mailings.

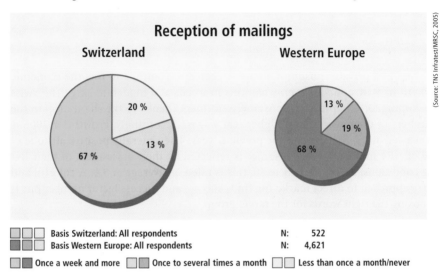

(Source: TNS Infratest/MRSC, 2005)

Reception of mailings

Switzerland   **Western Europe**

☐☐☐ Basis Switzerland: All respondents   N: 522
■■☐ Basis Western Europe: All respondents   N: 4,621

■■ Once a week and more   ☐☐ Once to several times a month   ☐☐ Less than once a month/never

Mailings go over well: 86% of recipients in Switzerland read advertising by mail. However, their response is more restrained compared with the rest of Western Europe: Only 8% of those who receive mailings and read them regularly respond frequently. The Swiss like it colorful (29%) and witty (26%) – a high-quality appear-

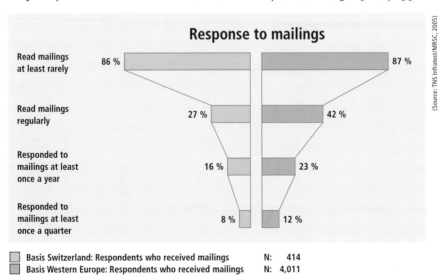

(Source: TNS Infratest/MRSC, 2005)

Response to mailings

Read mailings at least rarely   86 %   87 %

Read mailings regularly   27 %   42 %

Responded to mailings at least once a year   16 %   23 %

Responded to mailings at least once a quarter   8 %   12 %

☐ Basis Switzerland: Respondents who received mailings   N: 414
☐ Basis Western Europe: Respondents who received mailings N: 4,011

ance (18%) and fine paper (11%) tend to play a minor role. Overall, 66% of respondents feel design to be a very important element. Prize drawings (5%) are hardly a

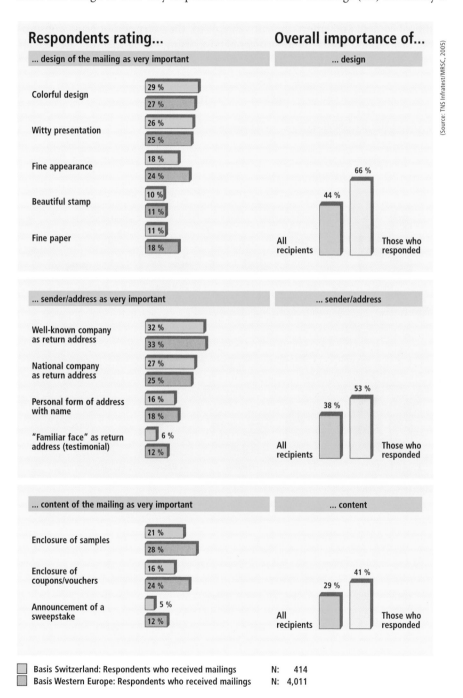

Respondents rating...

... design of the mailing as very important

Colorful design
- 29 %
- 27 %

Witty presentation
- 26 %
- 25 %

Fine appearance
- 18 %
- 24 %

Beautiful stamp
- 10 %
- 11 %

Fine paper
- 11 %
- 18 %

... sender/address as very important

Well-known company as return address
- 32 %
- 33 %

National company as return address
- 27 %
- 25 %

Personal form of address with name
- 16 %
- 18 %

"Familiar face" as return address (testimonial)
- 6 %
- 12 %

... content of the mailing as very important

Enclosure of samples
- 21 %
- 28 %

Enclosure of coupons/vouchers
- 16 %
- 24 %

Announcement of a sweepstake
- 5 %
- 12 %

Overall importance of...

... design

- All recipients: 44 %
- Those who responded: 66 %

... sender/address

- All recipients: 38 %
- Those who responded: 53 %

... content

- All recipients: 29 %
- Those who responded: 41 %

(Source: TNS Infratest/MRSC, 2005)

■ Basis Switzerland: Respondents who received mailings   N: 414
■ Basis Western Europe: Respondents who received mailings   N: 4,011

mean of achieving higher response rates among Swiss consumers – acceptance of them is well below the average for Europe (12%).

Print is way ahead of the other advertising media in terms of popularity, informational content and entertainment value. With the exception of print, consumers in Switzerland are far more critical of advertising media than the average for Western Europe.

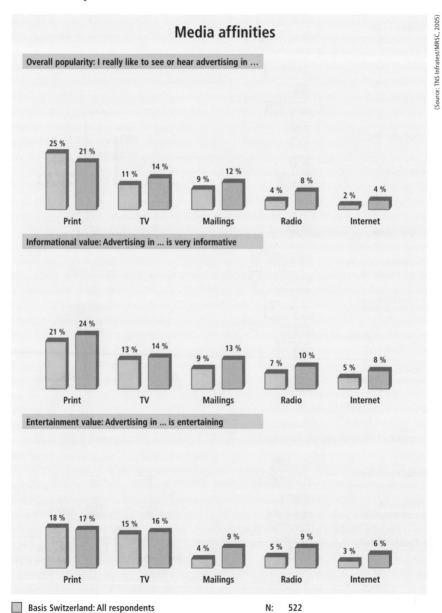

(Source: TNS Infratest/MRSC, 2005)

Consumer trends

Consumers in Switzerland are remarkably open: 53% state that they like trying out new products, demonstrating far more flexibility than their Western European neighbors (42%). In shopping, they decide in favor of a product on the basis of the brand (72%) and quality (69%). "Made in Germany" is regarded as a sign of quality by a good 29% of Swiss (Western Europe: 25%).

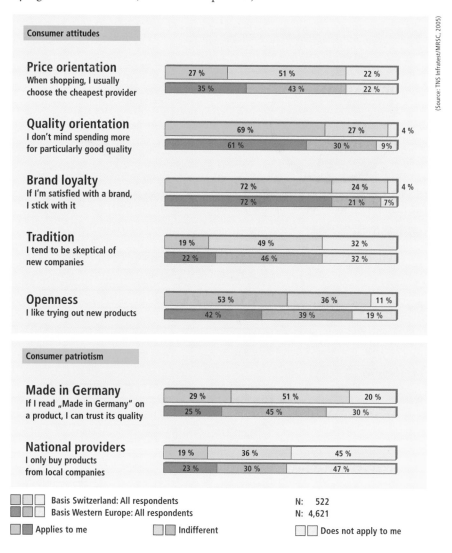

(Source: TNS Infratest/MRSC, 2005)

Consumer attitudes

Price orientation
When shopping, I usually choose the cheapest provider
27 % | 51 % | 22 %
35 % | 43 % | 22 %

Quality orientation
I don't mind spending more for particularly good quality
69 % | 27 % | 4 %
61 % | 30 % | 9 %

Brand loyalty
If I'm satisfied with a brand, I stick with it
72 % | 24 % | 4 %
72 % | 21 % | 7 %

Tradition
I tend to be skeptical of new companies
19 % | 49 % | 32 %
22 % | 46 % | 32 %

Openness
I like trying out new products
53 % | 36 % | 11 %
42 % | 39 % | 19 %

Consumer patriotism

Made in Germany
If I read „Made in Germany" on a product, I can trust its quality
29 % | 51 % | 20 %
25 % | 45 % | 30 %

National providers
I only buy products from local companies
19 % | 36 % | 45 %
23 % | 30 % | 47 %

Basis Switzerland: All respondents   N: 522
Basis Western Europe: All respondents   N: 4,621

Applies to me   Indifferent   Does not apply to me

Mail-order affinity

More than half of those surveyed shop by mail-order frequently or occasionally (55%), slightly above the average for Western Europe (49%). The Swiss have an affinity for the internet as a sales channel (20%) and also use this medium particularly often to order goods (43%). At the same time, ordering by order card (34%) is above the trend for Western Europe (30%).

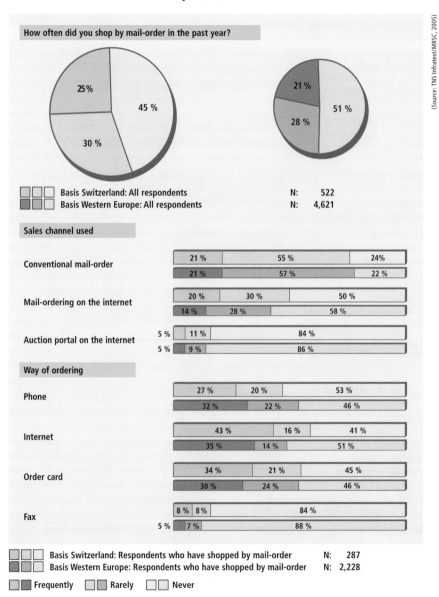

(Source: TNS Infratest/MRSC, 2005)

Denmark

17

Thanks to the sustained strength of private consumption and the rising investments, the Danish economy continued the positive growth evident in 2005. In particular, the strong demand for new cars, furniture and luxury goods kept consumer
spending at a high level. A comparison to the previous year shows that consumption in 2005 increased by about 5.6% and 2006 it is projected to grow by an additional 3.5%. The fact that the Danes are among the most satisfied people and the
country is one of the wealthiest in the world provides two more sound reasons to
pursue business in this country. A straightforward argumentation – in advertising
as in business – is the best way to convince the Danes.

Demographic data

Area	43,096 square kilometers
Population	5.4 million
Number of households	2.5 million
Average household size	2.2 persons
Number of households with internet connection	1.65 million
Major cities/metropolitan areas (residents)	Copenhagen (501,664), Aarhus (222,559), Odense (145,374), Aalborg (121,100), Frederiksberg (91,721)
Population age 0-14	1.0 million
Population age 15-64	3.6 million
Population age 65 and up	0.8 million

(Source: Fischer Weltalmanach 2005, Bundesagentur für Außenwirtschaft 2005)

Direct marketing trends

Only a quarter of Danish respondents receive direct mail at least once a week – the average for Scandinavia is 62%. In comparison, 41% of Danes state that they almost never receive mailings.

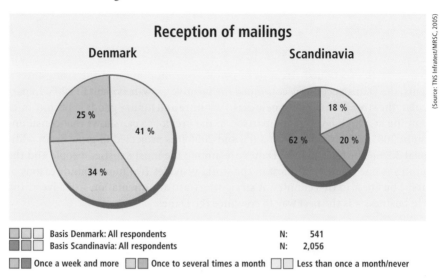

Danes' response to mailings is somewhat more reserved than their Scandinavian neighbors: Only 29% read mailings regularly (Scandinavia: 36%). 4% respond to direct mail several times a year – compared with an average of 13% for Scandinavia. 28% of all recipients and 33% of those who respond attach top priority to the sender

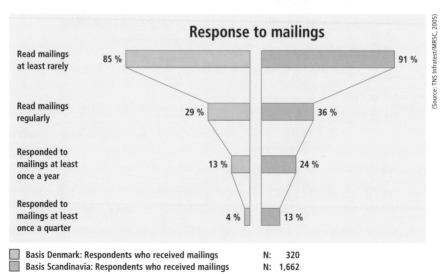

and form of address: A well-known sender or a company hailing from Denmark is a good mean of attracting 22% of respondents. Design is very important for 28%

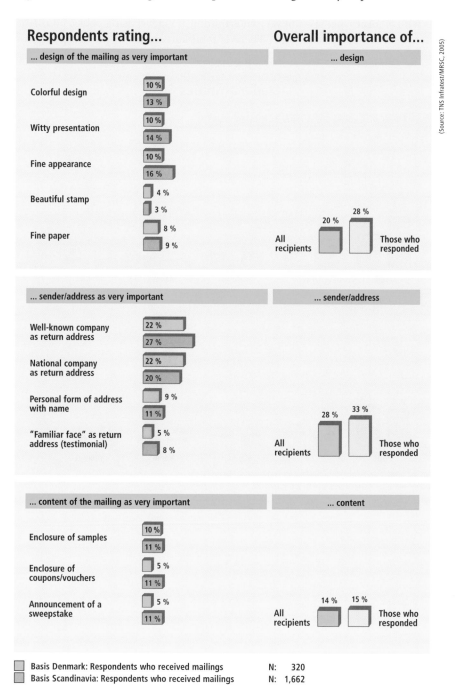

(Source: TNS Infratest/MRSC, 2005)

of those who respond: An average of 10% state that they prefer to receive colorful, high-quality and witty mailings.

The Danish respondents like print advertising and find it informative, although – as with all other media – not very entertaining. TV advertising polls a poor 10% in terms of entertainment value. There is total agreement on the acceptance of mailings: The Danes are right on the average for Scandinavia.

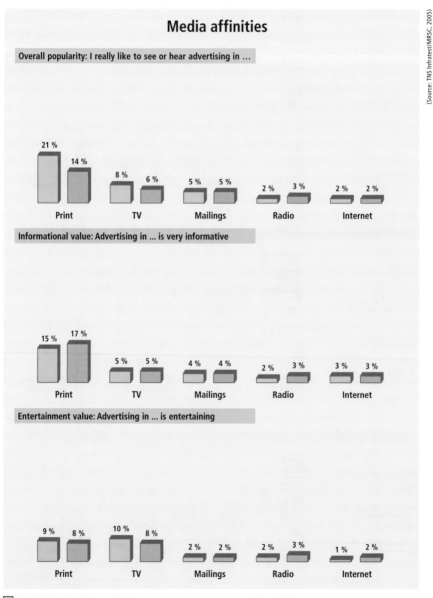

(Source: TNS Infratest/MRSC, 2005)

Consumer trends

Quality wins in the view of 66% of Danish consumers. However, price (61%) and the brand (60%) play an important role in the purchase decision. Danes are well above the average for Scandinavia (39%) when it comes to price orientation.

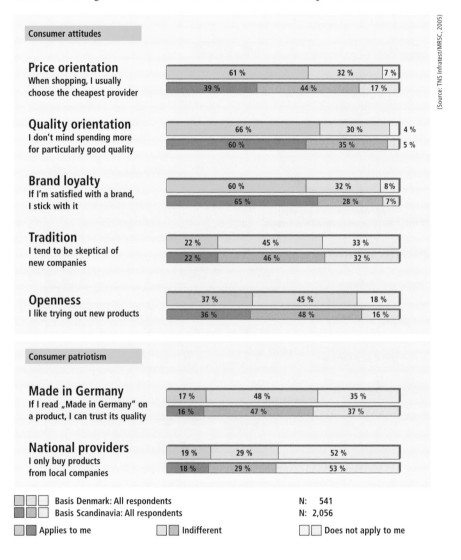

Consumer attitudes

Price orientation
When shopping, I usually choose the cheapest provider
- 61 % | 32 % | 7 %
- 39 % | 44 % | 17 %

Quality orientation
I don't mind spending more for particularly good quality
- 66 % | 30 % | 4 %
- 60 % | 35 % | 5 %

Brand loyalty
If I'm satisfied with a brand, I stick with it
- 60 % | 32 % | 8 %
- 65 % | 28 % | 7 %

Tradition
I tend to be skeptical of new companies
- 22 % | 45 % | 33 %
- 22 % | 46 % | 32 %

Openness
I like trying out new products
- 37 % | 45 % | 18 %
- 36 % | 48 % | 16 %

Consumer patriotism

Made in Germany
If I read „Made in Germany" on a product, I can trust its quality
- 17 % | 48 % | 35 %
- 16 % | 47 % | 37 %

National providers
I only buy products from local companies
- 19 % | 29 % | 52 %
- 18 % | 29 % | 53 %

Basis Denmark: All respondents   N: 541
Basis Scandinavia: All respondents   N: 2,056

Applies to me   Indifferent   Does not apply to me

(Source: TNS Infratest/MRSC, 2005)

Mail-order affinity

Mail-order in Denmark is slightly below the Scandinavian mean: 44% say they have shopped this way in the past year (Scandinavia: 51%). The internet (68%) ranks ahead of the catalog (56%) as a sales channel. 77% of consumers also order directly online – and 59% of them frequently.

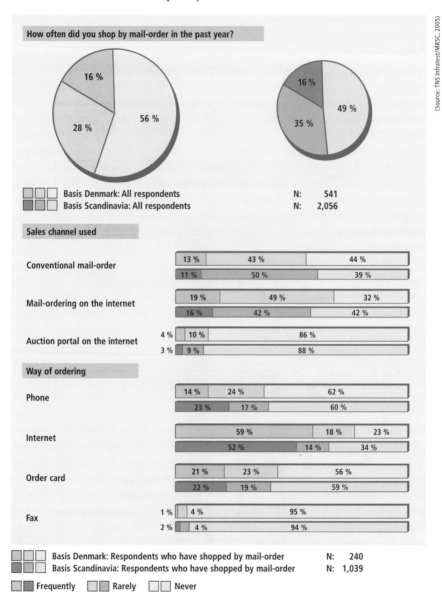

(Source: TNS Infratest/MRSC, 2005)

Finland

18

Finland's economy grows steadily even though the business situation in 2005 appears to have hit a slower period. Private consumption in 2005 increased by 3.4% and, for 2006, is projected to add another 3% compared to the previous year. The country is a world leader in the microelectronics and mobile telephone industries. Direct marketing is used on a wide scale here and the most popular mean of response is the order card.

Demographic data

Area	338,144 square kilometers
Population	5.2 million
Number of households	2.4 million
Average household size	2.2 persons
Number of households with internet connection	1.1 million
Major cities/metropolitan areas (residents)	Helsinki (559,330), Espoo (224,231), Tampere (200,966), Vantaa (184,039), Turku (175,059)
Population age 0-14	0.9 million
Population age 15-64	3.5 million
Population age 65 and up	0.8 million

(Source: Fischer Weltalmanach 2005, Bundesagentur für Außenwirtschaft 2005)

Direct marketing trends

Finland surpasses the average for Scandinavia in terms of mailing density: 69% of respondents state that they receive direct mail at least once a week (Scandinavia: 62%). Only 5% receive almost no mailings (Scandinavia: 18%).

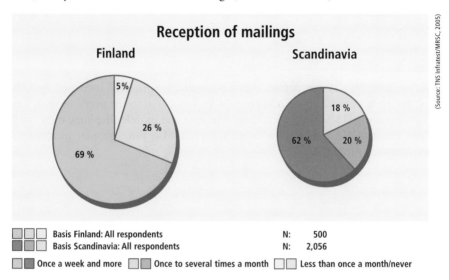

Reception of mailings

Finland

Scandinavia

Basis Finland: All respondents   N: 500
Basis Scandinavia: All respondents   N: 2,056

Once a week and more   Once to several times a month   Less than once a month/never

(Source: TNS Infratest/MRSC, 2005)

Finnish consumers are more willing to respond than their Scandinavian neighbors: 41% read their mailings regularly (Scandinavia: 36%). Of those who read them, 15% respond at least once a quarter (Scandinavia: 13%). The sender and form

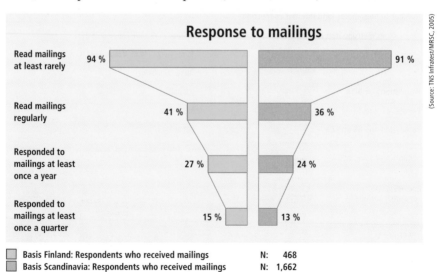

Response to mailings

	Finland	Scandinavia
Read mailings at least rarely	94 %	91 %
Read mailings regularly	41 %	36 %
Responded to mailings at least once a year	27 %	24 %
Responded to mailings at least once a quarter	15 %	13 %

Basis Finland: Respondents who received mailings   N: 468
Basis Scandinavia: Respondents who received mailings   N: 1,662

(Source: TNS Infratest/MRSC, 2005)

of address are crucial in the view of 63% of those who respond. As a result, Finnish consumers bear out a Scandinavian attitude, although their figure is above-

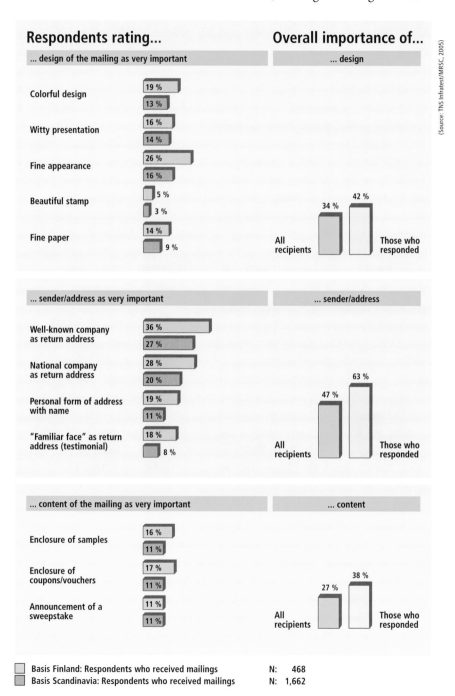

(Source: TNS Infratest/MRSC, 2005)

Respondents rating...

... design of the mailing as very important

Colorful design — 19 % / 13 %
Witty presentation — 16 % / 14 %
Fine appearance — 26 % / 16 %
Beautiful stamp — 5 % / 3 %
Fine paper — 14 % / 9 %

... sender/address as very important

Well-known company as return address — 36 % / 27 %
National company as return address — 28 % / 20 %
Personal form of address with name — 19 % / 11 %
"Familiar face" as return address (testimonial) — 18 % / 8 %

... content of the mailing as very important

Enclosure of samples — 16 % / 11 %
Enclosure of coupons/vouchers — 17 % / 11 %
Announcement of a sweepstake — 11 % / 11 %

Overall importance of...

... design

All recipients 34 % — Those who responded 42 %

... sender/address

All recipients 47 % — Those who responded 63 %

... content

All recipients 27 % — Those who responded 38 %

Basis Finland: Respondents who received mailings   N: 468
Basis Scandinavia: Respondents who received mailings   N: 1,662

average: 36% trust a well-known sender, compared with the Scandinavian mean of 27%.

Print media come out ahead in all three categories, especially regarding their informational value (26%). This means that with regard to mailings a creative approach with a little more entertainment value is needed to garner more attention in Finland.

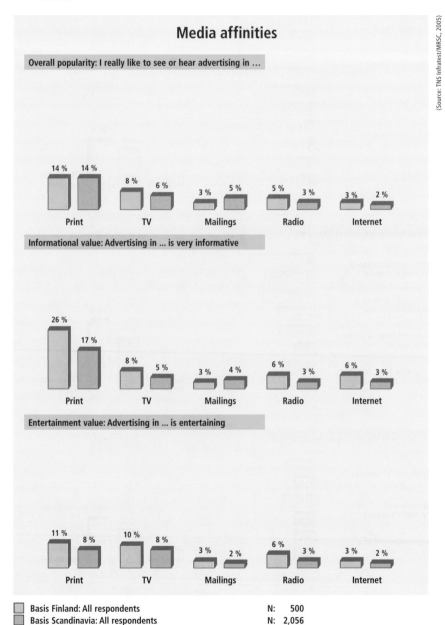

(Source: TNS Infratest/MRSC, 2005)

Consumer trends

Above all, Finnish consumers are loyal to a brand: 68% stick with a brand if they are satisfied with it – the Scandinavian mean is 65%. Good quality has its price: 54% are willing to spend more for it.

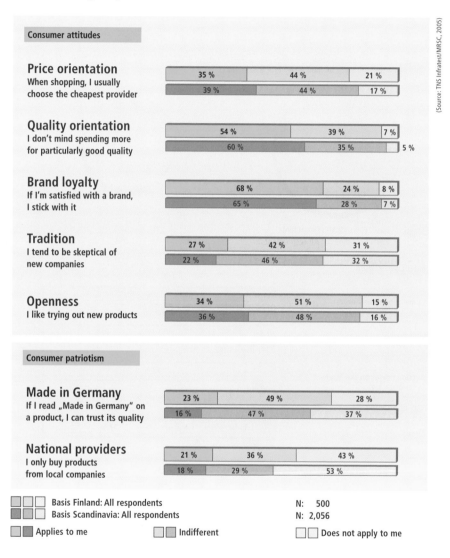

(Source: TNS Infratest/MRSC, 2005)

Consumer attitudes

Price orientation
When shopping, I usually choose the cheapest provider
35 % | 44 % | 21 %
39 % | 44 % | 17 %

Quality orientation
I don't mind spending more for particularly good quality
54 % | 39 % | 7 %
60 % | 35 % | 5 %

Brand loyalty
If I'm satisfied with a brand, I stick with it
68 % | 24 % | 8 %
65 % | 28 % | 7 %

Tradition
I tend to be skeptical of new companies
27 % | 42 % | 31 %
22 % | 46 % | 32 %

Openness
I like trying out new products
34 % | 51 % | 15 %
36 % | 48 % | 16 %

Consumer patriotism

Made in Germany
If I read „Made in Germany" on a product, I can trust its quality
23 % | 49 % | 28 %
16 % | 47 % | 37 %

National providers
I only buy products from local companies
21 % | 36 % | 43 %
18 % | 29 % | 53 %

Basis Finland: All respondents   N: 500
Basis Scandinavia: All respondents   N: 2,056

Applies to me   Indifferent   Does not apply to me

Mail-order affinity

Finnish consumers are divided about mail-ordering: 50% use it – 13% frequently and 37% occasionally – and 50% of respondents never shop this way. Of those who use this channel, a majority (68%) prefer conventional mail-order. 57% order the product over the internet. Second place is shared by the order card and phone (43% each).

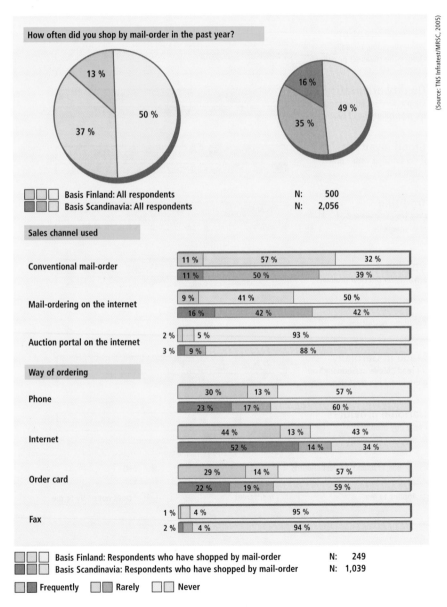

How often did you shop by mail-order in the past year?

13 %
50 %
37 %

16 %
49 %
35 %

Basis Finland: All respondents   N: 500
Basis Scandinavia: All respondents   N: 2,056

Sales channel used

Conventional mail-order
11 % | 57 % | 32 %
11 % | 50 % | 39 %

Mail-ordering on the internet
9 % | 41 % | 50 %
16 % | 42 % | 42 %

Auction portal on the internet
2 % | 5 % | 93 %
3 % | 9 % | 88 %

Way of ordering

Phone
30 % | 13 % | 57 %
23 % | 17 % | 60 %

Internet
44 % | 13 % | 43 %
52 % | 14 % | 34 %

Order card
29 % | 14 % | 57 %
22 % | 19 % | 59 %

Fax
1 % | 4 % | 95 %
2 % | 4 % | 94 %

Basis Finland: Respondents who have shopped by mail-order   N: 249
Basis Scandinavia: Respondents who have shopped by mail-order   N: 1,039

Frequently   Rarely   Never

(Source: TNS Infratest/MRSC, 2005)

Norway

19

The Norwegian economy continued to experience a strong upswing in 2005. The increase in the GDP for the year 2006 is expected to reach 3.4%; private consumption rose in 2005 and projections for 2006 are calling for about a 3.6% increase. Direct marketing is widely used in Norway and also widely accepted – above all when providing information about a quality product in a clever way and emphasizing the benefits of the product.

Demographic data

Area	323,759 square kilometers
Population	4.6 million
Number of households	2.0 million
Average household size	2.3 persons
Number of households with internet connection	1.2 million
Major cities/metropolitan areas (residents)	Oslo (521,886), Bergen (237,430), Trondheim (154,351), Stavanger (112,405), Baerum (103,313), Kristiansand (75,280)
Population age 0-14	1.0 million
Population age 15-64	3.0 million
Population age 65 and up	0.6 million

(Source: Fischer Weltalmanach 2005, Bundesagentur für Außenwirtschaft 2005)

Direct marketing trends

76% of Norwegian respondents receive direct mail at least once a week (Scandinavia: 62%). Only 14% say that they receive almost no mailings. This means the mailing density is well above the average for Scandinavia.

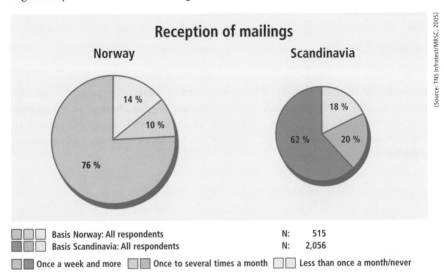

(Source: TNS Infratest/MRSC, 2005)

Norwegians have a slightly lower affinity for mailings than their Scandinavian neighbors: 90% read them occasionally and 30% regularly. Their response to them is somewhat more reserved: 9% respond several times a year (Scandinavia: 13%).

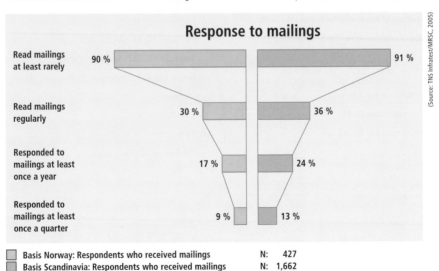

(Source: TNS Infratest/MRSC, 2005)

Compared with their Scandinavian neighbors, Norwegians have fewer priorities overall. 21% of those who respond attach great importance to the sender or

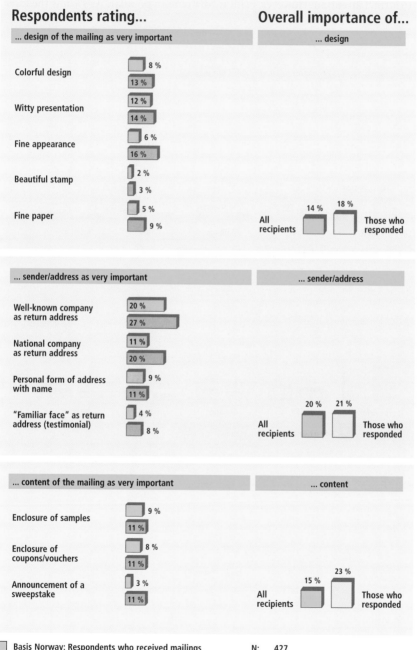

Respondents rating...

... design of the mailing as very important

Colorful design — 8 % / 13 %

Witty presentation — 12 % / 14 %

Fine appearance — 6 % / 16 %

Beautiful stamp — 2 % / 3 %

Fine paper — 5 % / 9 %

Overall importance of...

... design

All recipients 14 % — Those who responded 18 %

... sender/address as very important

Well-known company as return address — 20 % / 27 %

National company as return address — 11 % / 20 %

Personal form of address with name — 9 % / 11 %

"Familiar face" as return address (testimonial) — 4 % / 8 %

... sender/address

All recipients 20 % — Those who responded 21 %

... content of the mailing as very important

Enclosure of samples — 9 % / 11 %

Enclosure of coupons/vouchers — 8 % / 11 %

Announcement of a sweepstake — 3 % / 11 %

... content

All recipients 15 % — Those who responded 23 %

(Source: TNS Infratest/MRSC, 2005)

Basis Norway: Respondents who received mailings   N: 427
Basis Scandinavia: Respondents who received mailings   N: 1,662

address. A particularly decisive factor for 20% of mailing recipients is whether the company is well-known.

The Scandinavian trend is also reflected in Norway: It is not easy for advertising to attract attention. However, print media remain popular. At 9% it is the most

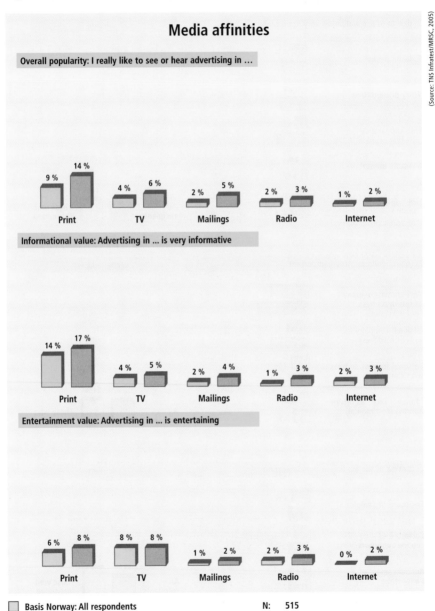

(Source: TNS Infratest/MRSC, 2005)

favored form of advertisement and at 14% the most informative. It is only beaten by TV advertising (8%) when it comes to entertainment value (print: 6%).

Consumer trends

Norwegian consumers are strongly swayed by brand (65%) and quality (61%). However, they also give new products a chance (39%) – only 13% of respondents are skeptical of new providers. Consumer patriotism is also not pronounced: Only 12% opt solely for "Made in Norway".

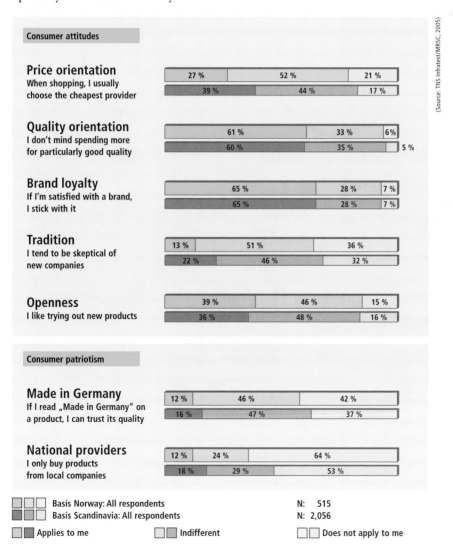

(Source: TNS Infratest/MRSC, 2005)

Consumer attitudes

Price orientation
When shopping, I usually choose the cheapest provider
27 % | 52 % | 21 %
39 % | 44 % | 17 %

Quality orientation
I don't mind spending more for particularly good quality
61 % | 33 % | 6%
60 % | 35 % | 5 %

Brand loyalty
If I'm satisfied with a brand, I stick with it
65 % | 28 % | 7 %
65 % | 28 % | 7 %

Tradition
I tend to be skeptical of new companies
13 % | 51 % | 36 %
22 % | 46 % | 32 %

Openness
I like trying out new products
39 % | 46 % | 15 %
36 % | 48 % | 16 %

Consumer patriotism

Made in Germany
If I read „Made in Germany" on a product, I can trust its quality
12 % | 46 % | 42 %
16 % | 47 % | 37 %

National providers
I only buy products from local companies
12 % | 24 % | 64 %
18 % | 29 % | 53 %

Basis Norway: All respondents   N: 515
Basis Scandinavia: All respondents   N: 2,056

Applies to me   Indifferent   Does not apply to me

Mail-order affinity

55% of Norwegian respondents state that they have ordered by mail in the past year –
and 17% of them frequently. The internet (58%) is just ahead of the catalog (56%) as
the preferred sales channel. However, most consumers also order directly online –
54% frequently and 12% now and again.

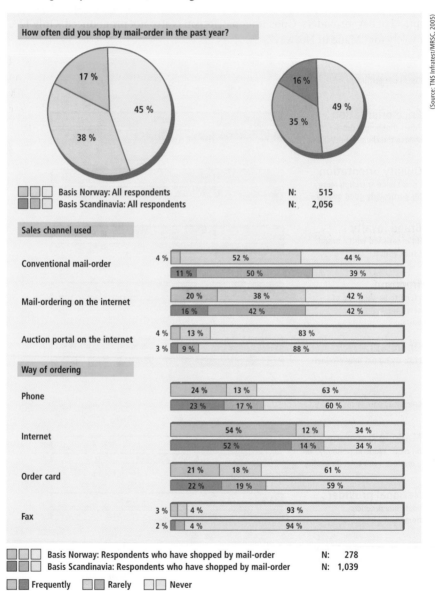

(Source: TNS Infratest/MRSC, 2005)

Sweden was unable to maintain the pace of the 2004 economic growth because of slower export sales. However, a rising level of private consumption provided an important impulse for the growth achieved in 2005 which was slightly below 3% and forecasts call for a further increase of 3.5% in 2006. Here, new records were achieved in direct marketing. Of all 24 countries in the study, Sweden leads in the response ranking: 26% of all recipients of direct mailings respond frequently.

Demographic data

Area	449,964 square kilometers
Population	9.0 million
Number of households	4.5 million
Average household size	2.0 persons
Number of households with internet connection	6.0 million
Major cities/metropolitan areas (residents)	Stockholm (761,721), Göteborg (478,055), Malmö (267,171), Uppsala (180,669), Linköping (136,231), Västeras (129,987)
Population age 0-14	1.6 million
Population age 15-64	5.9 million
Population age 65 and up	1.5 million

(Source: Fischer Weltalmanach 2005, Bundesagentur für Außenwirtschaft 2005)

Direct marketing trends

Sweden's consumers receive direct mail regularly – 80% as much as at least once a week, well above the average for Scandinavia (62%). Only 10% say that they receive almost no mailings (Scandinavia: 18%).

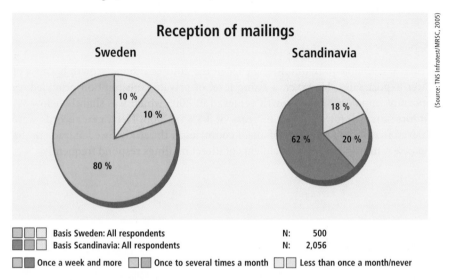

Swedes have a very high affinity for mailings: 93% read them occasionally and 45% even do so regularly (Scandinavia: 36%). Their response to them is also above the Scandinavian mean: A pleasing 26% respond to mailings at least once a quarter (Scandinavia: 13%). What is in the mailing counts: 34% of all recipients and 47%

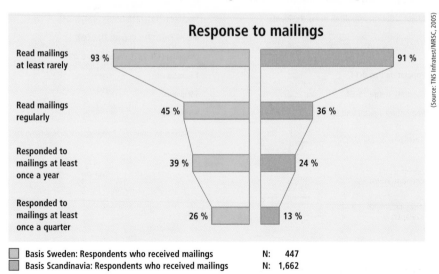

of those who respond to direct mail attach the most importance to content. Prize drawings are a big incentive for a quarter of those surveyed – far more than in the

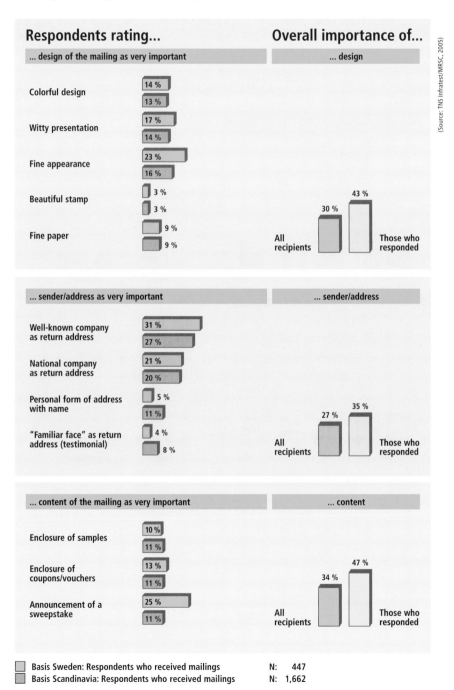

(Source: TNS Infratest/MRSC, 2005)

Basis Sweden: Respondents who received mailings   N: 447
Basis Scandinavia: Respondents who received mailings   N: 1,662

rest of Scandinavia (11%). A well-known company as the return address scores with 31% of Swedes.

Mailings are ahead of TV advertising in terms of overall popularity (10%) and informational value (7%); only print fares better. Overall, the Swedes have slightly more affinity for mailings than their Scandinavian neighbors – all the other advertising media meet with very little approval on average.

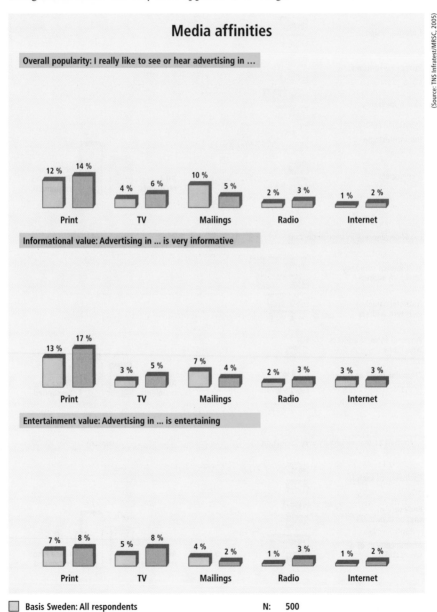

(Source: TNS Infratest/MRSC, 2005)

Consumer trends

The brand (68%) and quality (57%) induce Swedish respondents to purchase. Only one-third usually choose the cheapest product (Scandinavia: 39%). Companies from other countries are in a good position, as only 19% prefer national providers.

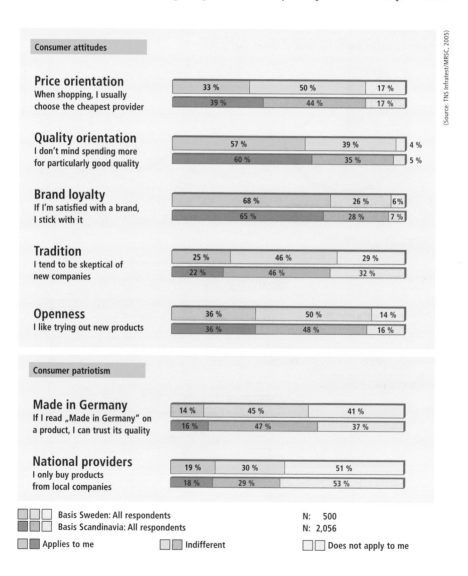

Consumer attitudes

Price orientation
When shopping, I usually
choose the cheapest provider

33 % | 50 % | 17 %
39 % | 44 % | 17 %

Quality orientation
I don't mind spending more
for particularly good quality

57 % | 39 % | 4 %
60 % | 35 % | 5 %

Brand loyalty
If I'm satisfied with a brand,
I stick with it

68 % | 26 % | 6%
65 % | 28 % | 7 %

Tradition
I tend to be skeptical of
new companies

25 % | 46 % | 29 %
22 % | 46 % | 32 %

Openness
I like trying out new products

36 % | 50 % | 14 %
36 % | 48 % | 16 %

Consumer patriotism

Made in Germany
If I read „Made in Germany" on
a product, I can trust its quality

14 % | 45 % | 41 %
16 % | 47 % | 37 %

National providers
I only buy products
from local companies

19 % | 30 % | 51 %
18 % | 29 % | 53 %

Basis Sweden: All respondents   N: 500
Basis Scandinavia: All respondents   N: 2,056

Applies to me   Indifferent   Does not apply to me

(Source: TNS Infratest/MRSC, 2005)

Mail-order affinity

More than half of Swedish respondents have used mail-order in the past year – 19% of them frequently. As a result, they are just above the average for Scandinavia. Most (63%) choose the goods they want using the conventional catalog. However, the Swedes prefer the internet as a mean of ordering (65%).

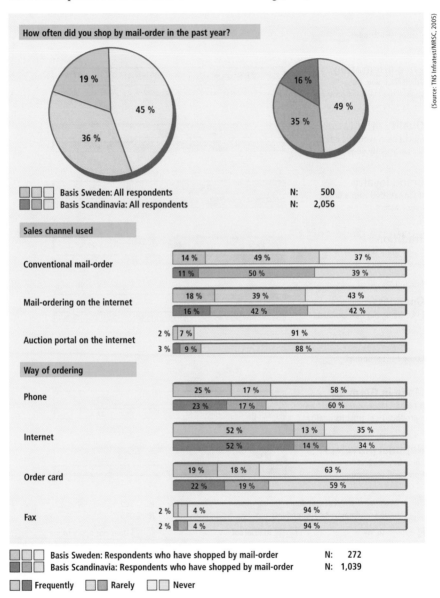

(Source: TNS Infratest/MRSC, 2005)

Czech Republic

21

The Czech Republic can look back on an exciting second year as a member state of the EU. GDP rose in 2005 in comparison to the previous year by 6%. The private consumption in 2006, as in 2005, should continue to grow by almost 3%. The statistically rapid rise may be attributed to the outstanding preparation by the business community for the membership in the EU. The automotive industry forms the foundation of this success. The results of direct marketing are also very respectable: in terms of popularity and information value, mailings rank higher than television, radio and internet ads. Every fifth recipient of a direct mailing replies frequently.

Demographic data

Area	78,866 square kilometers
Population	10.2 million
Number of households	4.0 million
Average household size	2.5 persons
Number of households with internet connection	0.6 million
Major cities/metropolitan areas (residents)	Prague (1,178,576), Brno (379,185), Ostrava (319,293), Pilzen (166,274), Olomuc (103,293), Liberec (99,832)
Population age 0-14	1.6 million
Population age 15-64	7.2 million
Population age 65 and up	1.4 million

(Source: Fischer Weltalmanach 2005, Bundesagentur für Außenwirtschaft 2005)

Direct marketing trends

65% of Czechs surveyed receive direct mail several times a month – and one-third state that they receive mailings at least once a week. As a result, mailing density in the Czech Republic is a little below the Eastern European average.

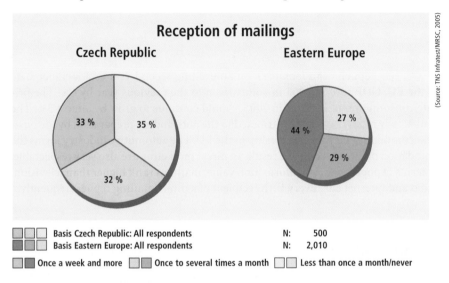

94% of Czech recipients of direct mail read it – and a majority (54%) do so regularly. Their response is very lively compared with Eastern Europe: An above-average 36% respond to mailings at least once a year and 20% even once a quarter (compared with 28% and 14% respectively in Eastern Europe). Design is key: 53%

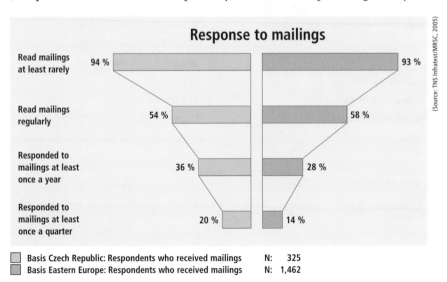

of respondents and 45% of all recipients in the Czech Republic attach great importance to the esthetics of mailings. In particular, a colorful design (33%) and fine

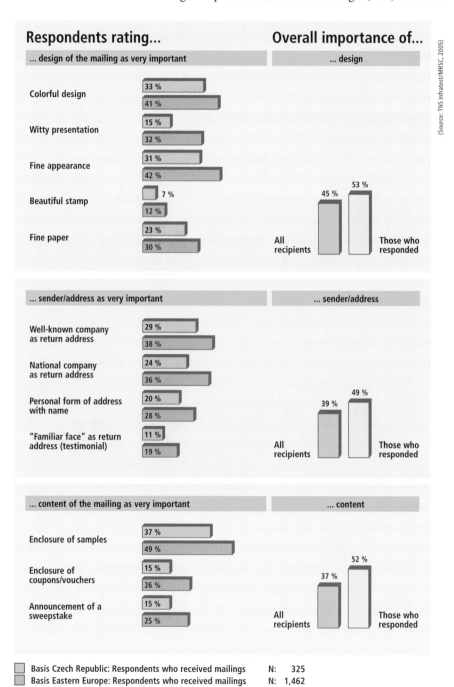

Respondents rating...

... design of the mailing as very important

Colorful design — 33 % / 41 %

Witty presentation — 15 % / 32 %

Fine appearance — 31 % / 42 %

Beautiful stamp — 7 % / 12 %

Fine paper — 23 % / 30 %

Overall importance of...

... design

All recipients 45 % — Those who responded 53 %

... sender/address as very important

Well-known company as return address — 29 % / 38 %

National company as return address — 24 % / 36 %

Personal form of address with name — 20 % / 28 %

"Familiar face" as return address (testimonial) — 11 % / 19 %

... sender/address

All recipients 39 % — Those who responded 49 %

... content of the mailing as very important

Enclosure of samples — 37 % / 49 %

Enclosure of coupons/vouchers — 15 % / 26 %

Announcement of a sweepstake — 15 % / 25 %

... content

All recipients 37 % — Those who responded 52 %

Basis Czech Republic: Respondents who received mailings   N: 325
Basis Eastern Europe: Respondents who received mailings   N: 1,462

(Source: TNS Infratest/MRSC, 2005)

appearance (31%) go down very well. With regard to content, 37% of those surveyed have a positive opinion of enclosed samples.

Although print dominates all the categories – popularity, informational content and entertainment value – ahead of all other advertising media, mailings come second in terms of informational content and popularity – before TV, radio or internet advertising.

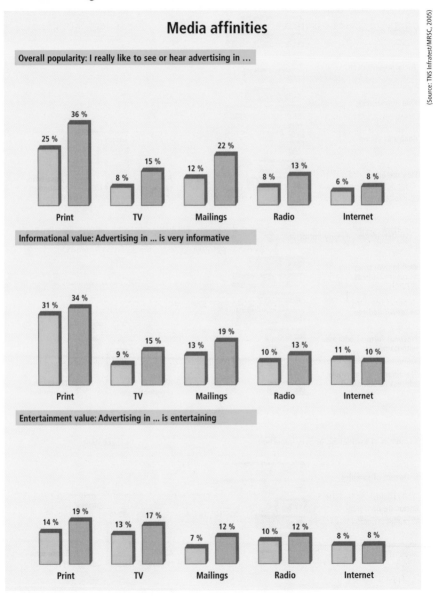

(Source: TNS Infratest/MRSC, 2005)

Consumer trends

76% of Czech consumers swear by brand loyalty – provided they are satisfied with the brand. Moreover, 60% of those surveyed are willing to spend a bit more for good quality (Eastern Europe: 55%). They are also very tolerant when it comes to choice of product: Only 16% are skeptical of new providers, whereas 37% state they like trying out new products. Good news for foreign providers: Few Czechs are patriotic in their consumption habits; just 24% only buy products from national companies.

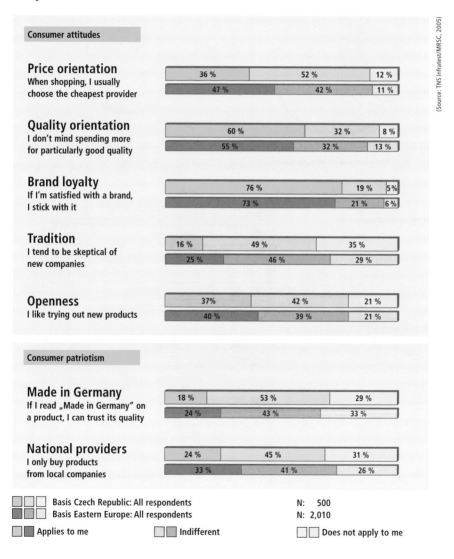

(Source: TNS Infratest/MRSC, 2005)

Consumer attitudes

Price orientation
When shopping, I usually choose the cheapest provider
- 36 % | 52 % | 12 %
- 47 % | 42 % | 11 %

Quality orientation
I don't mind spending more for particularly good quality
- 60 % | 32 % | 8 %
- 55 % | 32 % | 13 %

Brand loyalty
If I'm satisfied with a brand, I stick with it
- 76 % | 19 % | 5 %
- 73 % | 21 % | 6 %

Tradition
I tend to be skeptical of new companies
- 16 % | 49 % | 35 %
- 25 % | 46 % | 29 %

Openness
I like trying out new products
- 37% | 42 % | 21 %
- 40 % | 39 % | 21 %

Consumer patriotism

Made in Germany
If I read „Made in Germany" on a product, I can trust its quality
- 18 % | 53 % | 29 %
- 24 % | 43 % | 33 %

National providers
I only buy products from local companies
- 24 % | 45 % | 31 %
- 33 % | 41 % | 26 %

Basis Czech Republic: All respondents   N: 500
Basis Eastern Europe: All respondents   N: 2,010

Applies to me   Indifferent   Does not apply to me

Mail-order affinity

Compared with Eastern Europe, the Czechs are ahead by a nose in terms of affinity for mail-ordering. More than half (51%) state that they have shopped by this channel in the past year (Eastern Europe: 34%). Conventional mail-ordering, i.e., the catalog, is used by 83%; the internet trails well behind in second place (39%).

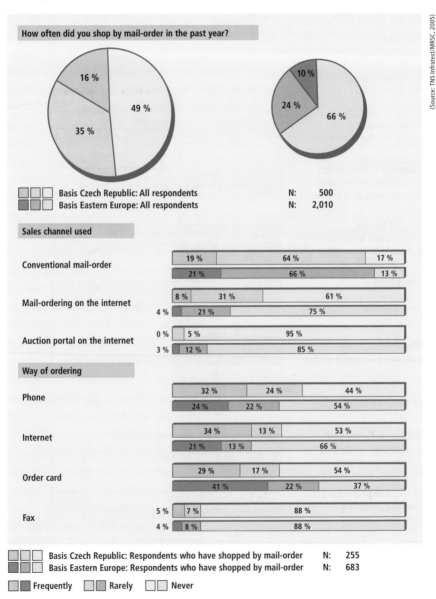

How often did you shop by mail-order in the past year?

16 % / 49 % / 35 %

10 % / 24 % / 66 %

Basis Czech Republic: All respondents   N: 500
Basis Eastern Europe: All respondents   N: 2,010

Sales channel used

Conventional mail-order
19 % | 64 % | 17 %
21 % | 66 % | 13 %

Mail-ordering on the internet
8 % | 31 % | 61 %
4 % | 21 % | 75 %

Auction portal on the internet
0 % | 5 % | 95 %
3 % | 12 % | 85 %

Way of ordering

Phone
32 % | 24 % | 44 %
24 % | 22 % | 54 %

Internet
34 % | 13 % | 53 %
21 % | 13 % | 66 %

Order card
29 % | 17 % | 54 %
41 % | 22 % | 37 %

Fax
5 % | 7 % | 88 %
4 % | 8 % | 88 %

Basis Czech Republic: Respondents who have shopped by mail-order   N: 255
Basis Eastern Europe: Respondents who have shopped by mail-order   N: 683

Frequently   Rarely   Never

(Source: TNS Infratest/MRSC, 2005)

Hungary

22

The economic growth expected to accompany EU membership and the start provided by development funds should begin to show clearly visible returns by the early year 2006. Growth industries of the future like biotechnology, information technology and logistics should support structural change in Hungary and move the country closer to EU levels in the near future. The private consumption shows a rise of 3.5 to 4.0% in 2006. Direct marketing enjoys a great popularity in Hungary and even ranks ahead of TV-ads. Nearly 70% of the recipients of direct mailings regularly take the time to read it.

Demographic data

Area	93,030 square kilometers
Population	10.1 million
Number of households	3.8 million
Average household size	2.6 persons
Number of households with internet connection	0.5 million
Major cities/metropolitan areas (residents)	Budapest (1,739,569), Debrecen (206,564), Miskolc (182,408), Szeged (163,699), Pécs (159,794), Györ (129,287)
Population age 0-14	1.6 million
Population age 15-64	6.9 million
Population age 65 and up	1.6 million

(Source: Fischer Weltalmanach 2005, Bundesagentur für Außenwirtschaft 2005)

Direct marketing trends

The mailing density in Hungary is astoundingly far above the Eastern European average: 72% of those surveyed receive mailings at least once a week (Eastern Europe: 44%). Only 7% say they almost never receive any mailings.

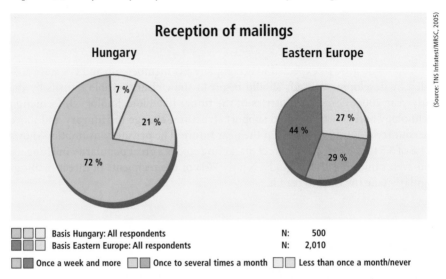

Hungarians respond with more curiosity to mailings than their Eastern European neighbors: 93% read them occasionally, and 68% even turn out to be regular readers (Eastern Europe: 58%). However, those surveyed prove to be more restrained in their response: Just under a quarter respond to mailings at least once a year (Eastern Europe: 28%). The design of a mailing is essential: 74% of all recipi-

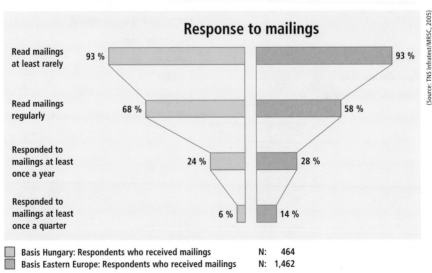

ents and 84% of respondents attach crucial priority to esthetics. It should also be colorful (56%) and witty (49%) and – particularly important – also have a fine ap-

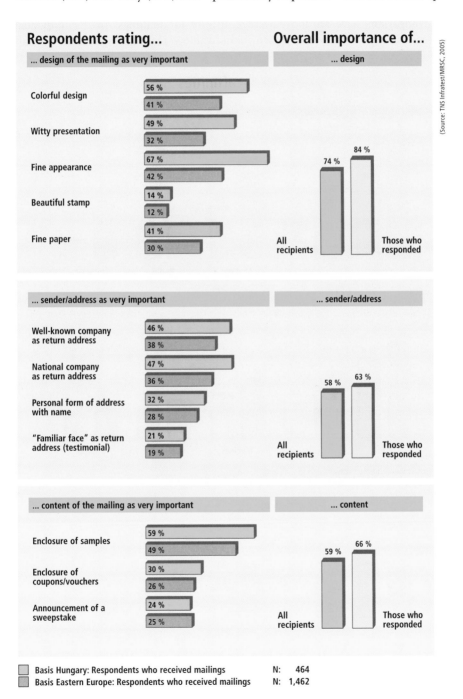

Respondents rating...

... design of the mailing as very important

Colorful design	56 % / 41 %
Witty presentation	49 % / 32 %
Fine appearance	67 % / 42 %
Beautiful stamp	14 % / 12 %
Fine paper	41 % / 30 %

Overall importance of...

... design

74 % All recipients — 84 % Those who responded

... sender/address as very important

Well-known company as return address	46 % / 38 %
National company as return address	47 % / 36 %
Personal form of address with name	32 % / 28 %
"Familiar face" as return address (testimonial)	21 % / 19 %

... sender/address

58 % All recipients — 63 % Those who responded

... content of the mailing as very important

Enclosure of samples	59 % / 49 %
Enclosure of coupons/vouchers	30 % / 26 %
Announcement of a sweepstake	24 % / 25 %

... content

59 % All recipients — 66 % Those who responded

☐ Basis Hungary: Respondents who received mailings   N: 464
☐ Basis Eastern Europe: Respondents who received mailings N: 1,462

(Source: TNS Infratest/MRSC, 2005)

pearance (67%), something that their Eastern European neighbors find much less important (42%). The enclosure of samples (59%) also meets with high approval among Hungarian consumers.

Hungarians have an above-average affinity for mailings: In the individual categories – popularity and informational value – mailings far surpass TV ad-

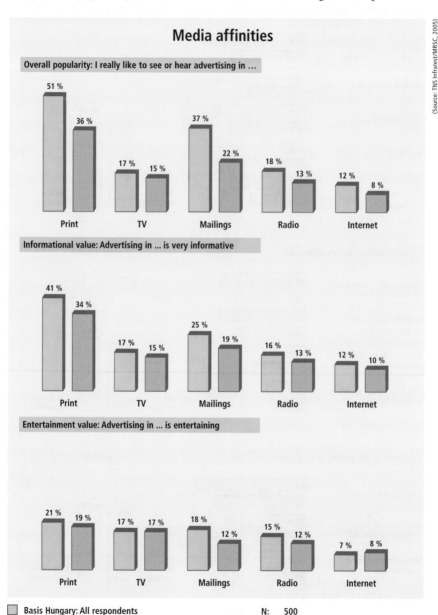

(Source: TNS Infratest/MRSC, 2005)

vertising. Only print (51%) enjoys greater popularity among consumers; the figure here for mailings is 37%.

Consumer trends

In terms of brand loyalty (75%), quality orientation (66%) and price orientation (57%), Hungarian consumers are above the average for Eastern Europe. 43% like trying out new products, although a striking 35% tend to be skeptical toward new providers (Eastern Europe: 25%). If the products are "Made in Germany", almost half of all Hungarians (47%) trust their quality.

(Source: TNS Infratest/MRSC, 2005)

Mail-order affinity

63% of Hungarian consumers state that they have never shopped by mail-order, just under the average for Eastern Europe (66%). One-third of those surveyed prefer the conventional sales channel, i.e., the catalog. The internet hardly plays a role – including as an ordering channel. The order card is well ahead here (49%).

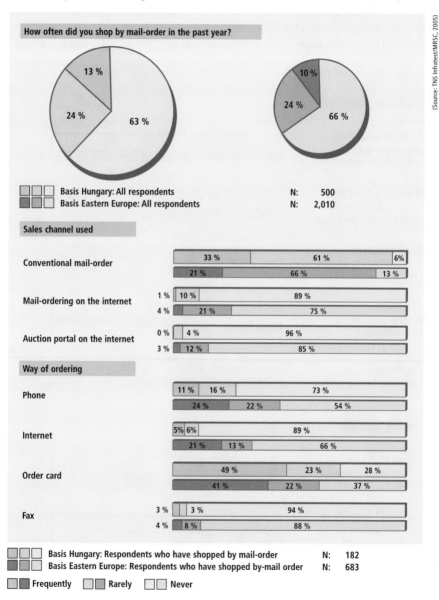

(Source: TNS Infratest/MRSC, 2005)

How often did you shop by mail-order in the past year?

13 %
24 %
63 %

10 %
24 %
66 %

Basis Hungary: All respondents   N: 500
Basis Eastern Europe: All respondents   N: 2,010

Sales channel used

Conventional mail-order
33 % | 61 % | 6%
21 % | 66 % | 13 %

Mail-ordering on the internet
1 % | 10 % | 89 %
4 % | 21 % | 75 %

Auction portal on the internet
0 % | 4 % | 96 %
3 % | 12 % | 85 %

Way of ordering

Phone
11 % | 16 % | 73 %
24 % | 22 % | 54 %

Internet
5% | 6% | 89 %
21 % | 13 % | 66 %

Order card
49 % | 23 % | 28 %
41 % | 22 % | 37 %

Fax
3 % | 3 % | 94 %
4 % | 8 % | 88 %

Basis Hungary: Respondents who have shopped by mail-order   N: 182
Basis Eastern Europe: Respondents who have shopped by-mail order   N: 683

Frequently   Rarely   Never

Poland

23

Given wings by its membership in the EU, the Polish economy has experienced uninterrupted growth. The GDP is projected to grow in 2006 by an amount somewhere between 4.1 and 4.7%. The rising private consumption, with 3.2% in 2005 and around 3.7% forecasted for 2006, further confirms the positive business situation in a country that is held up as a model among other new EU nations. The mailing density is still relatvively low in Poland, offering interesting opportunities for direct marketing campaigns. Aesthetic qualities in direct mailings are appreciated by the Polish consumer. Direct marketing is frequently used and effective, especially in the growing premium and luxury goods segment.

Demographic data

Area	312,685 square kilometers
Population	38.2 million
Number of households	13.3 million
Average household size	2.9 persons
Number of households with internet connection	3.5 million
Major cities/metropolitan areas (residents)	Warsaw (1,671,670), Lodz (789,318), Cracow (758,544), Wroclaw (640,367), Poznan (578,886), Gdansk (461,334)
Population age 0-14	6.6 million
Population age 15-64	26.6 million
Population age 65 and up	5.0 million

(Source: Fischer Weltalmanach 2005, Bundesagentur für Außenwirtschaft 2005)

Direct marketing trends

Compared with their Eastern European neighbors (27%), almost half of all Poles surveyed (48%) state that they receive direct mail rarely or never. In addition, only 21% receive mailings at least once a week (Eastern Europe: 44%).

90% of Poles read their mailings occasionally and 52% of them regularly – roughly on par with the average for Eastern Europe (93% and 58%). Response by Poles is slightly above-average: 16% respond at least once a quarter (Eastern Europe: 14%). Anyone wishing to attract Polish consumers should not underestimate

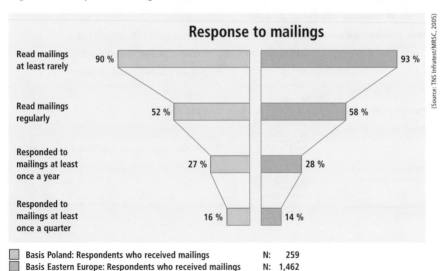

the relevance of the sender and address (80% of those who respond). For 46%, it is important to know the company and 39% expect a personal form of address. With

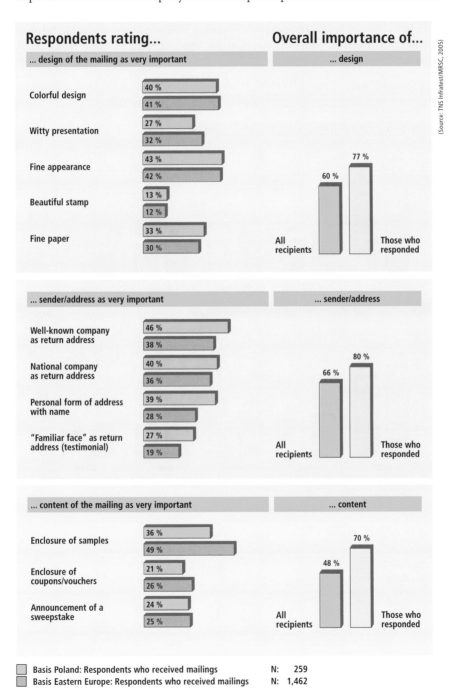

(Source: TNS Infratest/MRSC, 2005)

regards to design, they concur with their Eastern European neighbors: Color (40%) and fine appearance (43%) meet with general approval.

Print dominates in all categories and is above the average for Eastern Europe in popularity among Polish respondents. However, mailings come second in terms of popularity (19%) and informational content (18%) – before TV advertising. Mailings in Poland have some catching up to do when it comes to entertainment value.

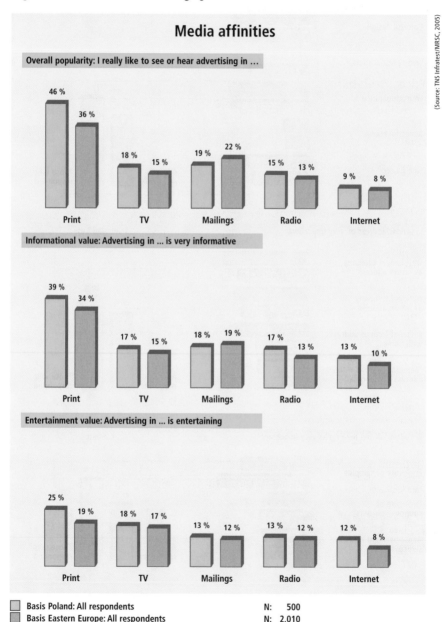

Media affinities

Overall popularity: I really like to see or hear advertising in ...

Print 46 % / 36 %, TV 18 % / 15 %, Mailings 19 % / 22 %, Radio 15 % / 13 %, Internet 9 % / 8 %

Informational value: Advertising in ... is very informative

Print 39 % / 34 %, TV 17 % / 15 %, Mailings 18 % / 19 %, Radio 17 % / 13 %, Internet 13 % / 10 %

Entertainment value: Advertising in ... is entertaining

Print 25 % / 19 %, TV 18 % / 17 %, Mailings 13 % / 12 %, Radio 13 % / 12 %, Internet 12 % / 8 %

Basis Poland: All respondents   N: 500
Basis Eastern Europe: All respondents N: 2,010

(Source: TNS Infratest/MRSC, 2005)

Consumer trends

The brand (79%) and quality (57%) incite Polish consumers to purchase. They are above the average for Eastern Europe in these areas (73% and 55% respectively) – and with regard to openness, as well: 43% state that they like trying out new products (Eastern Europe: 40%). At the same time, national providers enjoy particular sympathy among 43% of respondents.

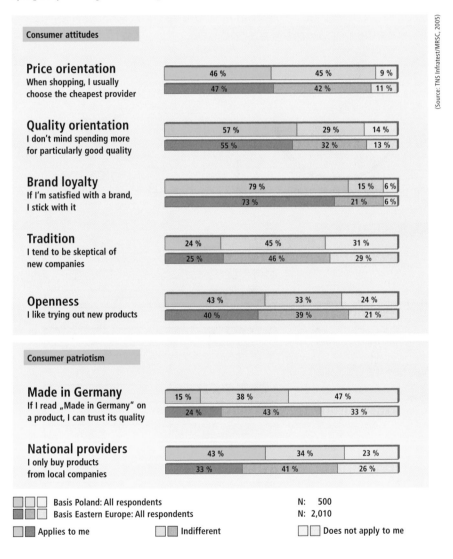

Consumer attitudes

Price orientation
When shopping, I usually choose the cheapest provider
46 % | 45 % | 9 %
47 % | 42 % | 11 %

Quality orientation
I don't mind spending more for particularly good quality
57 % | 29 % | 14 %
55 % | 32 % | 13 %

Brand loyalty
If I'm satisfied with a brand, I stick with it
79 % | 15 % | 6 %
73 % | 21 % | 6 %

Tradition
I tend to be skeptical of new companies
24 % | 45 % | 31 %
25 % | 46 % | 29 %

Openness
I like trying out new products
43 % | 33 % | 24 %
40 % | 39 % | 21 %

Consumer patriotism

Made in Germany
If I read „Made in Germany" on a product, I can trust its quality
15 % | 38 % | 47 %
24 % | 43 % | 33 %

National providers
I only buy products from local companies
43 % | 34 % | 23 %
33 % | 41 % | 26 %

Basis Poland: All respondents   N: 500
Basis Eastern Europe: All respondents N: 2,010

Applies to me   Indifferent   Does not apply to me

(Source: TNS Infratest/MRSC, 2005)

Mail-order affinity

Mail-ordering is not especially pronounced in Poland: Only 8% use this sales channel regularly, while 75% have never used it at all. Although catalog shopping dominates, Polish consumers prove that they have a greater affinity for the internet than their Eastern European neighbors. As far as the channel used for ordering is concerned, the internet (32%) is in first place, followed by the order card (23%).

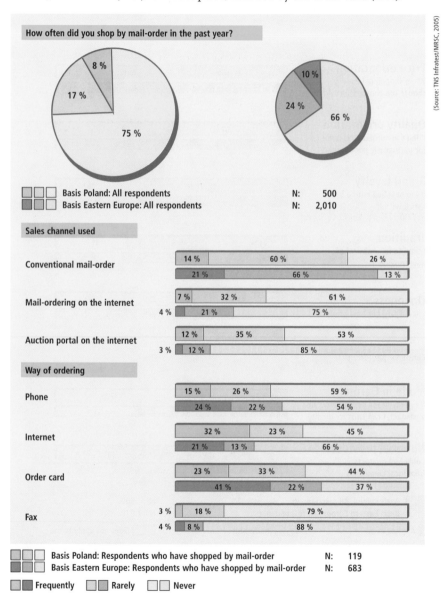

How often did you shop by mail-order in the past year?

Basis Poland: All respondents   N: 500
Basis Eastern Europe: All respondents N: 2,010

Sales channel used

Conventional mail-order
14 % 60 % 26 %
21 % 66 % 13 %

Mail-ordering on the internet
7 % 32 % 61 %
4 % 21 % 75 %

Auction portal on the internet
12 % 35 % 53 %
3 % 12 % 85 %

Way of ordering

Phone
15 % 26 % 59 %
24 % 22 % 54 %

Internet
32 % 23 % 45 %
21 % 13 % 66 %

Order card
23 % 33 % 44 %
41 % 22 % 37 %

Fax
3 % 18 % 79 %
4 % 8 % 88 %

Basis Poland: Respondents who have shopped by mail-order   N: 119
Basis Eastern Europe: Respondents who have shopped by mail-order N: 683

■ Frequently   ■ Rarely   □ Never

(Source: TNS Infratest/MRSC, 2005)

Slovakia

Private consumption – stimulated by an increase in real wages and lower inter-est rates – is driving the continued economic growth in Slovakia. Gross Domes-tic Product increased again by more than 6% in comparison to the previous year. Consumption is expected to be higher both in 2005 and 2006 by nearly 5% over the respective previous year. A positive mood among consumers is also good for direct marketing: mailings with product samples are met with approval by a large portion of the population and hold the promise of a high response rates.

Demographic data

Area	49,034 square kilometers
Population	5.4 million
Number of households	1.9 million
Average household size	2.8 persons
Number of households with internet connection	53,000
Major cities/metropolitan areas (residents)	Bratislava (428,094), Kosice (236,036), Presov (92,720), Nitra (87,308), Zilina (85,384), Banska Bystrica (82,961)
Population age 0-14	1.0 million
Population age 15-64	3.8 million
Population age 65 and up	0.6 million

(Source: Fischer Weltalmanach 2005, Bundesagentur für Außenwirtschaft 2005)

Direct marketing trends

More than half of the Slovakians surveyed (51%) receive direct mail at least once a week, a mailing density well above the Eastern European average (44%). Only 18% state that they almost never receive mailings (Eastern Europe: 27%).

Almost all Slovakian recipients of direct mail (93%) read it at least occasionally – the same figure as for their Eastern European neighbors. 56% are regular readers. Their response is around the average for Eastern Europe – a quarter of those surveyed respond at least once and 15% as much as several times a year. Samples

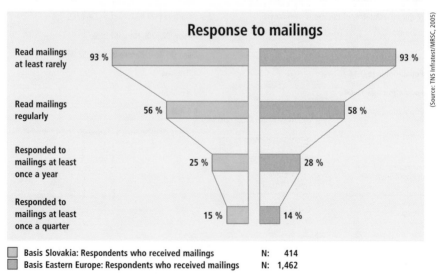

(63%), vouchers (38%) and prize drawings (36%) enjoy above-average popularity in Slovakia compared with the rest of Eastern Europe. 79% of respondents stress the

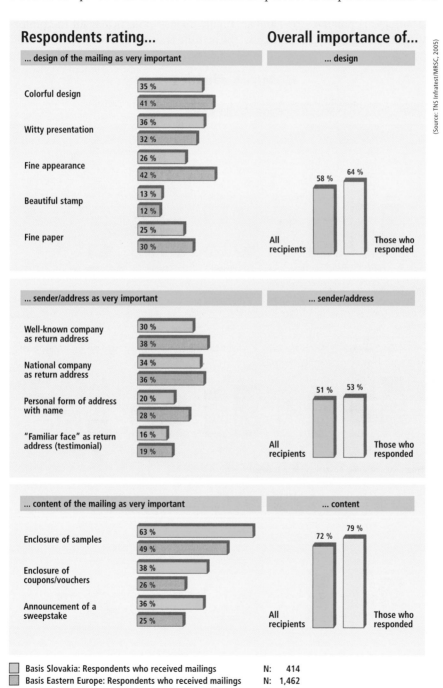

(Source: TNS Infratest/MRSC, 2005)

Respondents rating...

... design of the mailing as very important

	Slovakia	Eastern Europe
Colorful design	35 %	41 %
Witty presentation	36 %	32 %
Fine appearance	26 %	42 %
Beautiful stamp	13 %	12 %
Fine paper	25 %	30 %

... sender/address as very important

	Slovakia	Eastern Europe
Well-known company as return address	30 %	38 %
National company as return address	34 %	36 %
Personal form of address with name	20 %	28 %
"Familiar face" as return address (testimonial)	16 %	19 %

... content of the mailing as very important

	Slovakia	Eastern Europe
Enclosure of samples	63 %	49 %
Enclosure of coupons/vouchers	38 %	26 %
Announcement of a sweepstake	36 %	25 %

Overall importance of...

... design

All recipients: 58 %
Those who responded: 64 %

... sender/address

All recipients: 51 %
Those who responded: 53 %

... content

All recipients: 72 %
Those who responded: 79 %

Basis Slovakia: Respondents who received mailings   N: 414
Basis Eastern Europe: Respondents who received mailings   N: 1,462

special relevance of the content. A personal form of address (20%) or a well-known testimonial as the return address (16%) tend to be of lesser importance for those surveyed.

Mailings are popular (20%) and are highly rated – in particular for their informational content (21%). In these areas, the mailing is ahead of TV advertising – and

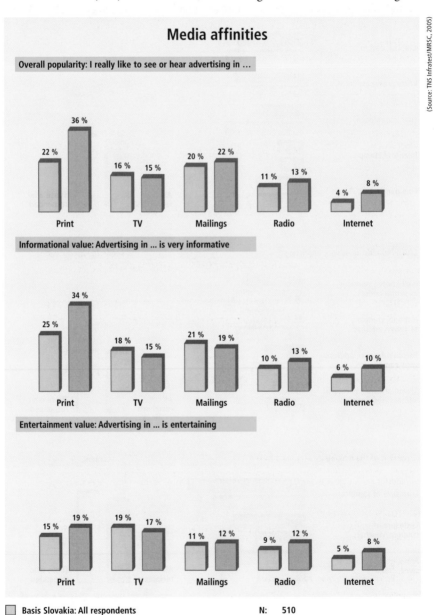

(Source: TNS Infratest/MRSC, 2005)

is only surpassed by print media (25%). Television wins in terms of entertainment value (19%).

Consumer trends

Although Slovakian consumers (61%) do not display the same degree of brand loyalty as the average for Eastern Europe (73%), it is still a clear determining factor in their behavior. Price orientation comes second (50%). Only one quarter (24%) of Slovaks are somewhat skeptical about new companies.

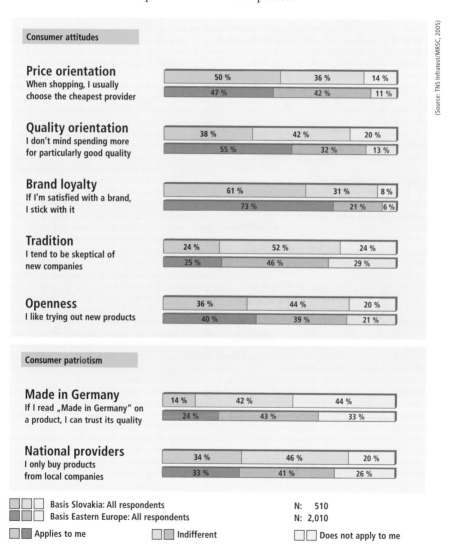

(Source: TNS Infratest/MRSC, 2005)

Consumer attitudes

Price orientation
When shopping, I usually choose the cheapest provider
- 50 % | 36 % | 14 %
- 47 % | 42 % | 11 %

Quality orientation
I don't mind spending more for particularly good quality
- 38 % | 42 % | 20 %
- 55 % | 32 % | 13 %

Brand loyalty
If I'm satisfied with a brand, I stick with it
- 61 % | 31 % | 8 %
- 73 % | 21 % | 6 %

Tradition
I tend to be skeptical of new companies
- 24 % | 52 % | 24 %
- 25 % | 46 % | 29 %

Openness
I like trying out new products
- 36 % | 44 % | 20 %
- 40 % | 39 % | 21 %

Consumer patriotism

Made in Germany
If I read „Made in Germany" on a product, I can trust its quality
- 14 % | 42 % | 44 %
- 24 % | 43 % | 33 %

National providers
I only buy products from local companies
- 34 % | 46 % | 20 %
- 33 % | 41 % | 26 %

Basis Slovakia: All respondents   N: 510
Basis Eastern Europe: All respondents   N: 2,010

☐■ Applies to me   ☐■ Indifferent   ☐☐ Does not apply to me

Mail-order affinity

Only 5% of Slovakian consumers shop regularly by mail-order and a full 75% have never ordered goods using this channel – a figure well above the average for Eastern Europe (66%). The few who order by catalog prefer to respond using the order card. 78% state that they have never used the internet for ordering.

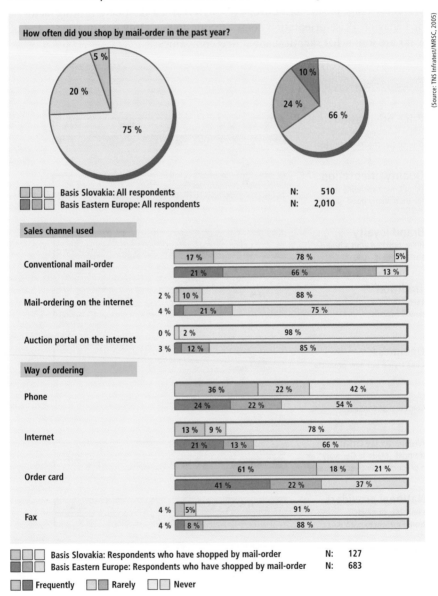

(Source: TNS Infratest/MRSC, 2005)

RECEIVED

JAN 1 7 2008

Golden Gate University, Univ. Library
536 Mission St., San Francisco, CA 94105